Half Famili
Whole Through Christ

◆

The Transforming Journey of Truth, Hope, and Love for Single Parents

Bev Frank

iUniverse, Inc.
New York Lincoln Shanghai

Half Families Made Whole Through Christ
The Transforming Journey of Truth, Hope, and Love for Single Parents

iUniverse books may be ordered through booksellers or by contacting:

iUniverse
2021 Pine Lake Road, Suite 100
Lincoln, NE 68512
www.iuniverse.com
1-800-Authors (1-800-288-4677)

The views expressed in this work are solely those of the author and do not necessarily reflect the views of the publisher, and the publisher hereby disclaims any responsibility for them.

Edited by Judy Bodmer

Cover design by Jim Fox

All scripture quotations, unless otherwise indicated, are taken from the HOLY BIBLE, NEW INTERNATIONAL VERSION®. NIV®. Copyright © 1973, 1978, 1984 by International Bible Society. Used by permission of Zondervan.

ISBN-13: 978-0-595-40535-0 (pbk)
ISBN-13: 978-0-595-84900-0 (ebk)
ISBN-10: 0-595-40535-5 (pbk)
ISBN-10: 0-595-84900-8 (ebk)

Printed in the United States of America

Contents

1

You Are Not Alone

You are not alone.

When I began my journey as a single parent, I thought I was alone. I certainly felt that way the weekend I took my sweet little boy and left my husband of nine years. I remember looking at my three-and-a-half year old son and thinking, "I cannot do this." I could not imagine raising him by myself. At that moment, memories of the past nine years, the pain of the present, and the perception of the overwhelming future responsibilities made me numb.

I was overwhelmed by both the turmoil of emotions arising from the separation from my husband and the magnitude of my economic responsibilities. I faced huge problems and I desperately needed answers. At times, the painful emotions from my separation overpowered me, intensifying my sense of being alone. How could I financially support my son and me?

I was not only alone, but I was lost. I had no answers. My partner was gone. My marriage was gone. What did I do now? I had been thrust onto a new road I had never before traveled. In fact, I felt like I was on a dark, dangerous road with no roadmap and no destination. I was now a single parent, and I was not prepared for this journey.

But the truth is I was not alone. Millions of women across this country were experiencing similar emotions and facing similar situations. Unfortunately, that truth still exists today. Whether you are separated, divorced, or facing life as an unwed mother, you are either embarking on or currently experiencing a new, sometimes harsh single parent journey filled with a whole range of emotions. It does not matter how you became a single parent; you understand the sense of being alone and the feeling of being lost on a dark road.

But you are not alone. You do not have to be lost on a dark, dangerous road. You do not have to wander through single parenthood without a destination. *For every single parent, there is a roadmap for the journey and a destination.* It is a remarkable journey with a surprising roadmap and an amazing destination. It is

1

true. I discovered this roadmap on my own single parent journey. My son is now an adult and I never remarried. I raised him by myself, but never was I alone. I may have been confused at times, but I was never lost on this journey. And I reached the amazing destination.

You also can experience a transforming journey that leads through truth, hope, and love. I will show you the way. But be prepared, this journey is not for single parents. It is for the mother in the Half Family who wants to be whole. I know that statement may raise a question in your mind. What is a Half Family? Before I answer, I need to shed some light on the truth about single parents.

The Truth

Every journey has a starting place and ours begins with the truth about single parents. You may know there are other single parents on this road with you, but have you looked around to really see them? If you are like me, you are probably so busy maneuvering through the day to day challenges of single parenting that you have no energy left to see anything or anyone else on this journey. So I want us to choose to stop a moment and look around us. There are other women facing the same road as you.

To help you see the vast number of women on this path, I am going to shine a light on the numbers and statistics about single parents in this country. Numbers and statistics do not lie. They reveal that there are millions, yes millions of single parents in this country.

One of the best sources for statistics on single parents is the 2000 U.S. Census. The census categorizes single parents as a family group. Interesting, the government refers to us as a family group. In fact, the government defines single parents as female householders with children. So I will use their terms. You are now a female householder with children.

Population of Single Parents in the U.S.

On the surface, there appears to be over 10 million female households with children.[1] Unfortunately, this number does not include all single parents. It does not account for a possible 1.5 million single mothers who are living with another family group like relatives or friends.[2] Many women, myself included, have had to live with relatives or friends just to survive.

The census also does not include the approximately 2.3 million adults and children who may be homeless in this country.[3] Over 67 percent of that homeless population is composed of single parents and the majority of them are women with children.[4] In other words, there could be over a million single mothers who are homeless.

Clearly, the census may not have captured the total number of single parents in this country. Some of the poorest women and children may have slipped through the cracks. Therefore, the single parent population of "female householders with children" could be closer to 13 plus million. The actual number is not as important as the truth that it reveals. You are not alone.

We are among a large and growing segment of the population. To put that statement in perspective, think about these numbers and statistics. There are approximately 26 million married couples with children in this country.[5] Since 1970, the population of female householders with children has grown to 16 percent of total households, but the population of married couples with children has decreased from 40 percent to 24 percent of all households.[6] In other words, the single mother with a child or children is part of a growing family group in our society, while the married woman with a child or children is part of a shrinking family group.

Characteristics of Female Householders with Children

Even though the number of female householders with children represents 50 percent of married couples with children, it would be wrong to assume that most single parents are divorced women. So who are these other women? Who is on the same dark road with you?

Those 13 plus million female households with children include separated, divorced, and unwed mothers. Approximately 18 percent of the mothers in these households are separated, 40 percent are divorced, and 42 percent are unwed.[7] In 1999, children born to unwed mothers accounted for 33 percent of all births in the U.S.[8] So whether you are separated, divorced, or an unwed mother, you are on the single parent journey. It does not matter how you became a "female householder with children," you still face a dark, dangerous road as a single parent.

We are even more diverse than our marital status. Female householders with children encompass many different ages and family sizes. We range in age from fifteen to fifty-four. The majority of us (60 percent) are above the age of thirty-four and the remainder (40 percent) are below. About 60 percent of us have two children under the age of twelve. The majority of us (88 percent) have a household size of four—a mother with three children.[9]

We are ethnically diverse. We are composed of Whites (52 percent), African Americans (30 percent), Hispanics (14 percent), and other races (4 percent). The

estimated breakdown among Whites is 18 percent are separated from their partner, 51 percent are divorced, and 31 percent are unwed mothers. For African
American women, 17 percent are separated from their partner, 18 percent are
divorced, and 65 percent are unwed mothers. Among Hispanic women, 27 percent are separated from their partner, 28 percent are divorced, and 45 percent are
unwed mothers.[10]

So as you can see, we cut across the fabric of this country. We are separated,
divorced, and unwed mothers. We are different ages, family sizes, and nationalities,
but we have one thing in common—we are all female householders with children.
We are single mothers raising children. Look again at those numbers. Are you surprised who is on this road with you? Numbers and statistics do not lie.

You are not alone. You may not believe those words at this moment. Even
though all those statistics revealed your fellow travelers, you feel alone. You may
want to believe the numbers, but you are a *single parent*. You feel single and isolated. Your road is dark and dangerous. And all the statistics in the world will not
change your view of your road. The truth alone is never enough; we need hope.

The Hope

We all need hope. Here is what I believe. *Hope is the difference between a single
parent and the mother in a Half Family.* Too many women are single parents,
walking a lonely road without hope. If you are facing the harsh truth about your
life every day without hope, you feel *single*: isolated and alone. You are a *parent*
with no sense of family. You don't feel like you belong anywhere and you struggle
to create a family with your children. You feel lost. You live at survival mode
financially. You are drained emotionally, physically, mentally, and spiritually.
Your single parent road is so dark that you feel like you are walking in circles and
you are tired and bloody from falling over obstacles in your way. The truth without hope is a cold, bitter single parent journey that does not lead anywhere.

But the truth surrounded by hope is a very different road. This hope transforms you from a single parent to the mother in a Half Family. What is a Half
Family? Good question.

When I became a single parent, that *label* nearly destroyed me. I was not single, I had a child. I no longer related to the single lifestyle. I was a parent but I was
more than that. When I was married, my husband, son and I were a family. Even
though I was divorced, my son and I were still a family. I was not a single parent.
That was a label that society had conveniently given me. I had been categorized
and stereotyped but it was not me. I felt I was stuck in the mud by this label with

no hope of changing my situation. It was only when I began to see myself through Jesus' eyes that I found the hope.

Jesus did not label me. He did reveal the truth but surrounded it with hope. There was no escape from the truth that my divorce split my family in two. My partner was now gone. But I was not single; I was a *half* of what used to be a *whole* family. I was still part of a family, a Half Family. And in that simple distinction, I found hope. Jesus revealed the truth and surrounded me in the hope that I could be whole. He showed me there was a road that could lead me to wholeness.

I gained hope to take one more step on this harsh road. Yes, the Half Family road is challenging and filled with obstacles just like the road of a single parent. But the mother in the Half Family has hope that she can maneuver the road and learn to live beyond survival. She has hope that empowers her emotionally, physically, mentally, and spiritually. Hope affirms that she is not alone.

If you choose to take this journey, you will be transformed from a single parent into the mother in a Half Family. You will have a roadmap and a destination. Be assured, the Half Family road is difficult but you will not get bloody from walking in circles. You will have the hope that insulates the Half Family journey from the cold and bitterness of the truth. Most important, you will have love to reach the wholeness destination.

The Love

As a mother in the Half Family, you will face the truth about your situation, access the hope to guide you on this harsh road, but it is love that leads you to your destination. It is love that makes your Half Family whole.

Concerning love, I will certainly not mince any words. Love truly is the key to successfully reaching our *wholeness* destination. However, it is not earthly love, it is heavenly. And heavenly love is on the opposite end of the spectrum from any form of earthly love. The only way to access this heavenly love is through Jesus Christ. This road to wholeness truly is a journey in love with Jesus. His love will forgive you, heal you, encourage you, walk with you, carry you and bless you. With his love, you will never be alone or lost. You only need to accept the free gift of salvation from Jesus Christ to access heavenly love.

I think that we need to stop right here for a moment because there two kinds of women who are reading this book. First, there are women who have accepted salvation through Jesus Christ. You know that Jesus is your refuge. You know that Jesus will guide you. I encourage you to continue to grow in his love.

But there are some women reading this book who have not accepted Jesus as their Savior. Some of you may have heard of Jesus, and you may have even been in church but have never accepted the free gift of salvation through Jesus. Some of you may have only a passing understanding of Jesus and salvation. Some of you may be totally confused. No matter where you are at this moment, I truly believe it is no accident you are reading this book. I believe it is a divine appointment with Jesus Christ. Please do not walk away from that appointment. Make a decision to keep an open mind and come on this Half Family journey with me. You will discover Jesus will meet you exactly where you are. You simply have to open your heart to him. My guess is you have tried everything else to survive the *single parent* journey and that is all you are doing: surviving a cold, bitter existence. Why not try a different road? What have you got to lose? Here is what you will gain: if you accept Jesus as your savior, you will gain a companion who will never leave you. His love has already overcome anything the world can throw in your path. For everyone who chooses to take this Half Family journey with love, there is much to gain. You can be whole.

Well now you know a little about the truth, hope, and love journey of the mother in the Half Family. I know the Half Family concept may twist your brain and challenge your thought process. You may want more information, which I cannot share with you now. I can't because *the transformation from single parent to the mother in the Half Family is not an event; it is a journey.*

But I can share a few things. For me, this Half Family journey has been brutal, painful, frightening, inspiring, full of joy, and an incredible learning experience. I am not the same woman who started down this road more than twenty years ago. I have made hundreds of mistakes. I have stumbled and fallen down. I have struggled to get back up and have sometimes chosen to just lie in the middle of the road. I have walked through incredible emotions and trials. I have seen the spectacular beauty of a road that was once dark for me. And the only constant in those twenty years has been the truth, hope, and love that kept me moving forward.

That forward movement has always been one step at a time. There is no skipping, running, or jumping ahead allowed on this journey. There are no magic wands to solve the problems that you will encounter from the road. Be assured, I do not have all the answers to your problems or your questions. Nor would I want to solve all of them or answer all your questions because in most respects, this Half Family journey is personal for each of us. All I have are the lessons I have learned from my own travels.

So if you choose to journey with me, given the dangerous nature of road, we will take one step at a time. Do not expect to embark on our travels immediately.

2

The Truth about
Our External World

With the hope that we are not alone, we are now ready to look at the Whole Truth Picture. We are going to shine light on the Whole Truth about our lives as single parents. You may think you already know the truth about your life. You may think I am not going to share anything with you that you don't know first hand. You know the economic challenges of raising a child or children on your own. You also know the range of emotions that can torment you, but those truths represent only part of the condition of your road. Do you see the Whole Truth?

Before you answer that question, I want you to think about the Whole Truth Picture as a mosaic. A mosaic is made up of thousands of small pieces of colored glass, or stone, which form a picture. If you stand too close to a mosaic, all you see are the individual pieces of glass, or stone, in front of you and they form no recognizable pattern. You know that you are looking at a mosaic, but you cannot see the image. Only when you stand at a distance do all those individual pieces form a clear picture.

The Whole Truth Picture for a single parent is like a mosaic. We are sometimes so close to the fragments of our lives and our shattered emotions we do not see the full picture, the Whole Truth. We see only the small dark colored stones of truth.

It is imperative we see the Whole Truth Picture, the whole mosaic. I spent many years ignorant of the Whole Truth and stumbled around on my dark road. Part of me did not want to look at it because it was painful. If the pieces of the truth were painful, I feared the Whole Truth would kill me. But there was no escape. At some point on the road, we all come face to face with the truth.

Therefore, we are going look at the condition of this dark single parent road one cluster of stones or one boulder at a time. As we examine the truth about each aspect of our lives, we will slowly begin to see the condition of our road. The fragments of our lives will reveal a mosaic that was always there. We simply were standing too close to see the Whole Truth. We did not see the Whole Truth Picture.

As we begin this process, you may have a strong desire to skip lightly over this part of the journey. In fact, you may want to ignore some of the truth about your life as a single parent. You may think that if you ignore the truth, it will just go away. I understand if you think this way, because I have been there, but the truth will not go away. We only delay the inevitable encounter with it. In fact, my own decision to ignore the Whole Truth made it more difficult and painful to face later down the road. In other words, as painful and difficult as it is to look at the Whole Truth now, it is even more painful and difficult to stumble over the truth on a dark road.

The bottom line is you can choose to look at the truth now or react to it later in the dark. The choice is yours. And remember, you have the hope that you are not alone.

What Is the External World of a Single Parent?

The first cluster of stones on the single parent road is the truth about our external world. What is the external world of a single parent? What does our external road look like? The answer is really a no-brainer for any mother who struggles to financially support a child or children. The external world of the single parent is made up of those economic challenges all mothers face who are raising a child or children alone. These challenges can just be stones in the path or boulders that block all forward movement. We all have faced the economic boulders that block our path as a single parent.

I would define our external world as *minimum income and maximum expenses*. Each day, each week, and each month, we are challenged to stretch our money to meet bills, which can be economic boulders. We live in an external world where the simple act of buying groceries or paying the electric bill can be financially challenging. Bills like the rent or a mortgage are worse and appear as boulders that block our path. Clearly, I am not defining anything that you do not already know, but the truth about the financial condition of the single parent road encompasses more than money or bills. The truth is larger. Therefore, we need to take one step back from this narrow focus and view three truths about minimum income and maximum expenses.

The Truth

It Is Not Personal.

That is right. If you are facing a road of minimum income and maximum expenses, it is not personal. Here is what I mean by that. I have traveled this difficult, sometimes impossible road of economic challenges. As a single parent in the dark, I have faced huge boulders in my way, and it was personal to me. When I was sitting at my kitchen table trying to decide between buying groceries and paying my electric bill, it was personal. It was *very* personal. We live in an obscenely rich country. Why should I be in this position? With a grocery store on almost every corner, how could my son and I be faced with hunger? My financial situation made me feel "single:" isolated, and alone. But the truth is millions of women and children across this country face this same dilemma every day. Unfortunately, that truth is a nice fact, but the daily financial struggle was still personal to me. No matter how hard I worked I could not pay some bill or buy some necessity. That may be how I felt, but I was missing the truth about the condition of the road. The majority of us face minimum income and maximum expenses. It is not personal. It is just a Cold Hard Fact.

The Cold Hard Facts

The truth about the financial condition of the single parent road is that it is not personal. Our external world of minimum income and maximum expenses is just a fact. It is just a Cold Hard Fact.

These Cold Hard Facts are scattered in front of us on this strange new single parent road. There is nothing personal about it. The Cold Hard Facts do not care whether we are separated, divorced, or an unwed mother. Race does not matter because the Cold Hard Facts are color blind. The Cold Hard Facts do not respect age or the size of your family. It is not personal; it is just a fact. If you are a single parent, you will face the Cold Hard Facts on your journey.

But what is the truth about the Cold Hard Facts of minimum income and maximum expenses? You may personally know some of the truth already. But are you standing so close to this part of the road that all you see is your personal situation? Do you really see the truth?

I discovered that the only way to see the truth is to step back and shine a bright light on this dangerous part of the road. That is exactly what we will do. We are going to look at the non-personal Cold Hard Facts in black and white. In other words, we are going to examine some numbers and statistics that represent the facts about income and expenses that the majority of us have in common. Those facts include income from child support, government assistance, and wages, and expenses from housing, food, childcare, transportation, and healthcare. We are going to learn the truth about our sources of income and the expenses that consume that income.

To give us some perspective on the financial condition of our road, I want to compare the Cold Hard Facts of single women with children with the Cold Hard Facts of married women with children. The economic condition of these two family groups could not be more different. Our road stands in stark contrast to the road of married women. In fact, if you wonder sometimes why a married woman with children has difficulty relating to your external world, all you have to do is look at the table to answer your question.

	Married Couples	Female Householders
INCOME		
The average income [1]	56% have an income of $50,000 and above	55% have an income of $25,000 and below
Child support income[2]	N/A	33% have received an average of $2,400 annually
Public assistance either cash or food stamps[3]	N/A	54% receive public assistance 23% receive cash --mean average distribution is $3,000 annually
Employment[4]	71% employed	75% employed
EXPENSES		
Housing		
Housing[5]	82% own home	48% own home
Mortgage as % of income[6]	20% estimated average	35% estimated average
Housing[7]	28% rent	52% rent
Rent as % of income[8]	25% estimated average	35% + estimated average
Food		
Food expenses as % of income for family with 3 children[9]	Estimated 15% (Family with 3 children)	Estimated 30% (Family with 3 children)
Childcare		
Child care expenses as % of income[10]	7%	16%
Transportation		
Automobile ownership as % of income[11] (87% of workers commute to work in auto[12])	Estimated 8-15% for used or new automobile	Estimated 17-30% for used or new automobile
Public Transportation as % of income[13] (5% of workers commute-public transportation[14])	1.5%	3%
Health Insurance		
Health insurance premiums as % of income[15]	0-12% (dependent on employer paid or self paid)	0-23% (dependent on employer paid or self paid)
Total Expenses as % of Income	**50-84%** income goes to expenses	**77-108%** income goes to expenses

These facts reveal what most of us already know. We are facing Cold Hard Facts. We have minimal incomes and maximum expenses. Unfortunately, the numbers only show the surface of these dark colored stones. We need to pick up each stone and examine it to understand the depth of our economic challenges. *What are the facts about minimum income and maximum expenses?*

Income. Let's start with an examination of annual incomes. But before we look at our sources of income, we need to take a look at overall income levels for single parents. This table only shows part of the truth. A whopping 85 percent of single mothers make less than $40,000.[16] An income of $40,000 may appear to be sufficient. However, if you are a woman raising three children and must spread your income to cover housing, food, childcare, transportation, and health insurance that income gets eaten up quickly.

To put that income in perspective: among married couples with children close to 70 percent make more than $40,000.[17] So the majority of us are living on annual incomes of less than $40,000 and the majority of married couples are living on annual incomes of more than $40,000.

If all single mothers' incomes hovered around $40,000, we would have a fighting chance to pay bills on time and actually have some money left over. The painful reality is that of the 85 percent making less than $40,000, 40 percent of those families fall below the established government poverty level.[18] Children under the age of 18 have a poverty rate that is higher than any other age group.[19] In other words, almost half of us are living in poverty. In fact, the poverty rate for single parents is five times higher than the poverty rate for married couples. Let me put a number to the poor. The designated U.S. poverty level for a mother with two children is about $13,874.[20]

If we further examine the numbers, we discover that about another 20 percent of single mothers, who are not designated as poor, are making less that $25,000 annually. Another 25 percent are earning between $25–40,000 annually and only 15 percent of single mothers make over $40,000 a year. So basically, the majority of us have minimum incomes. You are not alone. Now let's look at the sources of that minimum income.

Child Support

Unfortunately, there is a common perception that the majority of single parents receive child support payments, and that this income is adequate to support a family. Nothing could be further from the truth. Approximately, 56 percent of all single mothers with children have some type of support agreement.[21] The majority of those women have agreements due to divorce. Child support for unwed mothers is almost non-existent. For the women with agreements, 56.1 percent were White, 27.9 percent were African American, and 14 percent were Hispanic.[22]

However, a full 90 percent of these women with legal agreements have some child support due to them. They have an agreement, but they are either not receiving support payments or are receiving partial support payments. In 1997, only four million women with agreements received payments. The average award was $4,200 annually but the average distribution was $2,400 annually. In other words, most women do not receive the full amount of child support legally due. Of the parents who received all child support payments, their average income was $27,500. Of the 90 percent of parents who received partial child support, their average income was $20,400.[23]

Even though enforcement of child support agreements has improved since 1997, the numbers of single mothers living in poverty has not dramatically changed. Clearly, these women cannot support their families solely on child support payments and the majority of them receive no child support income.

Government Assistance

Given the staggering poverty rate among single mothers, another source of income should be government assistance. Again, the perception is not close to reality. Most of the single parents in need of government assistance are familiar with the Federal Food Stamp Program and TANF (Temporary Assistance for Needy Families). The Food Stamp Program is administered through the federal government. While a single parent does not receive cash for food, she does receive "vouchers" that can be used at any grocery store. TANF is a relatively new program that was established as a result of a new welfare law passed in 1996. TANF is administered through each state. The program does distribute cash to eligible single parents. A woman in need must meet the federal requirements for food stamps and the individual state requirements for TANF cash assistance.

The Food Stamp Program is the most widely used government assistance program by single parents. It is difficult to identify the actual number, but my conservative guess would be about 35 percent of single parents, or 4 million, have used this program. Unfortunately, the Food Stamp Program is not reaching the most needy families in this country. America's Second Harvest, the nation's largest hunger relief organization, reports that in 2001 only 30 percent of the individuals using their emergency food centers participated in the Food Stamp Program, but almost 75 percent were income eligible for food stamps.[24]

Eligibility for food stamps is based on a variety of factors such as gross and net monthly income, employment, and a social security number. Once a woman receives food stamps, she cannot use them to buy alcohol, cigarettes, nonfood items like soap, paper products, vitamins, medicines, and hot foods. The average monthly benefit for food stamps in fiscal year 2000 was $173.[25] According to a policy brief by the Brookings Institute, a single mother with two children who works thirty hours a week making $8 an hour is eligible for $134 a month in food stamps.[26]

TANF provides income assistance to needy families for a period of time. That assistance can come in a variety of distributions for childcare, medical care, etc. Eligibility for TANF has similar requirements to the Federal Food Stamp Program. I estimate that approximately 80 percent or 1.5 million participants in TANF are single mothers who receive some assistance on a monthly basis. According to the 1999 TANF report, work participation was mandatory for three out of every five adults. Only "9 percent were exempt from the work participation because they were single custodial parents with a child under twelve months."[27]

Only 4.2 percent of working adults received any subsidized childcare. Of the participants in the TANF program, 98.3 percent receive some assistance with medical care, 80.7 percent receive food stamps and 12.6 percent receive subsidized housing. The average distribution for cash and cash equivalents assistance was $357 monthly.[28]

Here is the truth in all these numbers. If you are one of the fortunate women who received the monthly assistance, your $173 for food and $357 of cash or cash equivalent is not going to stretch very far. The majority of single parents receive no assistance.

Wages

Even if a single parent gets an annual income from child support of $2,500 and the average government assistance (food stamps and cash) of $6,320, she is still below the poverty level. I estimate that a minimum of seventy-five percent of single mothers work.

Most single mothers are not receiving appropriate child support or maximum government assistance. Therefore, many single mothers are among the working poor. Many women make $13,000 annually or $6.25 an hour. Others earn the bare-bones federal minimum wage of $5.15 an hour or $10,712 annually.

Even if we assume that a single mother gets the average child support payment, government assistance and earns $9.50 an hour, she probably has an annual income around $23,000. Many women are in this situation and struggling to support their families. How do you support three children on that income? The truth is that most single parents face minimum income and maximum expenses.

Expenses. A single parent's income is minimal at best. We face the challenge of taking that minimal amount of income to pay the maximum amount of bills. Or as I like to say, "How do you stretch nothing into something?" So let's look at these expense stones on the road. We are going to look at five major areas of expenses that the majority of us have in common and that consume large portions of our income. Those expenses are housing, food, childcare, transportation, and health insurance.

Housing

Housing has always created the biggest challenge for me because it consumes the largest portion of my income. Whether you are part of the 48 percent who own a home or the 52 percent that rent a home, either choice nets out a possible 15–35 percent of income being diverted to pay for housing. But there is more to this Cold Hard Fact below the surface of this large, dark colored stone. Unfortunately, our true cost of housing is closer to 35 percent of our income.

According to the 2000 Census data, 55 percent of homeowners pay a mortgage between $700–1499 per month. If a single parent is making $30,000 annually, her $700 mortgage payment represents 28 percent of her gross monthly income.[29]

Unfortunately, the housing situation for that same single parent is getting worse. As of 2005, the national housing wage is now $15.78 per hour or over $32,000 per year for full time work. What does this mean to you? According to the National Low Income Housing Coalition, it means you would need this income to be able to afford a modest two-bedroom apartment in the United States. And that is the average. Some major cities require an income much higher.[30] In your external world, if you pay $600 a month in rent and earn of $22,880 a year, your housing expense is 31percent of your gross monthly income.

If you are facing those percentages, you are probably asking questions like how do I pay the electric bill, the gas bill, or the phone bill? And you pray that nothing in your house or apartment breaks down. According to a 1997 HUD report, more than 30 million households, including single parents, were facing major housing problems in this country. Fourteen million of the 30 million households in this country paid more than 50 percent of their income for housing payments and utilities.[31]

Food

Food is probably the second largest consumer of our income. The USDA indicates the average cost of food for a family of four is about $610 per month depending on the age of the children.[32] If you are only making $1,000 a month, you are most likely using food stamps. The truth about this Cold Hard Fact represents a very dark stone that comfortable two-parent families have never seen or experienced. That dark side is hunger in America. When we think of hunger, we think of third world countries, not our country. Sadly, hunger exists in America.

Given the gap between the average cost of food and income including food stamps, chances are you, as a single parent family, may have faced hunger. The government puts it another way: food insecure. How do you know if you are facing food insecurity? If you do not meet the definition below, you have faced food insecurity.

> *"Food security has been defined as access at all times to enough nourishment for an active, healthy life. At a minimum, food security includes the ready availability of sufficient, nutritionally adequate, and safe food and the assurance that families can obtain adequate food without relying on emergency feeding programs or resorting to scavenging, stealing or other desperate efforts to secure food."*[33]

The fact the government needed to define food security demonstrates there is a growing hunger problem in this country.

The government admits that the statistics on hunger in this country are not accurate. That fact is understandable. When my son and I were hungry, I would never have told the government. I did not want to jeopardize losing my child. With that thought in mind, the government numbers are still staggering: 36 percent of families at or below the poverty level reported food insecurity; basically, they were hungry. For children between the ages of two to five that are below the poverty level, 80 percent did not have a diet that was rated good or there was not enough food.[34]

Here are some statistics from America's Second Harvest (A2H): an organization that provides food for 25 million Americans annually.

Many A2H Clients are food insecure or are experiencing hunger

- 33 percent of their clients are experiencing hunger.
- Among households with children, 73 percent are food insecure and 31 percent are experiencing hunger.[35]

Whether you are one day away from being hungry or you are hungry right now, it is an extremely difficult Cold Hard Fact to swallow and accept. When your family is hungry, it is easy to take that fact personally. It is easy to blame yourself or blame others. Unfortunately, it is not personal. Hunger in America is just a Cold Hard Fact. If you are experiencing hunger, you are not alone.

Childcare

The majority of single parents who work either on a full-time or part-time basis need childcare. Some single mothers are fortunate enough to have a family member who will watch their children during the workday. Given the cost of childcare, some women opt to allow older children to stay alone at home after school. Most single mothers have no other option but to pay for this service.

What the numbers in our table below do not show is the true expense gap between two-parent families and single parents. In two-parent families, 46 percent spent less than 5 percent of their income on childcare, while 27 percent of single mothers spent more than 20 percent of their income on childcare.[36] The choice of a childcare facility is not only driven by cost but by quality of care. Quality care is expensive. A two-parent family is better able to bear a higher monthly cost than a single parent family. We can see that difference in this chart.[37]

	Two-parent families	Single parents
Percentage paying childcare	47%	52%
Cost per month	$297	$258
Percent of monthly earnings	7%	16%

Transportation

According to the U.S. Census about half of female householders with children live in urban areas and the other half live in the suburbs.[38] We would assume that there would be a 50/50 split with women in suburbs driving automobiles and women in urban settings using public transportation. That statement presupposes that there is adequate public transportation in all urban areas, which is simply not true. Many cities are sprawled, meaning that public transportation simply cannot adequately service an entire metropolitan area.[39] Therefore, an automobile can become a necessity for transportation.

Clearly, public transportation is less expensive than car ownership. Not surprisingly, the need for an automobile places a heavy burden on the single parent. The national averages for transportation costs as a percent of income are the following:

Income	$12,000 or less	$23,000	$38,000
Percentage for transportation[40]	36%	27%	19%

It is true that automobile expenses account for 98 percent of all transportation costs with public transportation costs at 2 percent.[41] Given the financial condition of most single parents, these women normally choose to drive a used car rather than a new one. So not only are they faced with a significant portion of their income being eaten up by a monthly automobile payment, they are also faced with high, fluctuating maintenance costs. For example in 2001, the average cost of owning, operating, and maintaining a 1996 model in southern California with 15,000 miles per year is $4,126 per year, or $343.83 per month; which includes, gasoline, oil, maintenance, tires, insurance, financing, depreciation, license, registration, and taxes.[42] But as of 2005, that average has increased significantly with the yearly cost around $6541 or about $545 per month not including gasoline.[43]

Health Insurance

Most Americans assume health insurance and adequate health care are available for everyone. Unfortunately, that assumption is not correct. Again the numbers do not lie. As of 2000, across the U.S. approximately 14 percent of the population did not have health insurance. Here is the statistic that hits home for single parents. Of the families making below $50,000, 39 percent do not have any medical coverage. There are 14 million children who have no health insurance.[44] But we assume everyone who needs health insurance can obtain it through the government i.e. Medicaid. Not true. Of the individuals who meet the government definition of poor, 30 percent have no health insurance. Among those individuals who are classified as near poor, 27 percent have no health insurance.[45] If you chose to obtain health insurance in the private sector, you could pay month premiums as high as $757 for your family.[46]

The reality is if you are poor and do not have health insurance, you will wait till the last possible moment to seek medical care. You probably will not go to the doctor, dentist or optometrist unless absolutely necessary. Why? You simply cannot afford the cost of medical care.

What Does It All Mean to You?

We have covered a lot of statistics and numbers, and it may have been overwhelming to you. If you are like me, it is difficult to read the numbers and know that you are one of those numbers. So what does all this information mean to you? What do all these dark colored stones mean to a single parent? Well let's put the pieces together and begin to look at this part of the Whole Truth Picture. In fact, I am going to create several pictures. I am going to take all these numbers and statistics, these Cold Hard Facts, and create several mosaics that reflect some truth about the external world of single parents. You decide which one relates to you.

Picture #1

First, we know that 40 percent of single parents fall below the poverty level. So let's look at the Cold Hard Fact picture for a poor single parent with two children. We will assume that she is among the working poor and receives no child support. She has an income $13,874 per year including wages, food stamps, and cash assistance. She is renting housing and may have one of the following problems: no hot water, no electricity, no phone, or limited bathroom facilities. She has no car. Since she lives in the city, she and her children use public transportation where available. Since 34 percent of these women pay close to 23 percent of their income for child-care, we assume she is one of those women. She has no health insurance. Finally, let's assume sometimes her children experience food insecurity.

Picture 1		
	Monthly Expenses	**Monthly Net Income** (annual income–$13,874)
Income		$1,000 including food stamps
Housing	$ 200 (subsidized)	
Food	642	
Transportation	100	
Childcare	200	
Health insurance		
Total	$1,142	$1,000
Variance		$ (142)

This woman is in the red every month a total of $142. This number is conservative because we have not included any costs for doctors, dentists, clothes, school supplies, or utilities.

Picture #2

Let's look at another single parent with three children. We know that approximately another 20 percent of single parents may live above the poverty level, but they make less than $25,000 per year. We will assume that she works full time and receives $2,400 annually in child support for her three children. She does not qualify for food stamps or cash assistance. She is renting a two-bedroom apartment in the suburbs and drives an older model car. Her company provides health insurance, but she has not been able to afford the premium. While she would not admit it, her children have experienced some food insecurity.

Picture 2		
	Monthly Expenses	**Monthly Net Income (annual income–$26,400)**
Income		$1,760
Housing	$ 600	
Food	642	
Transportation	343	
Childcare	258	
Health insurance		
Total	$1,843	$1,760
Variance		$ (83)

She also is in the red every month a total of $83. Again, this number is conservative because we have not included any costs for doctors, dentists, clothes, school supplies, or utilities.

Picture #3

Our next single parent is among the 25 percent of women who make between $25,000 and $40,000. We will assume she is on the high-end of this range. She works but does not receive child support. She has three children. She owns a home and drives an older car. Her company provides health insurance, and she contributes $200 per month to the plan.

Picture 3		
	Monthly Expenses	Monthly Net Income (annual income–$39,000)
Income		$2,438
Housing	$ 800	
Food	642	
Transportation	343	
Childcare	258	
Health insurance	200	
Total	$2,243	$2,438
Variance		$ 195

After paying these monthly expenses, she has $195 left. Again, we did not include clothes, school supplies, or utilities.

Picture #4

Our final single parent is among the lucky 15 percent of women who make more than $40,000 but less than $55,000 per year. That's right, she does not make more than $55,000. We will assume she works, receives child support, and her annual income is $50,000. She owns a home and drives a newer car. Her company provides health insurance.

Picture 4		
	Monthly Expenses	Monthly net Income (annual income–$50,000)
Income		$3,125
Housing	$1,000	
Food	642	
Transportation	450	
Childcare	258	
Health insurance		
Total	$2,350	$3,125
Variance		$ 775

She is fortunate; she has a positive income of $775, which could cover any clothes, school supplies or utilities.

According to the scenarios above, most single parents, or approximately 85 percent are living on the edge financially. Their external world is hard and very different from the lifestyle of a two-parent family. About 55 percent of married couples with children make $55,000 plus annually. In fact 67 percent of married couples with children make over $40,000 annually.

As we step back and look at these pictures, I want you to see in black and white that you are not alone. You may not fit exactly into one of these pictures, but you can relate to life on the edge financially. There are many other women in the same position as you.

I used to drive myself crazy trying to stretch money to cover all my bills. To make matters worse, people would tell me I just needed to budget my money more effectively. Good advice, but my problem was not budgeting. My problem was that I did not have enough money for my bills. You are not alone. You are just facing the Cold Hard Facts of your external world. It is not personal.

It is easy for me to say that the Cold Hard Facts are not personal. It is not so easy for you to understand and accept these truths about your external world. You may think accepting these truths is not going to help you maneuver the financial boulders in your path. But the only way to deal with this part of the road is to accept the truth that your external world is not personal and it is made up of the Cold Hard Facts. Only when we face these truths will we come to understand and accept the final dark truth. Yes, there is a truth that is hidden in the dark and it needs to be exposed.

Real Fear

Now that we have shown a light onto all the dark colored stones and boulders of your external world, are you frightened? Do you look at the truth in black and white about minimum income and maximum expenses and become fearful? Or better yet, are you terrified? If you answered yes, that is the right answer. It is the right answer because fear and terror is understandable and it is real. Do not listen to anyone who tries to tell you differently.

Think about it this way, if you are stuck in your car on the railroad tracks and a train is coming, you experience a *real* fear of being hit by that train. There is danger in your external world. That fear is good because it makes you get out of the car. This same example holds true for the Cold Hard Facts. If your electric bill is past due and your electricity is going to be shut off today, you have a Real

Fear in your external world. That fear is good because it will make you take action. We just need to learn to take the appropriate action.

The Cold Hard Facts create Real Fear. In fact, some Cold Hard Facts are not stones or even boulders on the road. They are terrifying landmines. Don't you think that you should be terrified of a landmine? Of course, you should. Daily, you face the dark stones, boulders, and landmines on your single parent journey. In fact, one of the key reasons why it is so difficult and painful for us to look at the truth of our external world is the Real Fear. The fear is normal.

But trust me, there is hope to deal with this Real Fear. I will help you learn how to deal with this fear so you can take appropriate action. At this point on our journey, cling to the hope that you are not alone.

The Truth about Our External World

We now know the truth about this part of our road. We have one cluster of stones that make up our external world. It is made up of three truths: 1.) It is not personal, 2.) The Cold Hard Facts of minimum income and maximum expenses and 3.) the Real Fear.

The majority of single parents have incomes from jobs or child support or government assistance that barely cover housing, food, childcare, transportation and healthcare expenses. These Cold Hard Facts can be stones, boulders or landmines scattered in front of us. We know that this section of the road creates Real Fear.

Choose to accept the truth about your external world and cling to the hope that you are not alone.

CHEAT SHEET

The Truth about Our External World

The Hope

1.   You are not alone.

The Truth

1.   It is not personal.

2.   The Cold Hard Facts represent minimum income and maximum expenses.

3.   The Real Fear represents real danger.

The Hope

1.   You are not alone.

3

The Self-truth about Our Internal World

The Cold Hard Facts of our external world clearly demonstrate that none of us are alone on the single parent journey. Numbers do not lie. You can see the facts in black and white. Unfortunately, the self-truth of our internal world is not always visible to the naked eye. The self-truth of our single parent existence can be just as devastating to us as the Cold Hard Facts. We live with it everyday and it is very hard to ignore. Therefore, if you are like me, you have tried to bury any truth about your internal world in the road, and chances are you have failed in this effort. Just like our external world, we need to face the truth about our internal world.

For that reason, we need to understand and accept three more truths, self-truths, about our lives as single parents in order to see the Whole Truth Picture. Though these internal truths may not be visible now, they are part of the condition of our road. These truths are part of the mosaic of the Whole Truth Picture. And just like the truth about your external world, you will discover the hope that you are not alone. When we expose the internal world of a single parent, we will see that we all face the same three truths.

The Truth

The Painful Wound

When I separated and divorced my husband, I believed I would just move on to a new life. When he was physically gone, I thought I was free of the relationship. My marriage was over, but I could not seem to move on to that new life. I may have had a divorce decree that said I was legally free, but I did not feel free.

I did not understand the self-truth that kept me trapped in my old life, unable to move forward. I did not understand that when I left my husband, I not only got a divorce, I killed a relationship. That self-truth does not mean I should have stayed in the marriage. It means I did not fully understand the consequences of divorce.

Divorce represents the death of a relationship. My divorce decree and for that matter my marriage certificate, were only external symbols of my internal world. They were symbols of a relationship. I had a relationship with my husband that existed in my internal world, not my external world. And when I divorced my husband that relationship died.

That death left behind two wounded people. Yes, I was wounded and I did not know it. My wound was not visible. I was not bleeding on the outside. But I was in excruciating pain on the inside, and no physical examination could determine the source of my pain. Unfortunately, I had a wound that could not be treated by conventional medicine. You see my husband and I were intertwined in our relationship. When we divorced, we were no longer the original people who had married years ago. I was part of him and he was part of me. Our separation was not a clean cut: it ripped, tore, and shredded each of us. The self-truth was the death of that relationship inflicted a severe wound on me, and I was hemorrhaging at the core of my soul.

But know this, the wound had nothing to do with a marriage certificate or a divorce decree. It had everything to do with the death of a relationship. Please understand this truth: *whether you are a single parent through separation, divorce, or an unplanned pregnancy, you will have a wound from the death of that relationship.* This will cause a wound for a couple married for twenty years or two weeks. If you have been intertwined with your partner and separate, your relationship will die, and the internal shredding of that relationship will result in two severely wounded people.

For too many years, we, as single parents, in this country have put ourselves in silos of separated, divorced, and unwed mothers. We have looked at the outward labels and have failed to see the universal self-truth. We all have a painful wound from the death of the relationship with our partner. I may have twisted your brain at this point. I understand. It took me many years to see the self-truth about our common painful wound. The truth is this wound occurs whether we are separated, divorced, or unwed.

Yes, it took me many years to understand and accept the self-truth that I had a painful wound from the death of my relationship. Even when I did not understand this self-truth, I could not deny the internal pain. I kept looking at that divorce decree, telling myself that the marriage was over. I kept looking at that outward label "divorced woman" and tried to bury the pain. But the pain could not be buried. The pain would emerge at the most inconvenient times. The problem was I did not understand my internal condition.

Here is what I have learned about this internal wound. Think about it this way. Assume your partner and you are in a car driving at high speeds on a narrow mountain road. The car spins out of control and rolls down a ravine. Your partner is killed and you are severely injured. How would you handle that situation? Well, after you were rescued, you would probably spend some time in the intensive care unit of your local hospital. Someone would take care of your children during your stay and assist you after your release from the hospital. It would take time for you to heal physically. At the same time, you would be grieving the loss of your partner or the death of your relationship.

Now assume you do not understand and accept the truth about the severity of your wounds or the death of your relationship. You acknowledge that something happened, but you ignore the impact of the event. You resume your life, assuming nothing has changed, and sometimes you wonder why you are in so much pain.

No woman in her right mind would ignore this situation and pretend like nothing happened. Yet that is exactly what many of us do. Our relationship is dead and we are wounded. However, we do not see the truth about our internal condition. We stumble around in the dark in pain and try to bury the pain, hoping that eventually it will go away.

Most of us do not ignore the wound from the death of our relationships on purpose. When I got divorced, no one told me my relationship died and I was wounded. Everyone around me was so busy giving me legal advice, paper work for government assistance, and providing options for housing, childcare, and jobs that they did not think about my internal condition. My external world became more important than anything in my internal world. I did not understand I had a wound. Sure, I was sad and depressed, but I was just emotional. True, but those emotions were the symptoms of my severe wound.

If you are a single parent, you know I speak truth. You have experienced the pain from your wound. You may have had difficulty describing the pain to others and may have been unable to find the source of the pain. You may have even been told by well-meaning friends and family to just move on with your life, the pain will go away in time. It won't; you have a painful wound. You are not just depressed or emotional. You have a severe wound and it will not heal with time.

In order for me to become the mother in a Half Family and journey to wholeness, I had to face this self-truth and accept that I had a painful wound from the death of my relationship. I had to stop trying to bury the pain. I had to cling to the hope that I was not alone. Other women must have experienced this same situation. Only when I came to a level of acceptance did I begin to see the next truth. In fact, I began to see how the next truth had been stalking me on this dark road.

Our Vulnerability to Nightmare Fear

Our painful wound makes us vulnerable to Nightmare Fear. To explain this truth, let's go back to the car wreck example. If you are wounded from the accident, you could be vulnerable to many situations. If you are left alone and wounded on a mountainside, you could "be vulnerable" to an attack by wildlife. If your leg is broken and you try to walk, you could "be vulnerable" to further injury. Without treatment and medication for a severe open wound, you might "be vulnerable" to an infection or pneumonia. Your wound will make you vulnerable to further injury. Normally, a severely injured person is rushed to the hospital and intensive care, which can eliminate much of that vulnerability.

Unfortunately, unlike our car wreck, we, as single parents, do not spend time in intensive care, no one watches our children and we have no time to grieve. Why? There is no transition time between the "car wreck" of separation, the death of our relationship, and the beginning of a single parent journey. We do not get the luxury of a fully-equipped intensive care unit to treat our wound. When your husband moves out of the house, you become a single parent. When you leave the hospital with that baby from an unplanned pregnancy, you become a single parent. We are thrust onto this dark road with no roadmap or destination and we are wounded. Therefore, we are extremely vulnerable. That is the truth. Every single parent begins her journey down this strange new road severely wounded and vulnerable.

We are vulnerable to further injury. Even after you understand and accept the truth about your painful wound, you will be vulnerable in many areas. But there is a vulnerability that poses the biggest threat. It is Nightmare Fear. This fear can take many forms. We can be afraid of the dark, afraid of driving a car, or afraid of leaving our house. But the one overwhelming fear of all single parents is the fear of the future fueled by the painful wound from our past. I call it: Nightmare Fear. Here is what I mean.

In our wounded state from the death of our relationship, we are vulnerable to Nightmare Fear. The throbbing pain from our wound can make any kind of movement on the single parent road seem impossible. In fact, we may look at our lives as single parents and tell ourselves "it is impossible" or "I can't do this." At times, we may not be able to control our emotions; we may cry daily or have fits of rage. We know that something is seriously wrong with us, but we cannot seem to locate the source of the problem, the source of our pain. If we cannot control our emotions, how can we possibly function in the world? We begin to doubt our ability to accomplish even simple tasks. How can we work or cook or clean or raise children? Then we begin to doubt our ability to find solutions to the big problems that we face on this dark road. We begin to doubt our ability to survive as a single parent.

This doubt seizes us and causes our perception of the situation to narrow. We can see nothing beyond our excruciating internal pain and our brutal existence as a single parent. Behind us the past is littered with the wreckage of our relationship, and before us the future looks bleak and ominous. And our present is not safe either. We begin to tell ourselves that we will never survive this journey. Our doubt has now turned into fear. We are trapped. We cannot retreat to the past, and we cannot go forward towards the future, and we cannot live in the present. We are wounded on an unfamiliar dark road with an unknown destination. We feel unable to protect ourselves. How will we protect our children? We begin to panic. We begin to see our lives as a living nightmare. We have just given birth to Nightmare Fear.

Nightmare Fear is a reality for every single parent because every woman enters single parenthood with a severe wound. Be honest with yourself, have you not had moments when you said to yourself, "I can't do this," "I can't go on," "It is impossible," and "I will not survive"? Of course, you have said similar things to yourself. Have you not focused so much on your painful past that you convinced yourself that the future will be exactly like your past? Are you filled with so much pain from the past and fear of the future that you have no idea what is happening today? If you can say yes to any of those questions, you are experiencing Nightmare Fear.

Okay so now you know that you have experienced Nightmare Fear that was born out of your painful wound. We know the truth that all single parents have this fear. We may now see this stone on our road, but we need to turn it over, examine it. Nightmare Fear is an extremely dangerous place to be on the single parent road. It causes us to narrow our focus. It causes us to stand so close to our painful wound that we cannot see the truth about our fear.

If we live in Nightmare Fear, we will not be able to separate it from Real Fear. If we are in panic convinced we will not survive, how effective will we be at maneuvering the Real Fear in the road? If you are convinced you are trapped, will you be able to take appropriate action when faced with the Cold Hard Facts? We have enough Real Fear from our external world without adding Nightmare Fear from our internal world to the journey.

There is a huge difference between Real Fear and Nightmare Fear. If there is no food in the house, the rent is due, or the electricity is going to be shut off, we are experiencing Real Fear. The Cold Hard Facts create Real Fear of the present situation in our external world. The Real Fear exists at one moment in time. Again, it exists in the present. It is good fear because it can motivate us to take action.

But Nightmare Fear is born out of our painful wound in our internal world. We feel and focus on the pain from our past, which causes us to see only a painful future. I would compare Nightmare Fear to something I was once told early in my own single parent journey: I was living in the future and dragging the past behind me. Do you do that? When we look at our present situation through the eyes of Nightmare Fear, we see only a bleak, dark future like a monster waiting to devour us. There is a big difference between Real Fear and Nightmare Fear. We may not have much control over our external world but we can gain control over our internal world.

Again, Real Fear lives in our external world in the present. Real Fear can motivate us to move. Nightmare Fear lives in our internal world, projecting the pain of the past into the future. Nightmare Fear can trap us.

I am some twenty-five years away from my wound, and I can still remember my Nightmare Fears. Those fears were very real to me. They kept me trapped and did not motivate me to take action. I understand the struggle to understand and accept the truth about Nightmare Fear.

When your child is afraid of the monsters in the dark closet and you turn on the light and open the door, what happens? Your child sees there are no monsters in the closet. Nightmare Fear is like a monster in the closet of our internal world and it does not like the light. Our fears can seem like huge monsters in the dark. In the light, our Nightmare Fears are not monsters and can become manageable. I am not saying these fears will go away immediately. The truth is Nightmare Fear will only go away when the painful wound heals. But if you choose to understand and accept you are vulnerability because you have a painful wound from the death of your relationship, the fear will become more manageable. It will not be a monster in the dark. You will begin to see the difference between Real Fear and Nightmare Fear. Trust me Nightmare Fear will shrink in the light of truth.

I know it is hard to manage Nightmare Fear as a new, raw single parent, but I am here to tell you it is not impossible. You can do this; there are solutions and you will survive. If I made it down this road, you can make it. The first step on this journey is to turn on the light of truth and let it shine on your Nightmare Fears. Only then will you begin to discover the third self-truth about your internal world.

The Lack of Margins

This final self-truth about our internal world may be a brain-twister for you. It certainly twisted my brain. It took me years to see this truth and even longer to verbalize it. I fell over these stones many times on my own dark road because I did not see the truth. This final self-truth is we, as single parents, lack margins.

Let me define a margin. *A margin is an extra amount beyond what is necessary.* Do you see where I am heading? Think about it. Your ex-partner was an extra margin of money, an extra margin of time, or just an extra body, like a babysitter. (As a side note, those of you who are struggling to think or say kind words about your now ex-partner, just think of him as an extra margin.) Do you ever say to yourself, "If I just had a little extra money, I could get caught up on my bills?" Or "If I could afford a babysitter, I would have some time for me," or "I could go to the movies with a friend"? Of course you have had those or similar thoughts.

The truth is you have lost margins because your partner is gone. The Cold Hard Facts of your external world show you have lost an extra amount beyond what is necessary to financially support yourself. You have lost that extra time for yourself.

Those margins are obvious. We can see them in our external world. And these margin losses may vary from woman to woman. We all have different relationships, financial situations, and available time for friends and ourselves. But there are some internal margins that are not obvious. These margins, or lack of, are common to all single parents. And these internal margins are much more important than any external margin. The truth is our painful wound and our vulnerability to Nightmare Fear have drained us emotionally, physically, and mentally.

We have lost emotional, physical, and mental margins in our internal worlds. Ever feel like you need extra space from fear, extra space from worry, extra energy, extra time to sleep, or extra brainpower. Your emotions may be so raw you have "nothing extra" inside to help you control your mouth so that you do not constantly yell at your child or children. You may be so full of fear you feel like you lack the physical energy to get out of bed in the morning. You may be so drained mentally you lack the extra brainpower to make sound decisions about simple things. If you can relate to these situations, you have lost some internal margins. We have all lost emotional, physical, and mental margins. Our painful wound and our vulnerability to Nightmare Fear have drained us of anything extra in our internal world.

You may not have thought about your journey as a single parent in terms of margins, but these internal margins are more important to us than anything in our external world. Remember, a margin is an extra amount beyond what is necessary. Actually, some of us would settle for just having "the necessary amount." And anything extra would be a blessing. So think about your condition; you are wounded and scared and facing a frightening external world. Doesn't an extra amount of anything sound great?

These internal margins may be starting to make some sense to you. In fact, you probably have felt the lack of emotional, physical, and mental margins. You may have even verbalized it. Even if we do see the truth, we simply classify our lack of internal margins as a low priority. Single parents do not think about themselves. We think about our children. We think about our ex-partner. We think about the Cold Hard Facts. We think about everything except us, and we get it backwards. We focus our emotional, physical, and mental energy, or lack thereof, on everything but us. And here lies the truth about our lack of margins.

Let me ask you an important question? What is the most valuable asset you possess as a single parent? What will you take with you on every step of this journey? It is not your money or even your children. The answer is you. If you are the most important asset on this journey and you are drained emotionally, physically, and mentally, you may have a problem traveling this road or reaching the destination. The truth is all single parents lack internal margins. Until we understand this, we will stumble around in the dark.

You may still be struggling with the idea you are the most important asset on this journey. It may be a strange and selfish idea to you. As a single parent, you are hopelessly focused on your external world. I understand because I have been there.

But here is some hope: the mother in the Half Family understands and accepts the self-truth about her internal world. She knows she is the most important asset on the journey. And that acceptance gives her access to new internal margins. Yes, a single parent may lack emotional, physical, and mental margins, but the mother in the Half Family has something extra needed to make it to her destination.

The Self-truth about Our Internal World

The self-truth about our internal world is that every single parent is severely wounded from the death of a relationship. We all have a painful wound. Our wound is not visible, but we are in pain. Unfortunately, we try to bury the pain. So our unattended wound makes us vulnerable to Nightmare Fear.

We look at the pain from our past and project our past situations into the future. We live in the future, dragging the past behind us. We feel trapped, hopeless, and afraid that there are no solutions to our problems. We give birth to dangerous Nightmare Fear. We do not see the difference between Real Fear and Nightmare Fear. Real Fear lives in our external world. The Cold Hard Facts can cause Real Fear in the present. This fear can motivate us to take appropriate action. But Nightmare Fear exists in our internal world. It may feel real, but it does not exist in the present external world. It is a nightmare that causes us to project the painful past into the future and makes us miss the present. It causes us to feel trapped and does not motivate us to take appropriate action.

Finally, we lack margins, that little extra beyond what is necessary. Our painful wound and our vulnerability to Nightmare Fear can drain us of anything extra emotionally, physically, and mentally. Unfortunately, on the dark single parent road, we either do not see this truth or we dismiss it as unimportant. We tend to focus on everything else but our most important asset for the journey. The truth is we, as single parents, are the most important asset.

For many of you reading this book right now, I have hit on some raw emotions with the self-truth about your internal world. You may want to stop reading because it is just too painful. I truly understand. For years, I could not face the self-truth about this single parent journey. I did not understand the truth about the pain from my wound, so I cried almost constantly. I did not understand the truth about my vulnerability to Nightmare Fear, so I reacted to my inner turmoil. I did not fully grasp my missing margins and became depressed about my lack of emotional control, physical energy, and mental lapses. In many respects, it was almost easier to look at my external world rather than face the self-truth of my internal world. Take courage and keep reading. Trust me you can choose to accept the truth now or fall over it later in the dark. These truths will not go away. They will surface at some point on your journey, and you will have to face the self-truth about your internal world.

I know I am painting a gruesome Whole Truth Picture. We have the Real Fear from the non-personal Cold Hard Facts in our external world. In our internal world, we have the truth about our painful wound, our vulnerability to

Nightmare Fear, and our lack of internal margins. I know that the picture so far is difficult to look at, but it is the truth. It is hard to see the truth in black and white and shine a light on the condition of your road.

So lean on the hope you are not alone…and that there is a Hope Roadmap. Yes, there is hope to deal with the truth about your external and internal worlds, and that hope is only one more chapter, one more step away. We are very close to the Hope Roadmap.

CHEAT SHEET

The Self-truth about Our Internal World

The Hope

1.   You are not alone.

The Self-truth

1.   Our painful wound

2.   Our vulnerability to Nightmare Fear

3.   Our lack of emotional, physical, and mental margins

The Hope

1.   You are not alone.

4

The Whole Truth Picture

The truth about the external world and the self-truth about the internal world of a single parent may not have been a surprise to you. The reality is you walk over and around these dark colored stones daily on your journey. I simply put words to the truth. I invited you to closely examine these truths and then step back and look at each cluster of stones in the light. So now you have a better understanding about the condition of this part of your road. But the truth about your external and internal world still does not represent the condition of the entire road, the Whole Truth Picture. We need to clearly see where these stones will lead us.

As a single parent, you may not have a roadmap or a destination, but you are walking in the dark in some direction. The non-personal Cold Hard Facts, the Real Fear, the painful wound, the vulnerability to Nightmare Fear, and the lack of margins will lead you somewhere. Unfortunately, without a Hope Roadmap and a clear destination, these truths, these dark stones, will lead to only one place, danger. And chances are good you do not see the danger on the road. I certainly did not see the danger on my own dark road until I stumbled over it. That danger is found in the last two truths about the condition of the single parent road. This dangerous cluster of stones completes the Whole Truth Picture. I call these truths Crisis Management and the Chasm.

Think about these truths this way. If you are burdened, wounded, and confused on a dark road, you are facing a crisis. You are not sure where to step, you do your best to manage the crisis in front of you. But you have limited vision and do not see a large gapping hole in the road, the Chasm only a few steps away. In the dark, you are in danger of panicking from this crisis and falling into a Chasm. The danger of a single parent road is that both our external and internal worlds can push us or throw us into Crisis Management and to the edge of the Chasm. You live with this danger on a daily basis. So let's shine our final light of truth and expose the condition of our road.

The Truth

Crisis Management

We, as single parents, tend to live in Crisis Management. If you disagree, let me describe it in more detail. Crisis Management is taught in every MBA (Master in Business Administration) program at every graduate school in this country. Each school may call it something different, but the content of the course is the same. Simply put, Crisis Management is a method for handling an unexpected critical situation or problem that requires immediate attention and a solution. Any business manager worth his or her salt knows how to effectively manage a crisis by gathering all the facts, clearly identifying the problem or crisis, carefully looking at the options to resolve the crisis, determining a logical recommendation, and making a clear-headed decision on the proper course of action.

But Crisis Management should be the exception, not the rule. If the executives of a company had to deal with daily Crisis Management, the company would not survive. If an executive, no matter how competent, had to daily manage a crisis by gathering all the facts, clearly identifying the problem or crisis, carefully looking at the options to resolve it, determining a logical recommendation, and making a clear-headed decision, he or she would not manage anything. Eventually, the stress and pressure would wear him or her down, and Crisis Management would evolve into crisis reaction. This executive would be spending all of his or her time reacting to a crisis instead of managing and growing the business.

We, as single parents, spend too many days dealing with crisis. We live in Crisis Management. Daily Crisis Management is a dangerous place to be. Now you may not think that you live this way. I did not think that I lived in Crisis Management mode until I really looked at my life.

Remember, a crisis is an unexpected situation. Have you ever had a situation where you received an unexpected bill that must be paid immediately like a car repair bill, or a doctor's bill? Ever been in that situation and have no cash or no room on your credit card to pay this expense? Guess what? You are in crisis.

Look again at the explanation of Crisis Management. It calls for a methodical, logical process to reach a clear-headed decision that solves the critical situation or problem. Are you equipped to manage this crisis? Or are you in danger of panicking and reacting to the crisis? If you are feeling your painful wound, will your emotions get in the way of a logical process to find a solution? If you are vulnerable to Nightmare Fear, will your fear of the future keep you from making a clear-headed decision? If you are drained emotionally, physically, and mentally, will you manage the crisis or react? In your present condition as a single parent, are you equipped for Crisis Management? No, you are not.

But here is the real danger for single parents. The example of an unexpected bill is almost an everyday occurrence for us. I truly believe that we, as single parents, have lived in Crisis Management for so long, we think this lifestyle is normal. It isn't. Crisis Management should be the exception, not the rule. If we are not equipped to handle an unexpected crisis, how can we expect to manage crisis on a daily basis? We can't. If trained professionals cannot daily manage a business in crisis, how can we who are wounded and fearful manage crisis daily on the single parent road? We can't. If we live in Crisis Management on a daily basis, we will manage nothing. We will react. No one can maintain the stamina to effectively manage a crisis day in and day out. The process will break down, and you will react to rather than manage the situation.

We are on a dark road in danger of crisis reaction rather than Crisis Management. Do you ever feel like you react to everything? Do you panic every time the phone rings thinking it's a creditor? Are you anxious just walking to the mailbox? Are you so tired and stressed you have a short temper with everyone in your life? No one can live with daily Crisis Management without eventually slipping into crisis reaction. If you are frustrated with your reaction, give yourself a break. If you react to a crisis rather than manage it, don't beat yourself up. Absolutely no one can handle daily Crisis Management without reacting. The fact that you can still make it through a crisis and raise a child or children is amazing. You are to be congratulated, not condemned. In fact, I think that the most courageous people in this country are single women raising children alone.

Even if you never thought of your life as Crisis Management, you now know it is true. Even if you never thought about crisis reaction, you now know the truth. You have felt the painful wound and experienced the vulnerability to Nightmare Fear that has confused your thought process in the middle of a crisis. You have been emotionally, physically, and mentally exhausted to the point that any decision is impossible. You understand crisis reaction rather than Crisis Management because you have lived it. Now you have a name for it. It is out in the light of day.

When we react instead of manage a crisis, it can push us and/or throws us into an extremely dangerous position on the dark single parent road. This last truth represents the most dangerous place for a single parent.

The Chasm

The Chasm is the last place you want to be on a dark road. We have all faced a great Chasm at one time or another on our journey. It is not just an obstacle in our way; it is a massive gaping hole in the middle of the road. This Chasm stretches out in front of us with no visible way around it. Standing on the edge of a vast, gaping hole is not some place any of us would choose to stand. On the edge of this Chasm, we feel trapped. We cannot go back or move forward, but we cannot remain on the edge. All single parents have faced this Chasm at some point on the journey.

There are many circumstances that can either push or throw us to the edge of this dark, ominous hole. The Cold Hard Facts can push us into daily Crisis Management. This day in and day out struggle to survive financially can push us to the edge of the Chasm. We can step on one or more unexpected Cold Hard Facts, landmines, which can throw us to the edge of the Chasm. And we are staring into the darkness with no visible way to cross this Chasm.

Our painful wound from the death of our relationship, the vulnerability to Nightmare Fear and the lack of margins can push us into Crisis Management. Our wound throbs as we think about the past and our Nightmare Fear of the future seems all too real. We feel trapped. We look down at the road and the Chasm opens up before us as a vast expanse of darkness. We stand staring at a situation or problem that has no solution, only a black hole.

In crisis, on the edge of the Chasm, we desperately search for a way across to the other side. We need to find a solution to that unexpected bill or loss of income. We need to get relieve from the pain and the fear. We need to find something extra, somewhere. We can't go back and we can't go forward. We are trapped in crisis, standing on the edge of the Chasm, staring down into the darkness with no way across to the other side. Ever face this situation? Ever feel like you are at the end of the road? Of course, you have. I have. What do you do?

I can tell you what I used to do as a single parent. I would stare into the Chasm looking for a solution to the problem that is causing a crisis in my life, but I never found a solution staring into the black hole. In fact, the longer I stared into the darkness of the Chasm, the deeper, wider, and more threatening it was to me. Logic and/or clear-headed thinking left me at that moment. I thought there was no solution. I was in crisis reaction mode. I was trapped. And once I embraced that trapped feeling, my emotions took over my thought process. My painful wound, my vulnerability to Nightmare Fear, or my lack of margins controlled me. I would begin to panic and my next thought would be, "If there is no viable solution, I need to find an escape route."

For a single parent in the middle of crisis reaction, escape is the real danger of standing on the edge of the Chasm. When you can no longer handle the pain and fear from your internal and external worlds, you will look for escape. Who in her right mind would not want to escape this situation? But escape is not a solution. Here is what happens if you focus on escape.

The desire for escape grows the longer you stay in crisis reaction and stand on the edge of the Chasm looking down. The longer you stare down into that vast darkness, the greater the danger you will jump into the Chasm. No way! It is true. You will begin to see the Chasm as an escape route. If we do not see a way to the other side, we will choose an escape jump into the Chasm. I know it does not make sense. I know we think we would never choose to escape by jumping into a black hole. Yet many of us do exactly that; we jump into our own personal Chasms.

At some point in the middle of Crisis Management, crisis reaction takes over and we begin to see the Chasm as an escape. That's right; if you stand too close to your Chasm, you will think "jumping in" is the only option, an "escape," from the crisis. You will think, "Clearly, there are no other solutions to my problems." "I cannot go any further. I have no other choice. Maybe, I am supposed to jump." It makes no sense that we would do such a destructive act. Sadly, if you are facing the brutal Whole Truth without a Hope Roadmap, you are vulnerable to an escape "jump" into the Chasm. Again, it is not a solution. It is an escape.

Still not convinced? Isn't it true we have all been tempted at times to jump into the Chasm of alcohol, drugs, promiscuity, an unwanted pregnancy, a marriage too soon after divorce, or overeating? If you are wounded, frightened, and facing a dark, brutal existence, have you not had the desire to escape into alcohol, drugs, food, or men? I have had that desire, and I have chosen to give in to the escape route. I have jumped into my own personal Chasm. And I am not alone. Many single parents have chosen to "escape" a brutal existence by jumping into the Chasm. We try to escape into something that will relieve the pain and fear.

But these escapes are not solutions. These escapes may feel "good" as we are free-falling off the edge into the Chasm. Alcohol, drugs, a man, and food will all give us some temporary relieve from the pain and fear. But we will hit the bottom eventually and will have to climb out of the Chasm. We will end up in rehab for the alcohol and/or drugs. We will end up raising another child or facing another divorce. We will end dealing health problems due to our weight. The Chasm is not a solution. Jumping into the Chasm is an escape with severe consequences.

The ultimate "escape jump" off the edge of the Chasm is suicide. Single parents can plunge to their death because they have no hope. The truth of their external and/or internal world is too much. They are on a dark road with no hope and no clear destination. The Chasm becomes an escape, they jump off the edge. I can understand this decision. I have been there. I have thought about that escape. When the pain from my external world and my internal world were so intense, I began to think death was my only way out. Obviously, I did not jump. I did not jump because I found hope. (I will share my experience with this ultimate "escape" jump later in our journey.) What I want you to understand and accept now is when we have no hope, we will choose escape. A mother in a Half Family has hope. When you are in crisis, standing on the edge of the Chasm, hope makes all the difference in the world.

We now have the last pieces of truth about the condition of single parent road. We know the truth about our external and internal worlds can lead us into danger. We can be pushed or thrown into Crisis Management and the edge of the Chasm. In our condition as single parents, we can easily slip from Crisis Management into crisis reaction. Standing on the edge of the Chasm, we can react and see an "escape jump" as a solution.

The Whole Truth Picture

The Whole Truth Picture reveals an extremely dangerous road for any single parent. We must maneuver a road filled with the truth about our external and internal worlds. There is the truth about the non-personal Cold Hard Facts that generate Real Fear in our external environment. We faced the self-truth about our painful wound that leaves us vulnerable to Nightmare Fear. And we faced our lack of margins. We know that anyone of these truths can either push us or throw us into Crisis Management and the edge of the Chasm. Unfortunately, all too often Crisis Management becomes a way of life for the single parent. Clearly, we cannot stay in Crisis Management mode on a daily basis. We will loose our ability to manage the situation with a methodical, logical process that leads to a clear-headed solution. We will react to the crisis and feel trapped on the edge of the Chasm. In that reactive condition, we will be in danger of jumping into the Chasm. We will choose an escape rather than a solution.

If you are a single parent, you are on this road. You have experienced all of these truths in the dark with no roadmap and no destination. Some women are among the fortunate few who do not daily face the Cold Hard Facts, but the painful wound and vulnerability to Nightmare Fear can still push them into crisis and the edge of the Chasm. For other women, poverty is a lonely, harsh road that results in daily Crisis Management and life on the edge of the Chasm. Every single parent will get pushed to the edge of the Chasm and be in danger of an "escape" jump. But no matter where you are on this dark single parent road, you have a choice right now. You can choose to accept the true condition of the road. I know that this picture is depressing but your courage will be rewarded.

If you choose to accept the Whole Truth Picture about the condition of the single parent road, you can have access to the Hope Roadmap. It is an amazing map that shows you how to maneuver this road not in the dark but in the light. It is a map that leads to a destination, which is only available to those who accept the Whole Truth.

Therefore, we have come to a crossroad on our journey together. You have a choice to make. You can choose to ignore the Whole Truth and continue to travel this single parent road in the dark, or you can choose to accept the Whole Truth and gain access to the Hope Roadmap and travel this road as a Half Family.

Believe me, you do not have to be alone in the dark. There is a Hope Roadmap and a clear destination for this journey. You can become a mother in the Half Family that is made whole through Christ. Choose hope.

CHEAT SHEET

The Whole Truth Picture

The Hope

1.   You are not alone.

Crisis Management

1.   The Real Fear from the Cold Hard Facts, the painful wound, the vulnerability to Nightmare Fear and the lack of margins can push or throw us into Crisis Management.

2.   The danger of daily Crisis Management is crisis reaction.

The Chasm

1.   The Chasm is a gapping hole in our road with no visible way to the other side.

2.   The danger of standing on the edge of the Chasm is an escape jump into it.

The Whole Truth Picture

1.   The truth about our internal world and/or external world can push us into Crisis Management and the edge of the Chasm

The Hope

1.   The Hope Roadmap

5

The Hope Roadmap

There is a Hope Roadmap that leads to our wholeness destination. You do not have to be lost on the single parent road. In fact, when you choose to equip yourself with this hope, you will be transformed from a single parent to a mother in a Half Family. You will no longer feel isolated and alone. You will no longer search for somewhere to belong. You will be part of a family: a Half Family.

Now I must warn you that this Hope Roadmap may surprise you. In fact, you may have been looking for something quite different. So before we begin to examine the hope for our journey, I want to explain what this Hope Roadmap is not. It is not a magical roadmap. This roadmap will not make the Cold Hard Facts magically go away. Those get-rich-quick schemes are just that: schemes. Nor will this roadmap provide a magic wand to heal your painful wound and vulnerability to Nightmare Fear. Those self-help ten-week courses to fix you will not work. I have no magic wands. Truly, sometimes I wish I did have one. I have looked and there are no magic wands.

Also, the Hope Roadmap is not designed for a single event. Single parenthood is not an event; it is a journey. In other words, if there is no magic wand to instantly make all our problems go away, then we will need to journey through our problems toward the solutions one step at time. The Hope Roadmap only works one step at a time. We cannot skip, run, or jump to our destination. We must choose to take deliberate steps on the Half Family road. You have heard that it is not the destination that counts; it is the journey. Whether we like it or not, that statement is true. The Hope Roadmap is designed for that journey: a journey of one step at a time into wholeness.

What Is the Hope Roadmap?

Now we know that this roadmap is not magical and that there is no skipping, running or jumping ahead allowed. So what is the Hope Roadmap? To answer that question, we need to first step back and look once more at the Whole Truth Picture. We need to look at the condition of the road and the danger on that road in order to understand our need for hope.

First, we have the condition of our external world. We have the Cold Hard Facts and the Real Fear. Even if I had not told you that there is no magic wand to solve your financial problems, you already know that truth first hand. The reality is the Cold Hard Facts will be with us on the Half Family road. We will still face the danger of Crisis Management and the Chasm. So how do we deal with minimum income and maximum expenses? How do we face Real Fear? How do we maneuver these stones and boulders? How do we avoid stepping on a landmine and being blown to the edge of the Chasm? We need a foothold on the road; we need hope.

Then there is our internal world. Our painful wound, the vulnerability to Nightmare Fear, and our lack of margins certainly do not help our situation. If we are in pain and fear, how do we move? If we are emotionally, physically, and mentally drained, how do we maneuver this challenging road? We need a foothold on the road; we need hope.

Finally, there is the danger of crisis reaction and an escape jump into the Chasm. We certainly need a foothold on the road to keep us from slipping into this dangerous position. We need hope.

It is clear we need hope we can maneuver the challenges that we will face on this road and make it to our destination. Therefore, in a sentence, the Hope Roadmap is designed to guide us on our daily travels over and around the stones, boulders, and landmines on the road and keep us away from the danger of Crisis Management and the Chasm. Sounds simple right? Well, I am going to twist your brain again.

What is Hope?

You may be thinking hope is the last thing that you want. You want answers. Whether you have verbalized it or not, you want a magic wand or a ten step program to "fix" your problems. Or maybe you want me to give you the solutions. After all I have traveled this road; therefore, I should have the answers. Sorry, I can only give you the Hope Roadmap. If you trust me for a little while, you will see that hope is exactly the right answer.

What is hope? It is hard to put into words, but I will try. Hope is intangible. You cannot touch it. For us, I guess I would describe it this way. Hope always follows the Whole Truth. When we shine light on the Whole Truth, we also receive the light of hope. If we shine a light on a huge boulder in our path, it also exposes a way around or over the boulder. When we think that there is no solution to our problems, hope is the foothold on the road. Hope exists in the present. Hope is the light that leads forward another step on the journey.

Hope is the operative word for our journey. I found this hope for our roadmap in an unlikely place. The light was there all the time. It was the one place where I actually had some control. I did not have control over the Cold Hard Facts or the Real Fear. I did not have control over the painful wound and the Nightmare Fear, but I had some control over my lack of margins. That's right; I found hope there. This light of hope was new margins, something extra. If I had something extra, a foothold on this rough road, I would have hope that I could make it to my destination. I needed new emotional, physical, and mental margins to give me a foothold on the rough road. I needed something extra, some hope.

Here lies the heart of the Hope Roadmap. If we can create emotional, physical, and mental margins to replace the ones we lost in the death of our relationship, we will find hope. We will have something extra to help us deal with the Cold Hard Facts and avoid slipping into crisis reaction. We will have something extra while we heal from the painful wound and get free from the vulnerability to Nightmare Fear. We will have something extra to keep us back from Crisis Management and the edge of the Chasm.

To be honest, at first I did not understand the value of creating new margins. I just did it to give myself something to occupy my mind. I did it to make me feel like I was moving forward. It took me a long time to understand and accept the gift of hope found in these new margins. What I have come to understand is that these margins were part of the roadmap that I needed on my journey. What I have come to understand is that the Hope Roadmap provides the self-care instructions for emotional, physical, and mental margins for the mother in the Half Family. What I have come to accept is that I am the most important asset on this journey.

The truth is you are the most important asset in your family. You are the only aspect of this journey you can control. Therefore, the hope in the Hope Roadmap is for you. Your emotional stability, your physical stamina, and your mental sharpness are crucial to successfully reaching the destination of wholeness. We need the self-care instructions from the Hope Roadmap. We need the light of hope found in self-care.

What is self-care?

Besides twisting your brain, I know that there is a nagging question floating in the air. If we focus on self-care for ourselves, isn't that selfish? What about our children? They are hurting too. It would be selfish to focus on us. You are right about your children. We cannot ignore them. We are the only full-time parent in the home. Besides, our children are hurting too. I agree. If we are selfish, we cannot be effective, loving, whole mothers. Selfish behavior is devastating to our role as parents. But there is a big difference between selfishness and self-care.

I submit it is selfish for a single parent to ignore her need for emotional, physical, and mental margins, get pushed into daily Crisis Management and the edge of the Chasm. I submit it is selfish to live that way and take an escape jump into the Chasm. Ignoring our need for emotional, physical, and mental margins will cause us to act selfishly and teach our children that behavior.

Here is what I mean by that statement. If you are consumed by pain, fear, crisis, and escape, you will be hanging on so tightly to yourself, you will be unable to hold on to your children. You will have nothing left to give them emotionally, physically, and mentally. You will have selfishly focused on your needs rather than your children. Our children learn from us. Our children are like sponges, and they pick up behavior patterns from our example. By ignoring our self-care needs, we are teaching our children that pain, reaction to fear, Crisis Management, and escape are an acceptable lifestyle. This pattern of behavior teaches selfishness. I know this pattern all too well. I have been there. For many years, I clung so tightly to myself that I did not see the truth. I never intended to be selfish, but I was. Is that what we want to teach our children? You have heard the phrase "the blind leading the blind." If you are an emotional, physical, and mental wreck living in crisis and escaping into the Chasm, you are leading your children down the same path. That is not the right roadmap for a Half Family.

Self-care is the absolute opposite from selfishness. Self-care gives us the emotional, physical, and mental margins that we need to take the Half Family journey. Our emotional, physical, and mental margins will promote healthy patterns for our children's learning experience. These margins will give us the ability to hold on to our children rather than our pain, fear, crisis, and escape. Trust me; self-care margins will promote healing and love for your children. The truth is selfishness and self-care cannot exist together. You are either hanging onto yourself or you are embracing your children.

I know this concept of self-care margins may seem strange. I know you may not want margins; you want answers. Trust me for a few more pages and see if this roadmap makes sense to you.

The Self-care Instructions for Our Margins on the Hope Roadmap

We now know that the Hope Roadmap does not provide a magic wand. We know that this roadmap requires us to journey into wholeness one step at a time. We know that hope is the light that gives us a foothold on this dangerous road. We know that the Hope Roadmap focuses on us, the most important asset in the Half Family. We know that hope is found in our emotional, physical, and mental self-care instructions. So let's look at the self-care instructions for our new margins that give us hope.

Emotional Margins

Find a Confidante. When the pressure from the truth of your external world and the self-truth of your internal world make it hard for you to breath, doesn't talking to someone else relieve it? When you are in Crisis Management on the edge of the Chasm, doesn't it help to have someone stand there with you? Always, always, always. We all need a confidante. I believe we all have an emotional need for relationship. Sometimes, we need to talk to someone. Believe it or not, you lost this margin in the death of your relationship. You may never have thought of your ex-partner as a confidante, but he was. Maybe, your ex-partner was not a good confidante, but there was some communication there. You need to replace that confidante relationship.

A confidante is extremely important for the mother in a Half Family. Often talking with another person will defuse the turmoil of our internal world. Another person's view can give us a new perspective. Sometimes having another person listen is more important than answers to problems. Human beings need to communicate.

I know that this need makes sense to us. In fact, we may think that we, as single parents, have many confidantes in our lives. But do we? Before we spill our guts to someone, we need to carefully consider this relationship and make an informed choice. We need to choose a confidante carefully.

First, we need to understand and accept the demands that we place on a relationship. A relationship is two-way communication. One-way communication, our needs only, would be a selfish margin. We want to create a self-care margin. Therefore, we need to consider our condition as we enter into this relationship.

We are very needy. We are very needy in our external worlds. Many of us live our lives at survival level. We want answers to our problems. A confidante can provide direction, and a good friend who has resources will share those resources with you. But a confidante is not a magic wand. A confidante will not have all the answers to the Cold Hard Facts. So we need to guard against putting that expectation on this person.

We are needy in our internal world. Our separation from our partner has created a bleeding wound. We were intertwined with this man. Again, it has nothing to do with a marriage certificate. This separation wound has left a painful hole inside of us. That hole screams to be filled with someone. Even if we do not understand it, we feel the need to fill that hole. Even a woman who has been a single parent for many years but has ignored the wound will try to fill that hole with someone. No human being can completely fill that hole or heal the wound. So we need to guard against putting that expectation on our confidante.

Also, we can easily suck massive amounts of time from a confidante as well as drain the emotions from them. We need to guard against relying too much on them. No one person will fill our every need, and every human being will fail us at some point.

Therefore, given the harshness of our lives and our painful wound, we need to choose our confidante wisely. Since just determining who to talk to can be overwhelming for us, I recommend a personal criteria list for choosing a confidante. Think about your condition. Think about your situation. Think about the condition and situation of the other person. And write down your criteria.

Here are some suggestions:

1. *Choose a woman confidante.* This criterion has been critical to the success of my close relationships. A man instinctively and culturally does not think like I do. He will never understand my emotions and perceptions at the level of understanding of another woman. He is simply different. I think about conversations with my son. I want to explain a situation in detail and share my feelings. He impatiently says, "Just get to the point." I want to take the full story journey and he wants me to get to the destination. I certainly never taught him this form of communication and my

son's father was not around during his maturation. My son is a man, and that is the way his mind works.

But there is a far more important reason to choose a woman. I learned this reason through my own experience. Like all single parents, in the early years of my journey, I had a hole inside. My hole came from the wound caused by the separation from my husband. My reaction was to fill that hole with another man. I wanted desperately to remarry and be rescued from my painful existence. I never verbalized this feeling, but unfortunately, I acted on this emotion. If a man was attracted to me, I would make him my confidante. I wanted to be rescued, but he did not necessarily want to rescue me; he wanted sex. My rescue took precedence over any kind of healthy relationship. The result was I, unknowingly, jumped into the Chasm. The man became my lover instead of a confidante. Choosing a man as a confidante is a wrong turn. My relationship felt good in the short term as my wound and fears were covered over by pleasure. Unfortunately, the internal turmoil did not go away and it resurfaced. Trust me, if you choose a man, this type of escape will hurt not only you but also your children. The truth is you are a wounded single parent; choosing a man as your confidante is selfish. Choose a woman. Remember, our goal is self-care margins not selfish margins.

2. *Choose a closed-mouth woman.* The definition of a confidante is a person trusted with one's secrets. Therefore, a closed-mouth confidante may sound redundant. I cannot stress this point enough. If you are exposing your internal world and external world to someone and making yourself vulnerable, you need some level of confidence that this information is in trusted hands. In other words, make sure your confidante is not a gossip. How do you know that someone is a gossip? Gossip is idle talk about another person's affairs. Simply put, a woman who shares her friend's secrets with you will share your secrets with someone else. You only need to be stung once to learn this truth. Also, remember that a relationship is two-way communication. Therefore, we should make sure we are not gossips. We should be willing to hold our friend's conversations in confidence.

3. *Choose a nonjudgmental, closed-mouth woman.* A judgmental woman will condemn your past and put restrictions on your future. She will make you feel trapped. For example, a single parent does not need to be

reminded that her divorce is the reason for her daily conflicts, nor does an unwed mother need to be reminded she should not have gotten pregnant. These women live with the consequences of their actions daily. A judgmental person will pepper her conversation with "you should" and "you can't," and she will talk more than listen. The reality is that a judgmental person will provide no hope. Instead this person will take part of the truth and beat you over the head with it. A nonjudgmental person will not ignore your past mistakes, but her advice will encourage, not condemn. She will speak the Whole Truth surrounded in hope. She will focus on the present, not the past or the future. She will listen more than talk. When she does speak, one of her favorite words will be "you can."

4. *Choose a truthful, nonjudgmental, closed-mouth woman.* The truth that comes from a nonjudgmental, closed-mouth woman can be a marvelous margin for the mother in a Half Family. For example, suppose my son falls of his bicycle and injures his head. He is covered in blood and seems to be disoriented. I panic and run this scenario through my head. He must have a concussion and needs to go to the hospital. I am sure the doctor will discover that it is more than a concussion and surgery will be necessary. What if there are complications? And I forgot, I have no insurance. I cannot deal with this...I call a trusted friend who happens to be a nurse. She calms me down and tells me he probably has a concussion. She tells me to go the doctor *now*. The reality is that my son is scrapped, bruised, and has a giant bump on his head which caused temporary amnesia (true story). Thank God for truthful friends.

Even though we, as mothers in the Half Family, face similar turmoil and emotions, we are unique personalities. Your criteria list for a confidante may not be the same as mine. However, this kind of personal examination of your relationship needs can provide a strong foundation for building a lasting friendship.

I cannot stress enough the importance of finding a confidante. Think about it. When people, in general, are disturbed by their emotions, they go to counseling. They are looking for a safe place to talk about their problems. They want their conversations to be confidential.

In fact, if you determine you need counseling, go find a good Christian counselor who will be sensitive to your financial condition. Also, there are some good single parent support groups. These groups are a good resource and will help you see that you are not alone. Be careful, some of these groups may be coed and not a good place to spill your guts. Therefore, you still need someone to listen to you, encourage you, and tell you the truth. Certainly, a confidante cannot fill the role of a professional counselor or a support group, but a good friend is worth her weight in gold.

Learn to Play. By far, the weakest area of my own margins is play. Play is a luxury. It is an unnecessary use of money and time for no valid purpose. Luxury is not part of my life and money and time cannot be wasted. That was the way I thought. Therefore, I spent years dismissing play from my life, and I was very misguided. Ask some of my friends and they will say that I still border on workaholic.

Webster defines recreation as play. Walking, gardening, and reading are recreation. Relating play to a sun-drenched two-week vacation on the golden beaches of Hawaii is only half right. Actually, I can play anywhere. It does not have to cost anything nor take massive amounts of time. But play is still a luxury. Is it?

Play is really a healthy escape from the pressures of the Cold Hard Facts and a wonderful emotional margin from internal pain and fear. When you are playing and laughing, it is hard to feel your pain and be afraid. If you are standing on the edge of the Chasm with no solution, choose to escape in play for a short time even fifteen minutes. Yes, play is escape: healthy escape.

My son has been my best teacher in the area of imaginative play and healthy escapes. He loves to play, creating new ways to have fun at a moment's notice. His ideas are limitless. When he was six or seven years old, he developed a great game loosely resembling baseball. I would pitch and he would hit the ball. After a few hits, he would run the bases. I, with ball in hand, was supposed to catch and tag him. Of course, he never stayed within any specific base lines. His rules were as subjective as the base lines. With no notice, he would decide we should switch positions. During this whole game, he would be giving a play-by-play commentary complete with crowd noises. This playtime cost nothing and I never considered it a waste of time. Was it a luxury? No, it was emotional therapy. It was a self-care emotional margin. For an hour or so, my son and I would run away from our harsh existence and have fun. It would cleanse my body of stress and change my perspective.

Not only did this play give me a margin, it enhanced my parenting. That special game was just between the two of us. It was our time and it strengthened our relationship. To this day, I wonder if my son's love of baseball was born during one of those play times. Was it a luxury? No, it was a necessity.

Physical Margins

You Are What You Eat. What I put in my mouth has a direct correlation to the health of my body. The saying, you are what you eat is true. It took me years to accept this truth. As a mostly exhausted single parent, I would buy prepackaged foods, frozen foods, or fast foods. It simplified my life and it filled the stomach. Isn't that enough? No. What is the most valuable asset you possess? The answer is you. Therefore, your body needs to be healthy. Why then, would any of us fill our bodies with salt, sugar, monosodium glutamate, xanthan gum, or propylene glycol, or any other chemical ingredients found in most packaged foods?

Too much salt in the diet can lead to high blood pressure and other heart-related conditions.[1] Too much sugar in the diet has been linked to a greater risk of tooth decay, obesity, and heart disease.[2] Chemical additives can cause hyperactivity in children. I am not a scientist, but I think that there is enough scientific evidence that we should not use these food sources as the staple in our diets. The wrong foods can give us false highs, exaggerated lows, create anxiety, and rob us of energy.[3] These effects do not promote a healthy margin for the already struggling body and mind of a single parent. If my mind and body break down, Crisis Management will reign. Emotional margins will not make up for the lack of this physical margin. Logically, proper eating makes sense.

I know food is a tough area to talk about for many single parents because many women have no options. If you are dependent on a food pantry or charitable food distribution center, you normally get the wrong kinds of food i.e., prepackaged foods, canned fruits with heavy syrup, vegetables with additives, powdered milk, and lots of sugary cereal. I have been there. Just do the best you can. If you are allowed to pick out your own food in that situation or even when you do your own grocery shopping, here are some suggestions to help you move toward healthy eating.

1. Look at the labels on cans and boxes and choose food that has the least salt, sugar, and additives. There are canned vegetables with less salt and canned fruit with less syrup (sugar).

2. When you use a food distribution center solely, you can ask for gift certificates for a local grocery store (many food pantries will now supply them). Use these certificates to buy fresh food.

3. If you supplement your income with a food pantry, you should use your money for fresh food like vegetables, fruit, milk, and eggs, not packaged foods.

As a mother, I know your concern is to fill those little stomachs in your household. Trust me, your children will have fuller stomachs with fresh food than packaged or fast food. Children's bodies need nutritional food. Nutritional food will satisfy the body's hunger. Packaged and fast food will only fill the stomach.

Remember, there are no magic wands. Therefore, you cannot change your lifestyle all at once. So take small steps toward eating healthy each day. Believe me, I am not a purist. Never will I give up my morning coffee or an occasional sweet. I am striving for balance. I eat fresh vegetables and fruit in some portion every day.

Besides the nutritional benefits of eating healthy, there is another reason for this physical margin. Unhealthy eating can lead to using food as an escape. Have you ever been in crisis staring into the Chasm and said to yourself, "I could really use something sweet" or "Fast food sounds great right now"? Have you ever wanted comfort food? We all feel this way at some point. But food should not be for comfort, it should be for nutrition. Food should not be an escape. That obscenely large double chocolate escape may taste so good going down, but the crash after a chocolate binge is not pretty. We all succumb to comfort food. I still do. But the danger lies in developing a compulsive overeating pattern. If we develop a diet of largely unhealthy comfort food, we will become overweight. Overeating does not create a self-care margin for the mother in the Half Family. I just heard a statistic on the news that 61 percent of Americans are overweight. Obviously single parents are not the only ones who need comfort food.

The key word for this self-care margin is balance. Nutritional foods can provide a natural high, a clear mind, abundant energy, and can actually reduce anxiety.[4] Those benefits can give us a great margin during a crisis.

Exercise Is Not a Dirty Word. After my twenties, my exercise routine was nonexistent until age forty. I was athletic in my youth, but as a mature adult, disciplined, scheduled exercise was for the rich and weird. That thought was an excuse, and it worked for me. It worked until I looked in the mirror one day and said, "What happened to my body?" It was sagging and bulging in all the wrong places. After a few weeks of feeling like I was a walking bowl of Jell-O, I decided to get in shape. Frankly, I wish I could say that my exercise routine was prompted by the reasons listed below. The truth is I was driven by vanity.

Facing the stressful lifestyle of single parenthood without exercise is like running my car at 90 mph and never stopping for a tune-up. At some point this machine will break down and so will my body. We all need the physical margin of exercise.

First hand, I have experienced the tune-up benefits of regular exercise. For me, I can diffuse internal pain, fear, depression, and anxiety through physical movement. While running around a track, it is difficult to remain emotionally paralyzed by internal pain or fear. I have found if I move in a disciplined direction for twenty to twenty-five minutes, I loose that trapped feeling from being on the edge of the Chasm. The muscles in my neck and shoulders pulled tight from stress begin to release. As I perspire, I feel a sense of accomplishment. I have control over something in my life and my perception changes. I see my road from a different perspective. Sometimes I see options or solutions that eluded me in my fearful condition. Exercise never fails to revive me.

Surprisingly, I am rarely exhausted after a workout. I am energized. Interesting. Pain, fear, problems, worry, and anxiety will rob me of energy and time. Exercise energizes me and gives me time. After exercising, I have actually gone home on a Friday night and cleaned my house. Without exercise, Friday nights were escape to my ozone layer as a coach potato in front of the TV.

Whether logic or vanity motivates you, I have some suggestions for beginning an exercise program.

1. *Start slowly.* When I started developing this physical margin, I was fortunate to have a free YMCA membership and sought counsel on exercising from a professional at the facility. A proper exercise program is developed according to your age, weight, physical condition, and work schedule. Do not skip over this education process. Successful exercise depends on knowing your body's strengths and weaknesses. Literally, I had to walk the track before I ran it.

2. *Do something you like.* Exercise is not a dirty word. If you think that, then you are focusing on an exercise you do not like. Exercise can be taking a walk with a friend on your lunch hour, an energetic aerobics class, or a bike ride with your children around the neighborhood. I am a solitary person. I prefer my own treadmill and some good music in the solace of my basement. Choose an activity you enjoy.

3. *Schedule a time and stick to it.* This suggestion is the toughest part of exercise. As I write this section, I am now much older than forty. I have not been as consistent in exercise as I was in the past. So I am going to take my own advice. Be realistic with yourself. If you can exercise Monday through Friday at night for twenty minutes, you should start there. If you only have time on your lunch, start exercising at this time. If you only have thirty minutes a day twice a week, start there. Just start and do

not beat yourself up if you miss a workout time. Remember, we are on a journey. I read somewhere that if you do something for twenty-eight to thirty days, it becomes a habit. So start building a habit of exercise one step at a time.

Mental Margins

The MHD. Everybody especially single parents need a MHD every once in awhile. A MHD is a Mental Health Day. A MHD is different from play. I would describe a MHD as run away for a day. Warning: do not forget to come back. A MHD is a healthy escape, and it can be anything that you want it to be. The choice is yours. So let your imagination run wild.

The only rules for an MHD are:

1. It must be self-care not selfish (everyday cannot be a MHD).

2. It must be healthy (nothing illegal, illicit, or immoral is permitted). (When my son was a teenager, I used to say these three words to him all the time. It drove him crazy.)

3. Do not take your children. (We will talk about a MHD and your children later in our Half Family journey.)

4. You must not forget to come back.

Examples of a MHD

1. Spend the entire day in bed. Only get up to take a bubble bath.

2. Spend the entire day at the beach, in the park, in the city, or in the mountains.

3. Write letters to friends or encouraging notes to other single parents.

4. Read a good book or two.

5. Watch funny movies on TV or rent them.

Do you get the picture? You give yourself permission to run away. It is amazing how a MHD can trick the brain into thinking it is on vacation. For that reason alone, a MHD is very important. Most single parents cannot afford to take a vacation. Yes, if we work, we may take time off during Christmas, spring break, or the summer. However, we normally take that time off because our children are out of school. Our time off is required to save money on childcare.

A MHD is wonderful healthy escape. I encourage you to schedule them appropriately throughout the year.

Positive Input for Positive Thoughts. The truth about our external world and the self-truth about our internal world do not promote positive thoughts. I can remember facing the Cold Hard Facts with a sick child and no job. It was hard to think positive thoughts. I am not suggesting we should ignore the truth and live in a "la-la" land of positive thinking. That attitude would not promote a good self-care margin or even a healthy escape. Here is my point. Our external world may be full of negative situations and we may have no control over that fact, but we do have control over the input into our brains.

We should be careful to avoid negative people: individuals who see nothing but doom and gloom in the world. When these people speak with burdened single parents, they feel like they are in a "doom and gloom" candy store. The last thing that you need as a single parent is someone fueling your Real Fear as well as your Nightmare Fear. In fact, we are fully capable of fueling fear all by ourselves; we certainly do not need someone else helping us in the process. We have a choice not to associate with a negative person.

Since we can be our own worst enemy concerning negative thoughts, I encourage you to examine the other sources of input into your brain like your TV viewing and reading material. The news on TV and in newspapers and magazines can be depressing. You have permission to turn off the news and ignore the print media. Despite the flood of information in our society, you really do not need the latest news every minute of every day. Sometimes that much input only overwhelms you rather than informs you.

The point is treat your mind like your body. Give it nutrition. You have heard the saying "garbage in garbage out"? It is true.

Therefore, we should choose to put positive thoughts into our brains. When you are staring at those Cold Hard Facts, tell yourself you can make it past these boulders. If you say you can't, you will sit down in the middle of the road, stare at the boulders, and feel trapped. How do you know you can't until you try? I truly speak from experience. I was the queen of "I can't statements." Now, I actually find myself saying, "I can do this" out loud.

Think back to our discussion about a confidante. Do you see the importance of the encouragement from a woman? A confidante can help you face the truth and provide the encouragement to walk through, over, and around that boulder in your path. Make a decision to surround yourself with positive people.

The Hope Roadmap

Since we are the most important asset on this Half Family journey, we need to be adequately equipped for the challenges and dangers on the road. The best way to equip us is to provide new margins to replace the ones we lost from the death of our relationships. The Hope Roadmap provides those emotional, physical, and mental margins for the mother in the Half Family.

The Hope Roadmap equips you as the mother in the Half Family to find solutions to your own life problems. There is no magic wand or self-help program that will make the Cold Hard Facts disappear and instantly remove the pain and Nightmare Fear from inside. Trust me, as you journey with me, you will find that this hope is so much better than any magic wand or self-help program. As we journey, you will find your own answers to problems.

Learning to use the Hope Roadmap by creating self-care margins is a process; it is not an event. So take small steps each day. Soon you will look back and see a new road from those daily small steps.

But our Hope Roadmap is not complete yet. We have one more self-care margin for our journey. In fact, this margin provides the most important self-care instructions for the journey. It is truly the core foundation for the Hope Roadmap. At the beginning of my journey, this margin was my least favorite part of my roadmap and now it is my most precious and valued hope of my road. It contains that hope which transforms us from single parents to mothers in the Half Families.

CHEAT SHEET

The Hope Roadmap (No Magic Wands—No Skipping, Running, or Jumping)

Emotional Margins

1. Find a confidante.

2. Learn to play.

Physical Margins

1. You are what you eat.

2. Exercise is not a dirty word.

Mental Margins

1. Take a MHD.

2. Use positive input for positive thought.

6

The Hope Roadmap—Crossing the Chasm

Now that we have a Hope Roadmap with self-care instructions for our emotional, physical, and mental margins to assist us on our Half Family journey and keep us from the danger of Crisis Management and the Chasm, I need to tell you that these margins are not foolproof. At some point, a confidante will fail you and play won't fix anything. The refrigerator will be empty and exercise will seem like an impossible task. A MHD will not be an option and you will not be able to distance yourself from negative people. Not exactly what you wanted to read, right? Don't get me wrong. Most of the time, these margins will provide trust-worthy guidance for traveling this challenging road. But what do you do when these margins fail to provide guidance? What happens when the day in and day out management of minimum income and maximum expenses pushes you into crisis reaction? What do you do when you are emotionally, physically, and mentally exhausted and teetering on the edge of the Chasm?

When every other margin fails you, there is one margin that will not fail you. In fact when you come to the end of yourself and are teetering on the edge of the Chasm, this margin is always available and able to guide you and protect you from any danger. This margin contains the most important self-care instructions on the Hope Roadmap because it contains the instructions for *crossing* the Chasm. It is true. When every other margin fails, this margin will extend across any Chasm that you encounter on the Half Family journey. This margin not only completes our Hope Roadmap, but it is the cornerstone of our roadmap. This margin is the rock-solid foundation that will faithfully guide us to our destination. This foolproof margin is the Spiritual Margin of Faith.

What Is the Spiritual Margin of Faith?

What is the Spiritual Margin of Faith? What is this foolproof margin that allows us to cross Chasms? Good questions. Let me answer this way. Did you ever see the movie *Indiana Jones and the Last Crusade*? If you have not seen it, you need to rent the video or DVD and view one scene towards the end of the movie.

Indiana Jones is an archeologist and is always searching for a rare artifact. In his search, he encounters obstacles and dangers on every road. In one of the last scenes in the movie, Indiana is close to obtaining his precious artifact; which appears to lie just beyond a booby-trapped cave. Naturally, he goes into this dark, ominous cave, dodges every conceivable booby trap, and then sees a light at the end of the cave. Quickly, he moves toward the light. But when he reaches the opening at the end of the cave, he finds himself standing on a narrow ledge, staring into a vast, seemingly bottomless Chasm. He can see the opening to another cave on the other side, but there is no way to cross the Chasm. He cannot go to his right or his left because he is standing on the only opening in a massive rock formation. He cannot go back because the danger behind him is too intense. He stares at the opening in the sheer rock on the other side, but there is no visible bridge over the Chasm. He is trapped. He gazes down at the small book of data and meticulous notes about the search for this artifact (his roadmap). He mutters to himself that no one could jump this Chasm. Then he says, "It's a leap of faith." At this point on his journey, the roadmap clearly states a "leap of faith" is necessary. He takes one more look around, puts his hand on his chest, and takes a step forward. Incredible! Miraculous! There was a bridge all the time. He could not see it because the bridge was the same color as the rock all around him. The bridge blended into the landscape and was only visible after he took a step forward, a leap of faith.

Indiana Jones is not the only one who faces booby traps, obstacles, and a Chasm. We often feel like we are traversing obstacles in a dark cave. We use our emotional, physical, and mental margins to effectively maneuver the road. Just when we think we see a light at the end of our cave, we may find ourselves on the edge of the Chasm. We are trapped. We can see the road on the other side, but there is no bridge. Just like Indiana Jones, when we look at our roadmap, we discover our instructions our clear. We must take our own "leap of faith." We must access the Spiritual Margin of Faith. Just like Indiana Jones, you will discover there is a bridge across the Chasm. When you step forward, you will step onto the invisible bridge of Faith. Faith is a rock-solid bridge. It is not visible, but when we take a step, it is always there. Faith is a spiritual margin between us and our perception of impending doom. It is the bridge across the Chasm. It is a solution not an escape. Faith is our most important margin because the Spiritual Margin of Faith is the "rock solid" foundation of the Hope Roadmap.

The Spiritual Margin of Faith will give us the wisdom to maneuver the Cold Hard Facts. The Spiritual Margin of Faith is the medicine, the balm, for our painful wound that will lead us to healing. It will banish Nightmare Fear from our path. It extends an invisible bridge across the Chasm.

Wait a minute. Maybe you could believe that some Spiritual Margin of Faith could lead to healing or even curb the fear. But the Cold Hard Facts are real. They are tangible. How can faith possibly help you? Do you have access to some spiritual grocery store or some spiritual financial resource to pay bills? Actually, those questions are valid. I have certainly asked myself those questions. Like you, I could understand the imagery of Indiana Jones stepping onto an invisible bridge. That is in a movie and we live in the real world. How can I possibly access an invisible bridge? How do I access the Spiritual Margin of Faith? We want to believe that there is a bridge across the Chasm, but it does not make human sense. How do I get this "rock-solid" faith? How do I cross the Chasm with faith?

It took me awhile to find an answer. It took me awhile because I was asking the wrong question. Before I can access faith to cross the Chasm, I must know what faith is. What is faith? I thought I knew the answer to that question, but I didn't. Actually I used to be confused about faith.

What Is Faith?

On my own Half Family journey, I can remember friends asking me, "How are you?" I would tell them about my lack of food, or late bills, or an eviction notice. Most of my Christian friends would say, "I will pray for you, just have faith." I would walk away saying to myself, "How will that help me? How do I just have faith?" I would tell myself to "have faith" and everything would be fine. These friends seemed to be fine. It was working for them. So it would work for me. But I failed to "have faith." Remember, I told you that there are no magic wands on this journey. Well, faith sounded like a magic wand to me. People waved it around in front of me like it was one. Is faith a magic wand? No. You cannot just have faith. This spiritual margin does not just happen.

Faith is much more than a word, and it is certainly not a magic wand. What is faith? Faith is a choice; it is action, and it is a journey. We must choose to step forward in faith. The Spiritual Margin of Faith requires a deliberate, conscious decision to take action and walk the invisible bridge. Faith is a journey. Faith is a living margin that grows and matures as you travel the Half Family road. Each time we choose faith and take a step forward on that invisible bridge, it grows a little stronger and matures a little more. This living faith is a choice, it is action, and it is a journey. In other words, faith is a lifestyle.

Lifestyle Faith

The Spiritual Margin of Faith is a lifestyle not an event. Here is what I mean by that statement. I used to think of faith as an event. I was saved so I had faith. I had the event of salvation, which is the birth of faith. When we recognize, accept and repent of our sin, we then accept the gift of salvation. And this birth means we have been born as a new creature in Jesus. And we are a "baby." We have a birthright to faith. But at birth, we do not yet know how to walk in faith. Would you expect a baby to stand and walk at birth? No, a baby must be nurtured and taught to walk. Would you want this baby to remain a baby? No, we want a baby to mature. The same is true for a "baby" born by salvation through Jesus Christ. We need to learn to walk in faith and grow into a mature Christ follower, and growing and maturing in lifestyle faith does not just happen. Remember, faith is a choice, it is action, and it is a journey. If we do not choose to grow and mature in faith, we will live our lives as "babies" and view faith as a magic wand.

We know what faith is, now let's go back to our original questions. How do we get rock-solid faith? How do we cross the Chasm in faith? We need to grow and mature in lifestyle faith. How do we do that? There are specific self-care instructions for this maturation process. We need a confidante to teach us about faith, food to nurture our faith, and exercise to grow and mature our faith. Just as we have self-care instructions for our emotional, physical, and mental margins, we have self-care instructions for the Spiritual Margin of Faith. We have an unfailing, perfect confidante, the perfect food, and spiritual exercise to grow and mature our lifestyle faith. These self-care instructions will build a rock-solid faith bridge across any Chasm.

The Self-care Instructions for our Spiritual Margin of Faith

Our Unfailing Perfect Confidante

Remember in the last chapter I told you that confidantes would fail you. Well, Jesus will never fail you. He is the unfailing, perfect confidante. We have no need of a criteria list because he is so much more than we could ever imagine. On this journey, you will discover for yourself the depth and breadth of a relationship with Jesus.

As our confidante, Jesus will teach us about lifestyle faith. Only through developing a relationship with this confidante can we learn to grow and mature in faith. We cannot see him, but our birth of faith through salvation gives us a birthright to walk into his presence. He is always with us on the Half Family journey to wholeness. In fact, he sees our wholeness destination when it is only a glimmer on the horizon for us.

He knows the whole road, including the invisible bridges that we will cross to reach our destination because Jesus is the architect of invisible bridges. He is the "author and perfector of our faith" (Hebrews 12:2). He holds the blueprints to this invisible bridge. We do not have to wander around aimlessly trying to have "faith." Jesus is always waiting to teach us and grow our faith. His faithful presence will never leave us, but we must take the first step. It is our decision to choose lifestyle faith and develop a relationship with Jesus.

I have learned much from this faithful companion and I am still maturing in faith. Amazing as it sounds, I am maturing not so much from anything new that I learn from Jesus. No, I am maturing because I keep doing the basics that he taught me. There are some basic instructions about faith that I just keep doing over and over. These instructions from my perfect confidante are clear and simple but not always easy.

The basics of lifestyle faith that Jesus has taught me are: Do not doubt, one small choice, and faith grows to trust.

Do Not Doubt. "Now faith is being sure of what we hope for and certain of what we do not see" (Hebrews 11:1). This passage is the definition of faith. It is not just the definition of the birth of faith, but the way we are to live our lives: lifestyle faith. As you read the passage above, it is clear that our Spiritual Margin of Faith requires something of us. We cannot just have faith. We must choose faith.

We must be "sure of what we hope for and certain of what we do not see." For lifestyle faith, we must believe that there is an invisible bridge across the Chasm. We must believe that when we take a step forward, we will step onto the bridge that Jesus built for us. In other words, faith requires that we make the decision not to doubt Jesus. The passage clearly states "sure and certain." There is no room for doubt. That does not sound like a magic wand to me. Nor does it sound like "just having" faith.

Not doubting is difficult. After the separation from my husband, I can remember in the early days being in excruciating internal pain from the death of my relationship and absolutely terrified of the future. Everything in my life was out of control, including me. I felt like I was going to be swallowed by some unseen monster. In those intensely frightening moments, I would shoot a cry to heaven, "God, help me." No one else could help me. Maybe God would remember me. But I assumed, as many people reinforced, I had committed the unforgivable sin, divorce. So I doubted that Jesus was listening to me. I doubted that Jesus was with me. I thought I was on my own. So I would escape into a glass or two of wine in the middle of the night to numb me and cry, "God, help me" as I fell back to sleep.

The truth of that situation was I was on my knees, clinging to my narrow ledge. I was looking down into the darkness of the Chasm and absolutely unaware that Jesus was standing right in front of me. Staring at the Chasm only fueled my pain and fear, making an escape jump an appealing option. Staring at the Chasm made me doubt. Since Jesus lives beyond my physical sight and I could not touch him, I doubted that the bridge was there. I could not see him or a bridge. Even if there was a bridge, I doubted Jesus' ability to guide me across the invisible bridge. Staring at the Chasm full of doubt made me unable to look up into Jesus' eyes. I was trying to hold onto doubt and faith at the same time. Doubt is holding onto the crisis and unbelief that there is a faith bridge across the Chasm. Faith is holding onto Jesus and believing that there is an invisible faith bridge. If we try to hold onto to both, we will be trapped. Jesus' words are crystal clear; I must have faith and not doubt. Jesus calls me to look up from the Chasm into his eyes, take his outstretched hand and walk across the Chasm.

Jesus was clear in his direction to me, "I tell you the truth, if you have faith and do not doubt…"(Matthew 21:21). Look, it says have faith, but it also says do not doubt. It is easy to have faith until you need to use it. If all your emotional, physical, and mental needs are met, it is easy to have faith. Only when you are faced with exercising faith as you stand on the edge of the Chasm, you are faced with the choice: do I believe Jesus or not? Do I believe that Jesus not only saved me, but he will guide me through anything? Or do I believe that Jesus saved me only to let me fall into the Chasm? Faith requires absolute allegiance, no doubt. Faith also promises the hope that Jesus is with us and has built an invisible bridge that leads all the way to our destination: wholeness. Faith requires we do not doubt the certainty of that promise. We cannot doubt and have faith at the same. It took me a long time to understand and accept this fact. I truly believe that faith vs. doubt is the most difficult part of lifestyle faith. Is it difficult for you? It was for me. Simply put here is the struggle we face.

My rules for the faith bridge:

1. Jesus, build me a visible bridge over the Chasm,

2. Then I will not doubt,

3. Then I will have faith.

Jesus' rules for the faith bridge:

1. Choose faith.

2. Do not doubt.

3. I built a bridge over the Chasm.

I have spent some time on this point for one simple reason. We will never access the Spiritual Margin of Faith unless we choose not to doubt. When you come face to face with this decision, it may seem overwhelming. In fact, when I came face to face with the depth of the commitment to a faith lifestyle, I did not think that I could succeed on this part of the journey. I was facing the Real Fear of the Cold Hard Facts strewn in front of me. I was in pain, feeling Nightmare Fear. I doubted everything. I hardly had enough faith that I could cross the visible bridges in my life like going to work and raising my child. Jesus is the unfailing perfect confidante who knows our frailty, so he has given very clear instructions for overcoming our doubt. He has surrounded the "do not doubt" with hope.

One Small Choice. Here is the hope. Jesus has a personal relationship with each of us and meets each of us exactly where we are. Not just at the moment of salvation but exactly where we are at any point on the Half Family journey. At this moment, he knows where you are on your journey. He knows every single boulder, landmine, and danger on your road. He intimately knows the pain and fear in your internal world. He knows exactly where to meet you on this road and provide an opportunity for faith.

But he also knows how difficult it is to have no doubt. So Jesus, who sits on the throne in the heavenly realms, does not shout down instructions to us on the road. No, he meets us at the edge of the Chasm, stands on the invisible bridge, stretches out his arms, and asks us to take one small step towards him. All he asks of you or me is for one small choice, one small step of faith. He knows how difficult it is for us to not doubt the existence of an invisible bridge across our dark Chasms. Therefore, he does not require us to run across the bridge or even take two steps. He does not even judge the quality of our steps. A faltering step without doubt is a step of faith. Jesus calls us to take one small step towards him.

As I said before, I was a slow learner concerning lifestyle faith. The words "have faith" used to ring in my ears, and I assumed I should stand tall and confidently walk across any invisible faith bridge. I should not falter or stumble. I should confidently keep walking. If I had enough faith, I could conquer any Chasm. True, but conquering the Chasm begins with one small step and *requires one small step at a time.*

Here is what Jesus said about faith. "If you have faith as small as a mustard seed, you can say to this mountain, move from here to there and it will move. Nothing will be impossible for you" (Matthew 17:20). Is that really true? Yes, it is. But don't focus on the mountain part of this passage: look at the mustard seed. In Jesus' time, a mustard seed was the smallest seed of any plant, and it could produce a tree ten feet tall. Jesus was saying that faith needs to start with one small seed, one small choice, and your faith will grow.

Here is the real pearl of wisdom hidden deep in faith. The reality is that lifestyle faith only works one small step at a time because *faith only lives in the present.* We choose faith moment by moment. We access faith with each step, it does not live in the past or the future. Let this truth sink into your mind, heart, and soul.

When we are standing on the edge of the Chasm, we struggle with living in the present. Now we may think we are living in the present. But are we? If we are focused on the pain and Nightmare Fear from the past and projecting Real Fear into the future, are we living in the present? No, we are living in the future, dragging the past behind us. In that condition, we will have doubt that there is a faith bridge because we are not living in the present. In that condition, we will be unable to take a step forward.

Whether we are rich or poor, healthy or dying, happy or depressed, everyone on the face of the earth has only this moment in time. The past is gone and the future is not here. We have only the present. Faith lives in this moment. Therefore, we have only this moment to take one small step forward in faith and onto the invisible bridge.

I have encountered this truth over and over on my own journey. In the beginning, I had only enough faith to surrender small things to Jesus. I would choose to take a small step towards Jesus and access the faith that he would help me not to cry all day. I would choose to take a small step towards Jesus and access the faith that he would help me not yell at my son. I would choose to take a small step towards Jesus and access the faith that he would help me to manage the Cold Hard Facts. Some days I lived in the present and some days I lived in the future, dragging the past behind me. Some days I kept my eyes on Jesus and some days I looked into the Chasm. I have walked, fallen, and tried to crawl on the invisible bridge of Faith. I have taken many small steps and walked across many Chasms over the last twenty years. I *still* take small steps because no matter how many times I stand on the edge of the Chasm, I still only have one moment in time. I still must live in the present and take one small step onto the invisible bridge. But one thing has changed over the years. My faith has grown to trust. I can surrender jobs, homes, my son, and "mountains" to Jesus. That's right; I am maturing into a trust relationship with Jesus.

Faith Grows and Matures into Trust. In the beginning of my walk in lifestyle faith, it was easy for me to doubt. I was walking into unfamiliar territory. It made no human sense that there was an invisible bridge. So I took small faltering, stumbling steps forward. And those small steps of faith have built a new past. I can look behind me and see the bridges I crossed. For example, at my separation I thought I would never be able to raise my son alone. On his eighteenth birthday, I looked back and realized I did it. But I was never alone. Now I can see the bridges Jesus led me across a step at a time. So I "trust" he's there and there is an invisible bridge over any Chasm in front me in the present. Does that mean I am not afraid? Absolutely not, sometimes I am terrified. That's right, even now Chasms can terrify me. I am only human. Sometimes, the unknown future can terrify me. However, I do not stay too long in the fear, staring into the new Chasm. I do not stay in fear because my faith is growing into a trust relationship with Jesus. When I choose to trust Jesus, I can overcome any fear. Does that mean that I do not have moments of doubt? Absolutely not; but the doubt leaves when I look back and see the bridges that I crossed with Jesus. Does that mean I run across the invisible bridge of Faith? Absolutely not, I still follow Jesus' instructions: I do not doubt, I take small steps, and I trust Jesus.

I cannot explain in words the sweetness of that trust relationship. I can tell you this relationship begins to grow the moment you do not doubt and take one small step onto the invisible bridge of Faith. Do you know what happens when you make that decision? You walk into the protective arms of Jesus. That is right, he immediately fills you with his presence. You may not see him or be able to physically touch him but you will know his presence. You will know peace like you have never known before. It is as if he reaches into your soul and calms the storm of turmoil from your painful wound and vulnerability to Nightmare Fear. You will know wisdom like you have never known before. You will see options and/or solutions to those Cold Hard Facts. You will know hope like you have never known before. Not a hope of positive thinking that we try to muster up ourselves. It is a hope that miraculously fills every fiber of your being. It is a hope that cannot be explained in human terms. When we do not doubt and take a step forward onto the invisible bridge of Faith, we are filled with hope.

Jesus knows the challenges we face on our Half Family journey. So not only has he given us his presence as our perfect confidante, but also he has provided the perfect food to grow and mature our faith into trust.

The Perfect Food

The unfailing, perfect confidante and the perfect food are inseparable. We cannot walk the invisible bridge and develop a trusting relationship with Jesus without the perfect food for our spirit. This perfect food will energize us, inspire us, encourage us, and strengthen us. This perfect food is the Bible. The words contained in the Bible provide us the perfect nourishment for this Half Family journey to wholeness.

Stepping out in faith onto an invisible bridge with an invisible confidante was not easy for me. I often needed encouragement, instructions, and road signs. It was difficult because at first I did not trust Jesus. I believed, but I did not have a trusting relationship with him. Even after the first few steps on my invisible bridge, I had only fleeting faith. I could not see Jesus or the invisible bridge. So Jesus gives me something to see and touch: the Bible filled with his words of encouragement, instructions, and road signs. He calls us to ingest those words and step out in faith. In fact, we cannot walk in faith without the Bible. We need the self-care instructions in this book to grow and mature in lifestyle faith.

We need to study the Bible. Think about this study as any other learning experience. If you wanted to learn something new, you would probably take a class on the subject. You might enroll in a course, and you would make a commitment to attend the appropriate classes to learn the subject. At your first class, you would be given a textbook. In order to learn the subject, you would study the textbook and then show up for the class. The instructor would teach with the understanding that you had studied the textbook. If you showed up for every class but never opened the textbook, would you learn anything? You might learn a little: probably just enough information to be dangerous.

Learning to grow and mature in lifestyle faith requires the same commitment. We need to study the Bible. We need to ingest the perfect food from Jesus. Trust me without the Bible, you will try to "have faith" but will never grow and mature your faith into trust. You cannot learn lifestyle faith from Jesus with out reading the Bible. You cannot build a trust relationship with Jesus without studying the Bible. I cannot stress this point enough. I spent too many years looking to people, yes, even pastors, to give me the answers to faith. While people and pastors could provide some guidance, I needed to personally ingest the Bible.

It is sad, but I was a Christian for a long time before I ever truly began to ingest the perfect food. Oh, I knew Bible stories about the creation, floods, oppression and deliverance, sin and redemption, and the birth of Jesus, but I had never allowed this perfect food to fill my spirit. So before I provide some self-care instructions for ingesting this perfect food, we need to grasp some truths about this amazing book.

The Bible Is the Holy Word of God. This is a powerful statement because of the word holy. As the word faith is waved around in Christian circles, the word holy is used with little or no understanding of its meaning. Can you define holy? I can't. Maybe there is a theologian that has clearly and accurately defined this word. But I doubt it. Our Holy God dwells in a place beyond our human understanding. There is no one on earth who has written a holy book and no human is holy. Therefore, we will never truly understand the word holy until we enter eternity with Jesus. We may lack the full knowledge of holy, but we do need to grasp the importance of the Holy Bible. And we need to strive to walk towards holiness knowing that we will know the fullness of a Holy God at the end of our earthly journey.

So as a starting point on this journey through God's Word, think of holy as pure or perfect. That means the Bible is pure. There are no lies, no mistakes, and no fantasies in God's word. Every word is true, every story is true, and every event is true. Do not take these statements lightly. As you travel through the Bible, you may be tempted to believe some parts and reject others. The whole Bible is true, pure, and perfect. The whole Bible is holy. Remember just as we are called to not doubt that Jesus has built an invisible bridge of Faith, we must not doubt that the Bible is God's Holy Word.

The Bible Is the Living Word of God. The Holy Bible is a living book. I cannot explain this concept. I only know it is true. When I am struggling for some spiritual direction, I have picked up my Bible and found the needed guidance.

Actually, more than guidance, it was as if a passage of scripture written two thousand years ago was written just for me. Often I read a passage or chapter that I have read many times before and find new meaning and understanding. The Bible is unlike any other book you will read. Your acceptance of Jesus as your Savior has given you access to the living Word. Yes, only Jesus' followers can breathe in living words from the Bible. If you have never experienced the nourishment from the living Word, you only need to believe and not doubt to experience the truth for yourself. You can open the Bible and find guidance that seems to be written just for you. You can read the same passage periodically over many years and find different encouragement each time. You can read the Bible every day from now until you die and find new meaning. Believe it and do not doubt. Accept that the Bible is God's Holy, living Word.

But how do we study the Bible? How do we ingest the perfect words from the Holy, living Bible? Just like trusting our confidante, we take in the nourishment from the Bible, one small bite, small choice, at a time. You may or may not study the Bible. You may have received suggestions from other people to start in the book of Matthew or John. You may have some personal study course. I recommend an approach especially designed for the mother in the Half Family. This approach has self-care instructions for two parallel study paths. Those study paths to ingest the perfect food for our Spiritual Margin of Faith are 1.) Meet your need and 2.) Know God.

Meet Your Need

We have a personal God. You may or may not believe that fact right now, but it is true. Jesus longs to personally meet our needs. Actually, we are not only needy, but sometimes we are desperate for help. We may be standing on the edge of the Chasm with no earthly way to cross this expanse of darkness. We are going to have to take a step of faith onto the invisible bridge and believe that Jesus has the answer. Sometimes we need encouragement to make that choice to step into the unknown. The Bible can meet our need for that encouragement, but choosing to pick up the Bible and reading the book of Genesis may not meet that particular need. Or choosing to read that personal Bible study course may give you biblical knowledge, but it may not meet your particular need. In fact, when you are in the middle of a crisis, reading the book of Genesis or a Bible study course may be like reading Greek for all the good it will do you.

I know the truth of that statement from first-hand experience. Sometimes I have felt like I was reading Greek in the Bible. I would get frustrated. I needed specific Bible guidance for my current crisis. That was when I decided to use the "meet my need" approach. There is nothing sophisticated about this approach, but it has provided the self-care instructions that I needed for stepping into faith.

So here is the process: find the concordance in the back of your Bible. Most Bibles will have a list of words and specific scriptures related to those words. All you need to do is select a word and look up the scriptures. If you are afraid, look up the word afraid. If you are angry, look up the word angry. If you are hungry, look up the word hungry. I guarantee that you will not encounter an emotion or situation that the Bible does not address. You will find answers to your questions. You may not like the answer, but you will get an answer. Some answers may confuse you and require that you seek godly counsel for an interpretation. The point is that all the answers to lifestyle faith are found in the Bible. Sounds pretty simplistic, right. Well it is.

We do not have to be a pastor or a biblical scholar to ingest the perfect food. In fact, Jesus said we need to be like children. We need to believe and not doubt. We need to take small faith bites. God honors those small bites of his holy, living Word with encouragement, guidance and road signs.

My process has changed slightly over the years. I have marked hundreds and hundreds of passages in my Bible with notations, dates, and insights. I have memorized many "meet my need" passages and used them as I stood on the edge of the Chasm. This "meet my need" approach has created a path through the Bible that has grown and matured my faith into trust. Each time I ingest the perfect food, it has been proven trustworthy in nurturing my spiritual body. When I get a word of guidance, I use it and it works. When I get a word of encouragement, I use it and I get hope. When I get a word about a road sign, I follow it and it is trustworthy. The Holy, living Word of God will meet each of our needs on the journey, but it is not enough to ingest these words to only meet our needs. We need to ingest these words to know God.

Know God

Mothers in the Half Family are not the only ones who read the Bible to meet a need. Many women may use a different approach from mine, but their goal is the same; they "need help." God wants us to look to him for guidance, encouragement, and road signs on a daily basis. Unfortunately, if we only read the Bible to meet our need, we will be creating a selfish pattern, not a self-care margin. We have a personal God who wants to meet our needs, but our God is also relational. Jesus longs for a relationship with us. Remember, relationship is two-way communication. Therefore, if we are only crying out to God in our time of need and taking from him, how are we building a two-way communication? If we are always taking, what kind of a message are we sending to God about our desire to have a relationship with him? Therefore, we cannot ignore our self-care instruction to know God. God wants to have a relationship with us and a relationship by definition is a two way street. No matter how needy we are, we cannot always only just take from the Bible. If we want to have a trust relationship with Jesus, we must make the decision to take small bites of the Bible to know God.

My own journey to know God has been bumpy. Hopefully, my experience can assist you in avoiding some of those bumps in the road. I had a deep longing to really know God, but I did not know how to do it. I would go to Bible studies, listen to biblical tapes from spiritual leaders and listen to biblical messages or sermons on Sunday, but I felt like I had pieces of God. I would see one aspect of God and then see another aspect and be confused. I was standing too close to the Bible. I could see beautiful pieces of God in Bible studies and sermons, but I could not see the whole picture. I knew I would never really fully know God until I got to heaven, but surely there was more to this earthly journey than fragments. Then I discovered the answer, which had been in front of me all the time: it was the Bible. Well duh, you know that. But do you?

The Bible is a book, right? You have read hundreds of books in your life. When you read, if you want to understand the whole story, do you read only pieces of the book? Do you listen only to other people's interpretation of pieces of the book? No. Sadly, that is how we often read the Bible. Have you ever read the last page of a book hoping to understand the story line? If you have done that, the last chapter or last page normally makes no sense because you do not know the story. Yet many people read Revelations, the last book in the Bible, and wonder why they don't understand a single word. My question to them is, "Have you read the whole book?"

The Bible has a beginning, middle, and an end. If you want to know God, you must read his Book. Back to our school example, would you read a textbook in pieces? No, it would be extremely confusing. The same holds true for the Bible. If you want to know God, you must read his Book from Genesis to Revelation.

After many years as a Christ follower, I made a commitment to know God. I took a two-year course that went from Genesis to Revelation and it transformed my life. Was it a difficult commitment for me? Yes, but I am still receiving blessings from that commitment made many years ago. Many confusing passages are now clear. Since I have read the whole Book, more often than not, I quickly know where to look for guidance, encouragement, and road signs on my own journey. Above all, I have a continually maturing trust relationship with my God. I know God not from the pieces of him but from the whole of him. I am beginning to understand the "Bible" story and know God. I say beginning because knowing God is a journey. Each day is a new revelation about my God revealed to me in his Holy, living Word. It is a journey where I keep repeating the basic instructions. I keep reading the Book. So guess what? Even as I write to you, I am rereading the Bible from beginning to end.

Making a choice to know God is difficult because it requires commitment and time. Choosing to know God requires a step of faith. Make a choice to not only ingest the perfect food to meet your need but to know God.

But it is not enough to have Jesus as the unfailing, perfect confidante and ingest the perfect food from the Holy, living Bible to meet our need, and know God. We need to learn to communicate with Jesus. We need to exercise our spiritual muscles of faith through prayer. Our final self-care instruction for the Spiritual Margin of Faith is prayer.

Spiritual Exercise

Just as the physical margin has self-care instructions for exercise to strengthen our bodies, we have self-care instructions for prayer from the Spiritual Margin of Faith to strengthen our spiritual body. Prayer is stretching our spiritual muscles in communication with Jesus. Through this spiritual exercise, we can get access to specific "invisible" bridge instructions or road signs for the journey. I know that talking to an invisible confidante and receiving answers may sound a tad mystical. Actually, without the self-care instructions for our unfailing, perfect confidante, Jesus, and the perfect food, the Holy, living Bible, prayer is nothing more than mystical. The spiritual exercise of prayer that I want to share with you is not mystical. It is not a magic wand. This self-care instruction for lifestyle faith is spiritual communication that must be born from a relationship with Jesus and grounded in the Holy, living Bible. Jesus, the Bible, and prayer are inseparable.

So how do you start? Well, I could give you guidelines for praying or I could give you a process for this communication. I don't think so. This spiritual exercise is much more than guidelines or a process. Prayer is not about techniques; it is about communication and relationship with Jesus. Do you have one-size-fits all guidelines for communicating with your earthly confidante? Do you have a process for communicating with her? Of course not, and neither is there a one-size fits all guideline or process for communicating with your heavenly confidante.

If I do not have any prayer techniques, maybe I should just share my prayer experience with you. In fact, I could write pages on the experiences of my own prayer life. And those experiences may be interesting to you, but they are personal to me. The point is prayer is personal. Your prayer life will be personal for you.

And the only way to truly exercise your spiritual muscles in prayer is to get alone with Jesus. You are the only one who can use your self-care instructions for exercise from your physical margin to build a healthy body. And you are the only one who can use the self-care instructions for prayer from your spiritual margin to grow a healthy spiritual body. You are the only one who can make the decision to communicate with Jesus.

I may not have techniques or experiences to share with you, but I do have some self-care instructions to recommend. Prayer, spiritual exercise, is simple. You talk to Jesus and then you listen to him. It truly is that simple. Of course, prayer is not always easy.

Jesus lives beyond our physical sight. If we cannot see Jesus, how do we know when and where to talk to him? More importantly, how do we listen? Guidelines and a process are sounding better all the time. Actually, all we need to know to pray are two self-care instructions for this spiritual margin: 1.) Jesus is always listening and 2.) listening takes practice.

Jesus Is Always Listening. There was a point at the end of my abusive marriage that I would shoot arrows to heaven, "God help me; God help me." Over and over, I would cry out. You see, I had salvation. I was a child of God. Jesus was my savior, but I was not on the road of lifestyle faith. I had wandered off the road into dangerous territory. Even in that state, Jesus heard my prayers. How do I know? Twenty-five years later, I am alive, healed, and writing this book. Given the last few months of my marriage, I could and should have been a statistic on a page, just another victim of abuse. I am here because Jesus was listening. That is the promise that he has made to his children, "I will never leave you nor forsake you" (Joshua 1:5). In fact, even if you have not accepted Jesus as your savior, he knows that you are reading this book and he is listening. He is waiting for you to call to him. He is waiting to embrace you.

Jesus never takes a break. His communication lines are always up and available for anyone. You will never get a busy signal. You will never experience an outage. No matter the time or the circumstances, no matter the form or content of your prayer, Jesus is always listening. If you can only manage "God help," he hears your cry.

In fact, it is no accident that Jesus is always listening. I think there is a glorious hope in that fact. He longs for constant communication with us. Prayer is communication. Therefore, prayer is not an event, it is a lifestyle. If you are like me, I had always thought of prayer as an event. I would struggle to find the appropriate time during the day to pray. I would look for the right words and techniques. I was missing so much with that approach. If Jesus is always listening, doesn't it make sense that he might want more communication than a onetime event? The answer is yes.

Prayer is a lifestyle of communicating with Jesus who is always listening. And we do not have to measure our words or take a course in the right words for prayer; we just need to desire to communicate with him. In fact, our desire is more important than the words. If we believe and do not doubt that Jesus is listening, and our desire to communicate with him causes us to simply say "God help," Jesus hears us. He is interested in our heart's desire for communication. The reality is that Jesus knows what you are going to say before you say it. So just talk to Jesus and believe he is always listening. He wants us to bring all our needs to him in prayer.

Remember, Jesus longs for constant communication. He listens to our heart, not our words. But talking to Jesus is only one-way communication. We must be also willing to listen.

Listening Takes Practice. Just as we should not only read the Holy, living Bible to meet our need, we cannot simply exercise our spiritual muscles by talking to Jesus. This spiritual exercise of prayer is about communication and relationship. Communication means that Person A talks and Person B listens, then Person B talks and Person A listens. In other words, we need to listen to Jesus.

This aspect of spiritual exercise takes practice and more practice. Most of us do not need any practice asking for help. Once I learned I could cry out to Jesus at anytime, it was like a gift from heaven. I found it easy to spill my guts, which is extremely important but it was only one-sided communication. Listening to Jesus was a challenge.

I could not hear anything after I spilled my guts. I was distracted by my internal and external worlds. I knew that Jesus was probably trying to give me encouragement, instructions, or road signs, but I only heard static.

We will only learn to listen and hear Jesus with practice. How do we practice? Well, if prayer is stretching our spiritual muscles in communication, then we must create a consistent, disciplined exercise program. We need a program that we can practice over and over to get spiritually fit to listen and hear Jesus. We would not expect to strengthen our physical muscles without exercise and neither can we strengthen our spiritual muscles without it.

Therefore, we need to schedule time with Jesus. We cannot just shoot words to heaven and spill our guts and expect to hear anything but static. Not because Jesus does not want to give us instruction, encouragement, or road signs, but because we do not know how to listen. When we learn to listen through a disciplined prayer life, we will get instructions, encouragement, and road signs for our lifestyle faith journey.

If you are like me, you may need some help with listening. You may want to try: 1.) listening to the Bible and 2.) giving our best to Jesus.

Listening to the Bible

How do I listen to Jesus? How do I hear him? But more importantly, how do I know what I am listening for? How do I know what I hear is from Jesus? I must admit that for me it was the simple things that I stumbled over on this road of lifestyle faith. The answers to my questions were in front of me all the time. When Jesus left this earthly world, he left behind his Holy Spirit for us. His spirit speaks to us. Mystical? Magic wand? Without the Bible, his spirit will seem mystical. Remember the Bible is the Holy, *living* Word of God. The Holy Spirit speaks to us from those pages.

Listening to the Holy, living Bible is the most important lesson I learned in my daily prayer life. Here is what I mean. Prayer is not some mystical process of communication. Yet that is exactly what I used to do. I figured out that I should talk to Jesus and then listen. However, when I tried to listen, I had no idea what I was listening for. Was I going to get an answer to my problems? How would I know if it was the right answer? If I asked other people to pray for me, how did I know they heard the right answer? I went down a lot of wrong roads and missed a lot of road signs because I was on some mystical path.

Just as we need Jesus for prayer, we cannot exclude the Bible. The Bible has all the answers, and Jesus will direct us to those answers in prayer. Jesus, the Bible, and prayer are inseparable.

From personal experience I learned the power of the Holy, living Bible in prayer. Often times on my own Half Family journey when I faced crossing the Chasm, my mind and emotions overwhelmed me. All I could do was cry and babble incoherently to Jesus. There was no way I could hear anything else but my own painful moaning. In those moments, I would read the Bible out loud and hear the words. More often than not, these living words would calm my mind and emotions. I heard peace and hope. Now I may have gone into prayer with a different agenda than peace and hope. I may have wanted the Chasm to go away. By listening to the Bible, I received God's agenda: a calm spirit so Jesus and I could communicate. I could then receive the instructions to cross the Chasm and the strength and courage to walk in faith.

In other moments, when nothing that I read in the Bible made sense to me, I would simply pray scripture to God. Can you imagine how pleasing it is to God's ear to hear one of his children speak his Holy Word to him? In my darkest moments, one of my favorite scriptures to pray is Ephesians 6:10–18. It talks about the fact that our perceived earthly battles are really spiritual battles. Therefore, we should put on the armor of God and we will win the battles. When I have been standing on the edge of the Chasm, I have often put on the armor of God. So the next time you are in that position, pray Ephesians 6:10–18. It does not matter if you understand it. Take a step of faith and watch Jesus move in your life. If you want to listen to God, just read his Holy, living Word out loud.

I have memorized scriptures so I can have constant communication with Jesus. In those hours away from the solace of my scheduled prayer times, I can listen and hear Jesus in the scripture stored in my mind.

Listening takes practice. We need to learn to listen to the Bible and the only way to do that is to make a decision to give our best to Jesus.

Giving Our Best to Jesus

Do you ever try to talk to your children while they are playing a video game or watching TV? Do they hear you? No, you need their undivided attention. They may hear a portion of what you have to say, but it will probably be distorted into what they want to hear. Listening to Jesus is no different. If we are distracted by the cares of this world, how can we clearly hear Jesus' words? We can't. Therefore, if we want to hear Jesus, we need to give him our undivided attention. We should give Jesus our best time. In other words, don't give your unfailing, perfect confidante your leftover time. If Jesus, who sits enthroned in the heavenly realms, can extend his best to us by always listening, we should give him our best. If the Spirit of the living God is waiting to speak to us, we should give him our undivided attention. This choice to listen is important because listening to Jesus is not always about us. Listening to Jesus is about getting to know him and building a relationship. We should not just listen to Jesus to make us feel better or get some answer. How rude! How selfish! Remember, we are creating self-care margins, not selfish margins. No, we need a two-way communication line.

Here is the reality about listening to the Bible and giving Jesus our best time. It is the only way to really hear Jesus. The Spirit of the living God speaks to us through his living Word in those moments that we are focused on listening. There is nothing mystical about listening to Jesus. Learning to listen and hear Jesus is a choice and it takes practice. I had to choose to read the Holy, living Bible to meet my need and know Jesus. I had to choose to listen to those words.

Listening took practice. Sometimes, I would fall asleep listening to the Bible. Other times my mind would wander or I would look at the Chasm. Sometimes I heard nothing but silence. Sometimes I heard something, but it made no sense. I would ask myself was that really God, so I would go to Scripture to test it. Important point about listening, you will never hear something from the Spirit of the living God that contradicts the Bible. Jesus would never instruct you to lie, cheat, steal, murder, take drugs, or alcohol to escape.

This point is crucial for us to understand. In my early days of learning to listen to Jesus, I would also listen to other people. Sometimes people would tell me something that had come to them in prayer. I would listen and accept it without prayerfully testing that message against the Bible. Don't make that mistake. Prayer begins in the Bible. Jesus does not give cosmic messages that float around in the universe. Jesus speaks the truth grounded in the Bible.

Once I learned this, I started to get better at listening and hearing the Spirit of the living God. I truly do receive encouragement, instructions, and road signs from Jesus. Trust me, if you stay faithful and learn to listen, you will be amazed by the guidance, the answers, the direction, the peace, the joy, and the miracles that come from listening to Jesus.

Just remember, prayer is two-way communication with Jesus. He is always listening to hear our cries for help, but he also waits for us to listen to him. In order to hear Jesus, we must listen to the Bible and give him our best time. Jesus, the Bible, and prayer are inseparable.

The Spiritual Margin of Faith

Our Spiritual Margin of Faith provides self-care instructions for accessing lifestyle faith through our unfailing, perfect confidante, the perfect food, and spiritual exercise. We have Jesus as our confidante. He tells us not to doubt that there is an invisible bridge of Faith. He tells us to take one small step forward and promises that those small steps of faith will grow and mature into trust. We have the perfect food, the Holy, living Word of God. We can study the Bible and ingest these living words to grow our faith. Finally, we have the spiritual exercise of prayer. We will learn to communicate with Jesus and listen to him. The Spiritual Margin of Faith completes our Hope Roadmap. So guess what?

We Are Ready

We are ready for the *Half Families Made Whole Through Christ* journey. We know the truth about the condition of the road. We have the Whole Truth Picture. Based on the condition of the road, we have the complete Hope Roadmap. It contains the self-care instructions for our emotional, physical, mental, and spiritual margins.

So now we are ready to see "where the rubber meets the road." In other words, the Whole Truth and the Hope Roadmap are great information and maybe some of it has already helped you. Actually, none of it is really trustworthy until we use it. We need "real world" experience. We are going to take the Whole Truth Picture and the Hope Roadmap and take a walk into reality through the toughest spots on the Half Family road.

Therefore, no single parents are allowed beyond this point. You now know the Whole Truth and have access to the Hope Roadmap. So you are no longer a single parent. You are no longer single. You are not alone. Other women are with you. More importantly, Jesus is with you. You are no longer a dark road with no roadmap and no destination. You have a roadmap and a destination: wholeness. You are now officially the mother in a Half Family. We will no longer utter the word single parent. We are now Half Families on a journey to wholeness through Jesus Christ.

We are going to pick up the Hope Roadmap and take our first step forward as the mother in the Half Family. And our very first step on this road will be to pick up our children. Before we can truly embark on the journey, we need to prepare our children to walk with us on the road to wholeness.

CHEAT SHEET

The Hope Roadmap—Crossing the Chasm

The Spiritual Margin of Faith

1. It is a choice; it is action; it is a journey.

2. It is lifestyle faith.

Jesus, the Perfect Confidante

1. Do not doubt.

2. Make one small choice.

The Holy, Living Bible—the Perfect Food

1. Meet your need.

2. Know God.

Prayer—Spiritual Exercise

1. Jesus is always listening.

2. Listening takes practice.

7

Equipping Our Children for the Journey

We have spent some time equipping ourselves for the Half Family journey. As the guide and the most important asset on this journey, we need to be prepared for the challenges along the way. But we are not alone on this road trip. Our children travel with us. Doesn't it make sense that they also need to be equipped for the journey? Yes. After all, we are equipped with the Hope Roadmap for the journey based on our Whole Truth Picture. Shouldn't we do the same for our children? Yes, but what do our children need? Well, our Hope Roadmap is based on our Whole Truth Picture. Therefore, it only makes sense that we need to first understand the truth about our children's external and internal worlds before we identify the appropriate equipment for the journey.

Now obviously, our children have much of the Whole Truth Picture in common with us. In their own way, they see the Cold Hard Facts. Minimum income and maximum expenses impacts everyone in the Half Family. They too can experience Real Fear from their external world.

Do our children have a painful wound and a vulnerability to Nightmare Fear in their internal world? Are they wounded and fearful? Yes. Have they lost margins in the death of the relationship? Yes.

Certainly, our children share in the experience concerning the truth about our external world. But it is the truth about the internal world of our children that has the greatest impact on their journey as part of the Half Family, and we need to examine this truth closely. If you think about it, you would probably agree that your children are wounded and fearful. That makes sense. Do you really believe they are wounded and fearful? I think that many of us operate under a false assumption and make a mistake in assessing the truth about our children's internal world. This causes us to miss our children's true needs: the right equipment for the journey. I certainly made this mistake.

Quite honestly, right after my separation, I had trouble identifying the truth about my internal world let alone determining the truth about my son's internal world. Therefore, I operated under a false assumption that my son was broken and he needed to be fixed. I did not verbalize this assumption, but my behavior said, "My son is broken and needs to be fixed." My false assumption caused me to miss meeting my son's real need.

My False Assumption

About a year after my divorce, I began to make faltering steps at improving my parenting skills. I knew I needed to be there for my son. Unfortunately, my preoccupation with my painful wound and my Nightmare Fear caused me to, at best, neglect my son's true needs. I did the basics for my son such as food, clothing, shelter, and school. Sadly, I was hanging on so tightly to myself that I did little else. I knew I needed to do more, so I decided to take a small step towards parenting my little boy. I took missteps because I did not see the truth about his internal world. I saw only the symptoms. I only saw my son's misbehavior and my own overreaction to his actions.

From the moment of separation from my husband, my son began to act out through erratic and irritating behavior. Since I had only superficial emotional stability, I would explode in anger. Yelling became my main discipline tactic, which only fueled his actions. I could see the wheels turning in that little brain, "I want to watch Mom get red in the face." Distressed by my obvious lack of control, I sought counsel on how to defuse my volatile temper. It was suggested that before yelling at my son, I should count to ten. This method would give me time to gain some perspective. It sounded logical to me. So I began counting to ten many, many times during the day.

Along with his behavior eruptions, my son had some poor eating habits. It was difficult to get him to eat a full meal. I knew I had to improve his nutrition, so I began feeding him vitamins. Faithfully, every morning, I would put the tablet next to his breakfast plate and sit him down to eat. I would leave him at the table and I would go finish dressing for work. When I returned to the kitchen, the food and the vitamin would be gone. I was very pleased with myself. We were making progress with his nutrition, or so I thought until one Saturday morning.

While cleaning the living room, I moved the couch. There, to my horror, hidden beneath the couch were piles of tablets. Realizing that my son had not eaten even one vitamin, I became furious. I did not count to ten. I yelled, "Darius Albert Frank." He cautiously entered the room, knowing that anytime that I used his full name he was in serious trouble. He put his hands on his hips and stared at the vitamins. Then he looked at my red, boiling face complete with fiery eyes and said, "You better count to ten real fast." I was speechless long enough to defuse my anger and hide a smile.

The Truth

There is a Whole Truth Picture hidden in that story that took me a while to see. I had to step back and see that my son was not broken. You see I had read a book and even heard some counselors talk about the brokenness of children from divorce. Unfortunately, in our society children of unwed mothers or from divorced homes are considered broken. Who was I to doubt the experts? Therefore, I thought that my son was broken, and I kept trying to find some "fix him" repair kit. I was focused on techniques and gimmicks to repair his brokenness, and I was making little progress. In fact, he was wise to my count-to-ten gimmick. The problem was that the gimmicks were designed to "fix" the symptoms and not the core problem. I was not seeing the truth of his internal world. The erratic behavior and poor eating habits would never change until I saw the Whole Truth.

The Painful Wound

My son was not broken; he was wounded just like me. If divorce ripped and tore me apart, what did I think that it did to him? He was not part of a relationship by choice but by blood. He was physically, emotionally, and mentally part of my husband and part of me. The death of the relationship, the marriage, had deeply wounded him. If I had confusion about my condition, he had confusion. If it took me time as an adult to realize that I was wounded, how could a child come to this realization? If I had trouble dealing with the pain, how did I expect a four year old to react? My son was wounded. He was not broken.

This wound from separation occurs in a child of any age. Babies, toddlers, adolescents, and teenagers will feel the pain from the wound. The child's age may define their reaction to the wound, but all children will feel the pain. Babies can sense the loss and the stress from a mother and may cry constantly. Toddlers will act out in erratic behavior. Adolescents may do poorly in school. Teenagers will verbalize the pain. Our children are wounded. They are not broken.

The Vulnerability to Nightmare Fear

If our children are wounded, then our children are also vulnerable to Nightmare Fear. Guess what? Their most prevalent Nightmare Fear is the fear of the future, but it is not the same nightmare as ours. Their future fear is a life without us. Most children cannot verbalize this fact, but the fear of being abandoned is overwhelming. They have already lost one parent. Will they loose the other one? They were an innocent victim, a backseat passenger, in the "car wreck" of the relationship. They have experienced the death of the relationship and one parent is gone. If you have read any books about the impact on children from the death of a relationship or been in any support groups, you have learned about the fear of abandonment. That does not sound broken to me. It is true that all children face this fear. Again, this fear comes from the vulnerability caused by their painful wound. And remember, the painful wound and the vulnerability to Nightmare Fear have nothing to do with a marriage certificate but has everything to do with the death of a relationship.

After the separation from my husband, I came face to face with my son's fear of abandonment. Two days after I left my husband, my son and I flew halfway across the country to stay with my parents. A month later, I needed to fly back to my home state and take care of some business. I could not take my son with me. I will never forget the day that I was preparing to leave for the airport. My son was absolutely hysterical. He kept screaming, "Mommy, don't go. Mommy, don't go. You won't come back." No amount of verbal reassurance would comfort or calm him. I had to go, so I left him crying. At that moment, I knew he was wounded, and he was afraid of loosing me. I had hurt him and I clearly saw his fear of being abandoned. It still grieves me deeply to recall that moment. I had failed my son.

Just like us, our children need to face the pain from the wound and the vulnerability that causes Nightmare Fear. Unfortunately, many children carry their pain and fear into adulthood. If I had continued to view my son as broken, I would have continued to use gimmicks and he would have become a wounded adult. Our children are not broken. They are wounded and afraid. And they have lost a margin.

The Lost Margin

Our children have lost margins such as their physical home, and emotional and mental stability. However, the primary margin they lost was a father. That margin may be a husband or an unmarried partner to us, but to a child that margin is father. That father was another body in the house. It does not matter the age of the child whether infant or teenager. The father was a presence in the home and a part of that child is now gone. The relationship may have been decent or abusive, but there was a relationship. Our children are the grieving victims from the death of a relationship. They are not "products of a broken home." Forget for a moment about your feelings for your ex-partner. For a child of any age, a father is a devastating margin to loose.

My son's wounded, fearful condition without a father was never more apparent than in his rare quiet moments. In those times, he would sit down to color and would draw pictures of black monsters. No amount of encouragement could dissuade him from these pictures. In truth, I could relate to the "black monster."

Only my son knows his feelings in those moments, and I can only imagine the turmoil inside of him. He was the innocent victim in the death of the relationship. He was a passenger in the "car wreck" of the divorce. In his mind, he loved and trusted both of us. Now his daddy was gone. His world was turned upside down. It was not safe. What was happening? Did a monster do this? Did a monster swallow up his dad? Was his mother next? Was he next?

My son was never broken; he was wounded. His Whole Truth Picture was very similar to mine. In his internal world, he had a painful wound, vulnerability to Nightmare Fear, and he had lost a significant margin, his father. Therefore, my son was on the edge of his own Chasm, his black monster, and his erratic behavior and poor eating habits were his feeble attempts to escape. Sound like anyone you know?

The Chasm of Parenting

My son may have been standing on the edge of his Chasm, but he was not alone. I was standing right there with him. As his mother, I knew he needed my help, but clearly my gimmicks and techniques were not working. I could not find a "fix-him" kit because my son did not need to be repaired. He needed to be healed. He needed hope and I was not equipped to handle this situation. I could not cope with my own pain and fear, how could I cope with his inner turmoil? Yet, there was no one else.

We were standing on the edge of a Chasm: the Chasm of parenting. The view may have looked different to my son, but we were staring at the same Chasm. I was wounded and he was wounded. We were both afraid of the future. He was afraid that the only remaining parent would leave him, and I was afraid that the only remaining parent, me, was incapable of parenting anybody. The parenting road that I was on during my marriage was gone and all that was left was a dark, bottomless pit. As I stared into the Chasm of parenting, I felt completely alone, unable to raise my son and convinced that this task was impossible. I could not do it.

Intuitively, I knew my son needed a "whole" mother, and I was at the end of myself. I could not give him what I did not possess. I was facing the dark Chasm of my own "black monster." We were in serious trouble. Somehow I realized that I must find a solution to my parenting dilemma.

The Hope

When I began to see the Whole Truth Picture that my son had a painful wound, was vulnerable to the Nightmare Fear of abandonment, and that he had lost the margin of a father, I really needed some hope. When I came to the realization that I did not want my destructive behavior to impact my son and that I could not do it alone, I went to Jesus for hope and help.

I wish that I could say that my early encounters with Jesus on this journey were driven by my great spirituality. Unfortunately, I was normally desperate for parenting answers and chose Jesus as my last resort. Despite my motives, Jesus was there for me. Since my first "parenting" prayer, I have never stopped going to Jesus for help. I have spent many long hours with Jesus and the Bible in prayer for my son over the years. Anyone who has a teenager knows that those hours normally stretch into days of prayer. What Jesus impressed on me in those early days has stayed with me. Those desperate hours of prayer profoundly changed my parenting forever.

When I came to the end of myself and believed that there must be a way across this parenting Chasm, I took small steps of faith onto the invisible bridge towards Jesus. In the beginning, Jesus gave me the needed guidance for parenting my son. The counsel was unexpected. I was still looking for gimmicks and techniques for him. I wanted a one-size-fits-all solution for my unique little boy. I wanted a magic wand to fix him, but the answer to my prayers was not gimmicks and techniques. I did not get a one-size-fits-all solution or a magic wand for parenting. I did not get these things because my son was not broken. My son was wounded, afraid, and had lost his father. Jesus gave me the needed guidance, the answer to my unasked question: how do I parent a wounded, frightened child? The answer was love. The answer was that he would lead me into love for my son.

The Leader

Jesus is not only my unfailing, perfect confidante, he is the leader of my Half Family. We are to take encouragement and instruction from Jesus and follow his road signs. We then are to travel the road guiding our children with Jesus as the head of our household. Do you know what a relief it was to know that I am not the leader? When I looked at the devastating truth of my son's condition and my own overwhelming personal truth, I gladly handed the leadership for this Half Family to Jesus. My statement that "I cannot do this alone" is true. If I had tried to be the leader, I would have failed. What a marvelous hope that I can lean on Jesus as the leader. I am responsible for faithfully following his parenting counsel, but I am *not* responsible for healing the wound and chasing away the Nightmare Fear. Only Jesus can accomplish this task. He is the leader so that is his responsibility.

Now, we need to be clear on this leadership; Jesus is the leader of the Half Family, but I still have the responsibility to guide my son. Jesus' leadership means that I am not alone, but I am still required to walk the invisible faith bridge across my parenting Chasm. So what is our parenting responsibility? How do we guide our children across the parenting Chasm? If we have to discard our gimmicks and techniques, what do we use? How do we equip our children for the rough road? We equip our children with love. Our responsibility is to love our children. We need to guide our children across the parenting Chasm in love. We are to use love with our children, not gimmicks.

Choosing to Love Our children

As mothers, we want the best for our children. No mother wants to see her child or children in pain and fear. I was no different. I could accept that Jesus was the leader. I did not want the job. And it took me a short period of time with Jesus to figure out that my son needed to be loved. Clearly, there must be more to parenting than love. How do I guide my son in love; how do I equip him with love? I was confused because I still thought love was a repair kit for my son. I did not understand love.

See, if you had asked me, "Do you love your son?" I would have said "Yes, of course." But I had a shallow, superficial love based on the world's definition. My love was emotional; it was conditional and at times, manufactured. I would "feel" love for my son and say the words, "I love you." But sometimes I was more concerned about my pain than my son's. At times, my own painful wound and vulnerability to Nightmare Fear made me think of my son as a burden. Sometimes, I thought of my son as a responsibility and a constant reminder of a failed marriage. I was more concerned about escaping my own pain than parenting my son. What horrible thoughts. I did not want to think or feel that way. I wanted to be a loving mother. I wanted my son to "feel" that he was loved, and I thought the words "I love you" were enough. All too often, my actions and behavior did not always reflect those words. In my prayerful moments, I knew that left to my own creative devices, I would fail. I would read all the right books, heed the advice of experts on parenting, and give my son gimmicks and techniques, but I would fail because love was absent. The truth was I felt unlovable. I did not "feel" any love inside of me. I had failed at my marriage and would probably fail at parenting my child. How could I give my son something I did not possess?

In my confused state, I would sit with Jesus trying to get an infusion of love from him. I wanted to feel love so I could love my son. As always, Jesus faithfully revealed himself to me and gave me what I really needed. I did not get an infusion to "feel" love; I got the definition of love. I had to learn that love it is not "what I felt for my son," but "who I am for my son."

> *Love is patient, love is kind, it does not envy, it does not boast, it is not proud. It is not rude, it is not self-seeking, it is not easily angered, it keeps no record of wrongs. Love does not delight in evil but rejoices with the truth. It always protects, always trusts, always hopes, always perseveres. Love never fails.*
> (1Corinthians 13:4–8)

When I first read this definition, it surprised me. It surprised me because it had nothing to do with me "feeling" love. I had always thought of love as an emotion, a feeling, or a magic wand. Love like faith is another word that is waved around like a magic wand. This definition of love had nothing to do with magic wands.

This passage clearly shows that love is a choice and it is action. Each time I choose to love it grows and matures. Sound familiar? Look at the passage above, love is not a feeling and it cannot be manufactured. Love is a choice. We choose to be patient, and kind. Love requires action to protect and persevere. And like faith, I have learned that we grow and mature into love. There was no way that I could just "feel" love. This love requires that I choose to be patient and that I practice patience. And love grows and matures.

As I have chosen love over the years, I learned that it is not about me but is all about other people. When I thought about my gimmicks, I realized that my parenting was void of this love. I failed in my count-to-ten technique not only because it was a gimmick. In reality, it was for me not my son. I said that I wanted to fix my son. Actually, I was more concerned about my reaction, my needs, and my peace and quiet. Jesus' definition of love indicates that we focus on others not ourselves. Love is all about other people not me.

We struggle with this concept because we have the definition for love backwards. Our human definition of love is an emotion. We want to feel loved. So when we get a "feeling" of love, we want to hang on to it. Why? Well, if we give our love feeling to someone else, we may not get that love back. What if that person will not love us in return? Therefore, we selectively give our emotional love to safe people. As long as someone will love us in return, we will love him or her. So we try to possess love. Basically, our human definition of love is subjective, selfish, and based on self-gratification.

But Jesus' definition of love is the absolute opposite. Love is deliberate, selfless, sacrificial acts to meet the needs of others. Therefore, we must choose to love. We must choose the love that focuses on others, not ourselves. We cannot subjectively choose only safe people to love and we definitely cannot possess love.

I truly struggled with this definition of love. I wanted to know what do I get out of choosing to love someone else? I needed love. I "felt" unlovable. I wanted to be loved in return. I wanted my son to love me, but the return of love did not seem to be part of the definition. It was difficult to trust Jesus with this definition and choose to love. I wanted someone to love me.

But I was looking for love in the wrong place. I was looking for another human being to make me feel loved when all the time Jesus' perfect, unfailing love was waiting for me.

My distorted view of love kept me from understanding that I was loved; Jesus loved me. You see the Biblical definition of love reflects the way that Jesus loves each of us. I can now see Jesus' love for me in his daily patience, kindness, protection, faithfulness, hope, perseverance, and unfailing presence over the years.

I want to let you in on a little secret about love. It is one that I learned further down the road into the journey of wholeness. I will tell you now because I think it will help you in those moments when choosing love may be difficult.

Jesus' love cannot be accumulated and stored up in us. Love is not ours to possess. Love flows through us. Only through Jesus, the Bible, and prayer can we have access to love. When we make a choice to access that love, Jesus will allow it to flow through us to another human being. Love is a difficult choice because it requires us to let go of ourselves and unconditionally embrace another human being. And here is the secret. *When we allow love to flow through us, love will flow back to us.* It is absolutely amazing. As you let go of yourself and allow the love of Jesus to flow through you, you will begin to understand and know that the God of the universe loves you. It will not matter so much if you "feel" love because you will know love. Love will flow back to you.

Love is not easy, but we must continue to choose it. And we will begin this learning process with our children. We will equip our children with love for the Half Family journey. And this love will grow as we travel down this road.

The Love

Parenting Our Children in Love

I truly believe that the only thing I did right as a parent was to continually learn from Jesus to love my son. As with faith, Jesus led me into love one step at a time. In the beginning, I had no idea that this Half Family journey should begin with loving my son. I would periodically slip back into techniques or gimmicks. But in his patience, Jesus showed me love's path. Loving our children is a journey. It is not an event. Parenting in love is one moment, one minute, one hour, or one day at a time. Love truly is all we need to give our children for the rough road. First Corinthians 13:4–8: simple instructions but not always easy to follow.

Love Is Patient. I love Webster's definition of patience. Patience is calm endurance without complaining or losing self-control and a willingness to put up with waiting, pain, trouble. If patience is a key ingredient of love, Webster's definition certainly eliminates any possibility that love is a feeling or an emotion. There have been hundreds of times in communicating with my son that I have not felt calm, like using self-control, or willing to put up with pain or trouble. Patience is not emotion. It is a disciplined action. I think that God must have a good sense of humor. He begins his definition of love with the one action that absolutely demonstrates that love is not an emotion. We are to parent our children with calm endurance, without complaining or losing self-control, and with a willingness to put up with waiting, pain, and trouble. My son will attest to my ability to mess up this action of patience. (Just wait until he has children.)

So instead of creating a count-to-ten gimmick for dealing with an unruly child, shoot a silent prayer to Jesus for patience. In your Bible study times, learn to know God, read about God's patience with us, his children. In your scheduled prayer times, pray for patience. Take a step in love and trust that Jesus will flow patience to you.

Love Is Kind. *It does not envy, it does not boast, it is not proud. It is not rude, it is not self-seeking, it is not easily angered, it keeps no record of wrongs.* When I read this passage, I realized afresh how clearly Jesus knows us. He does not tell us what kindness is; he tells us what kindness is not. I am creative and can find loopholes in almost anything. This passage takes away all my loopholes.

Think about people who you consider kind. Their presence, their words, their actions and their touch make you feel warm and valued. They are not envious, boastful, proud, rude, selfish, easily angered, and they do not hold a grudge. They touch your heart with their kindness. There is the key to kindness. It is an inside job. Love is action that comes from a heart surrendered to Jesus' definition of love.

Kindness will lead our children to a deeper understanding of love. Children will learn kindness from our example. A kind touch, a kiss, a heart-felt hug, and an encouraging word can empower a child to rise above the harshness of their environment. Kindness is truly found in the simple acts of our daily lives. I used to grieve because I could not give my son the material things that other children possessed, his own room, a backyard to play in, new clothes, and the latest toys. In reality, the kindest thing that I did for my son was to give him my presence.

Trust me, our children need our kindness more than any material object that we can buy for them. A material object may distract them for a while from their painful wound and vulnerability to Nightmare Fear, but the distraction will last only a short time. In fact, if we are not careful those material objects can become an escape, a jump off the Chasm. An act of kindness has a lasting effect. A kind word or a kind touch can sooth the pain and fear and move a child towards healing and wholeness. Kindness will not cost us anything financially. It requires that we deliberately, selflessly, and sacrificially chose to meet our children's needs with an act of kindness.

Love Does Not Delight in Evil *but rejoices with the truth. It always protects, always trusts, always hopes, always perseveres.* Love embraces the Whole Truth and rejoices in that truth. With love, the truth will set you and your children free. Look at this passage closely, Jesus is telling us that truth is always delivered surrounded in love. In other words, we do not lay the truth on our children and walk away from them. We do not tell our children the truth of their wrong actions or behavior and let them suffer the consequences of their mistakes. Is that the way Jesus deals with us? Does he say, "You have divorced your husband, or have had a child outside of marriage. That is wrong, so you are on your own now. You will suffer the consequences." It is true we must face the truth about our wrong actions or behavior. It is true there may be consequences for our actions or behavior. It is not true that we are on our own. Jesus forgives us and then he uses the truth to point us in a new direction. He longs to protect us, trust us, give us hope, and encourage us to persevere. We need to provide protection, trust, hope, and encouragement to our children in all situations.

Our goal is to use the truth to lead them to wholeness, not to use the truth to break their spirit. Therefore, we must be long-suffering with our children. We must be willing to stand with them in the truth surrounded by protection, trust, hope, and encouragement. No matter how unlovable they may be at times. We must always protect, always trust, always hope, and always persevere. There is a deep truth hidden in these verses. Our human definition of love implies that it grows the more that we feel it. Jesus' definition of love grows and matures in those moments when we do not feel like loving someone but choose to love despite our feelings. In other words, Jesus' love truly flows in the moments that we have to choose to love someone who we view as unlovable, just as Jesus loves us despite the world's view or our view of ourselves as unlovable.

If you are struggling with a child who is in deep pain and absorbed in Nightmare Fear, put down all your techniques and gimmicks. Pray to Jesus for the flow of love. Choose to forget about your own pain and fear for a moment and meet this child where they are. Stand in front of them with truth surrounded in protection, trust, hope, and encouragement. Reach out to them and allow Jesus' love to flow through you.

Love Never Fails. Beyond a shadow of a doubt, I know the truth about throwing away all the gimmicks and techniques and learning to love my son. It is a journey, a personal journey. I stumbled a lot in the beginning. Despite my mistakes, Jesus honored my heart decision to allow love to flow through me to my son. And the love flowed back to me in wonderful ways, not just from Jesus but from my son.

I began this chapter talking about my son's erratic behavior, his poor eating, and his quiet moments of drawing "black monsters." During his year in kindergarten, I began to allow Jesus' love to flow through me to my son. My progress was slow and certainly not as easy as using a gimmick. At first, I did not see anything tangible to demonstrate to me that this love was soothing my son's pain or relieving the Nightmare Fear. However, towards the end of my son's school year, Jesus gave me a very special gift to show me the power of even small of amounts of his love.

Near Mother's Day, my son came home from school with a present for me. It was a tall drinking glass with a simple painting wrapped around it. The little painting was encased in a protective plastic covering around the glass. I looked at the glass and painting in amazement and said to my son, "Who drew this picture?" He said, "I did, Mommy." I cried. There before me was a colorful little painting full of red, yellow, and pink flowers with brilliant butterflies flying through the picture. Across the middle was engraved, "I love you, Mommy." Jesus' healing touch of love had embraced my little boy. And that love flowed back to me. It is absolutely true that love never fails.

The Journey of Truth, Hope, and Love

This love for our children will not only equip them for the journey, but this love will empower us at every stop on the road. At every rough spot on our journey, we may selectively use different self-care instructions from the Hope Roadmap, but we will always use love.

Now that we have equipped our children, we are ready to take a journey through truth, hope and love that will lead us to wholeness. On our journey, we are going to walk through the toughest spots on the road. At each stop on the way to our destination, we will look at the truth about the rough road and then use the appropriate self-care instructions from our Hope Roadmap and love to keep us moving towards wholeness.

There are three important rules for this road trip. Number 1, it is a journey. We take one step at a time, one situation at a time, one problem at a time, one healing at a time, one joy at a time, and one precious moment of love at a time. No running allowed.

Number 2, the self-care instructions from the Hope Roadmap are designed to serve us, not for us to serve them. In other words, this roadmap is a guide; it is not a one-size-fits-all "fix-it" kit. I do not have all the answers. We are all unique. Therefore, you may not agree with my recommendation for dealing with a particular rough spot on the road. So I encourage you to refine the self-care instructions to meet your personal situation.

Number 3, love is everything. It covers the Whole Truth in grace. Love empowers the Hope Roadmap. Love is the healing touch for our children and us. Ultimately, love will make the Half Family whole. I encourage you to grow into love as we journey.

Now there may be one more question you have before we embark on the Half Family journey. That question is what is wholeness? What does the destination look like? Well, I am not going to answer those questions. You cannot truly understand or see wholeness until we reach the destination. But I will tell you this: I have been there and it is a marvelous destination. It is a place where you will be healed, be whole, and have the desires of your heart. So let's begin the journey.

CHEAT SHEET

Equipping Our Children for the Journey

The Truth

1. Our children are not broken.

2. Our children have a painful wound and our vulnerable to Nightmare Fear.

3. A father is the lost margin.

4. We face the parenting Chasm.

The Hope

1. Jesus is our leader.

2. Choosing to love our children.

The Love

1. Parenting our children in love.

2. Love is defined in 1 Corinthians 13:4–8.

8

Embracing Forgiveness

Fortunately, we are well equipped with truth, hope, and love for this Half Family journey to wholeness. We have the Whole Truth Picture, the Hope Roadmap with self-care instructions, and love. We have everything that we need for the journey. It is now our choice to accept the truth and hope empowered by love for each stop on the road. I caution you again that we are on a journey. I have no magic wands. I have no ten-step "get fixed" repair program. What I have to offer is my own experience in using truth, hope and love from my own Half Family journey.

Yes, it is fortunate we are well equipped because our first stop on the journey to wholeness involves embracing forgiveness as related to the death of our relationship. If you are like me, you would probably like to begin this journey anywhere else than here. The very word, forgiveness, makes your stomach knot. For many of you, I may have stirred up all your inner emotions by just mentioning this word. For some those emotions are intense anger focused squarely on your ex-partner, which makes your painful wound throb. For others those emotions may be suffocating guilt about the death of your relationship, which only fuels your vulnerability to Nightmare Fear. I understand those emotions. I have been there.

Why do we have to start this journey with forgiveness? Why do we need to embrace forgiveness now? Let's revisit the Whole Truth Picture to find the answer to those questions. What is the one piece of the Whole Truth that we can change? We may have little control over our external world, but we can exercise some control over our internal world. The answer is we can change ourselves.

What aspect in our internal world can we change? Or a better question might be, what in our internal world has the most negative impact on our journey? The answer is the painful wound and the vulnerability to Nightmare Fear. And how can we change this situation and what can move us towards healing of the wound and relief from Nightmare Fear? The answer is embracing forgiveness.

The Reality about the Half Family Journey

The truth is our internal world is not only the most logical starting place for this journey it is the only starting place to begin the journey. We may say that we need to focus on our external world first, but we will never effectively maneuver the Cold Hard Facts until we relieve the pain and fear in our internal world. The management of the Cold Hard Facts requires clear thinking. If you are in constant emotional turmoil, how effective will you be in that management? You will not be effective.

Here is the reality of the Half Family journey: *It is an inside out trip.* This Half Family journey to wholeness requires we begin this road trip at the core of our internal world, our painful wound and the vulnerability to Nightmare Fear, and then slowly travel to the outer edges of our external world, the Cold Hard Facts. Our journey takes us from our internal to our external world. We must travel from the inside out.

This approach may seem logical to you, but emotionally you may be looking for another approach, another roadmap. Trust me, I understand. I tried for years to avoid this forgiveness part of the trip. I would rationalize that when everything in my external world calms down, I would think about this internal stuff. I knew that forgiveness meant I would need to forgive my husband. In my opinion, he was a monster. He did not deserve to be forgiven. No, I would not forgive him.

Also, I thought maybe I would need to ask Jesus for forgiveness for something. Even though I saw myself as the victim in this divorce, I knew that divorce was a sin. In fact, I had the clear perception from many Christians that it was the unforgivable sin, second only to women who had children outside of marriage. So I was a victim who had committed the unforgivable sin. I could ask Jesus to forgive me for divorcing my husband, but chances were good Jesus would probably not forgive me.

You know what I did? I simply dug my heels in and refused to move forward toward forgiveness. I sat down in the middle of the road. But deep down somewhere, I wanted to be whole and free from pain and fear. Sitting in my little hole, I tried to find another way around the pain and fear other than forgiveness. There must be a gimmick that I could use. Be assured, the truth is the only way to become whole and free from pain and fear is to embrace forgiveness.

Forgiveness is the intensive care unit for our wound and vulnerability. Our painful wound will never heal and our vulnerability to Nightmare Fear will never leave us until we embrace forgiveness. Trust me, you can either decide to take this part of the journey now or later, but you will have to travel through forgiveness to be whole.

My own journey to embracing forgiveness was extremely messy. I kicked up dirt and dug holes in the road. I occasionally made mud pies to throw at anyone who suggested I forgive my ex-husband. A gimmick would have been cleaner. Actually, I think we like gimmicks and techniques because we can stay clean. They are sterile, and the Half Family journey to wholeness is messy. You will get dirty on this road. I speak from experience of getting filthy at this forgiveness stop on the journey.

I warned you we would visit the roughest spots on the road. Well, here is the first rough spot. You have a choice to make. Will you choose to learn to embrace forgiveness or are you going to sit down in the middle of the road? The choice is yours. We must choose to pick up our Hope Roadmap and use the self-care instructions from the Spiritual Margin of Faith to walk across the invisible bridge and embrace forgiveness.

The Truth

Our Need for Forgiveness

When I finally surrendered to the forgiveness path, I wanted to skip through the truth that I needed forgiveness. I had done nothing wrong. I was an innocent victim in the death of my relationship. For years sitting in the middle of the road, I compared my actions to my husband's. I compared my behavior to his. I compared my words to his. In my opinion, I looked like an angel compared to him. Therefore, he needed to ask me to forgive him.

I actually liked the victim role. I did not feel loved, so as a victim I could get attention. I would tell my divorce story to anyone who would listen and they would feel sorry for me. In some sick way, I thought this attention was as close to feeling loved as I would ever feel. For a brief moment, that "feel sorry for me" feeling would dull the pain and fear. But the pain and fear always came back. As I sat in the dirt, I tried to convince myself I was an innocent victim.

But I was sidestepping the truth. Jesus, my unfailing confidante, slowly and gently revealed the truth to me without my asking. I was comparing myself to my ex-husband. No wonder I did not think I needed forgiveness. I really believed his sins were much more serious than any I had committed in the marriage and divorce. In God's eyes sin is sin. You see the comparison I needed to make was to look at myself in relation to a Holy God. My actions, my behavior, and my words looked very different from that perspective. I had to examine my responsibility in the collapse of my marriage.

The truth made me squirm. First, I went into my marriage as a Christian. I was saved, but I lacked a devoted lifestyle as a Christ follower. My husband was not a Christian. I knew what and whom he was when I married him. I was so desperate to feel love I ignored any signs that I should not marry him. There were plenty of them. I even had a member of the church that I was attending at the time boldly tell me not to marry him. I ignored the warnings. You see as a Christian, I still did not have a clue about Jesus' definition of love. As a Christian, I had access to that definition, but I chose to be selfish. So I chose to accept the world's definition of love. I wanted to be loved and I was not really concerned about loving my husband. If he loved me, I would love him. I went into that marriage with selfish motives and my rules for love.

Second, I enabled my husband's behavior. I think somewhere in the back of my sick mind, I thought I could save him. He was not a Christian, and I thought I could change that situation. That thought was only a justification for my marriage. I wanted what I wanted. I wanted to be loved, and I was not interested in his spiritual condition. Early in our marriage, I should have confronted some of his abusive behavior and sought counseling for both of us. I should have prayed, sought fellowship with mature Christians and found a confidante. I did none of those things. I quietly sat by and enabled my husband's behavior by doing nothing and saying nothing. I was so focused on my selfish desire to be loved and be married that I ignored his cries for help. Yes, I believe the abuse was a cry for help. I ignored the cry and enabled him until the end of the marriage when it was too late to do anything but escape.

I had done wrong. I had sinned. I had acted selfishly. I ignored the possible consequences of my selfish acts. I needed Jesus to forgive me for my part in the destruction of this marriage and the wounding of three lives: mine, my husband's, and my son's. The heart of Jesus' love is selfless relationship. In relation to my husband, I had violated that definition of love. I had offended my God and I needed to be forgiven.

Forget about divorce for a moment. If you are an unwed mother, look at your motives in the relationship that led to a child. I am going to go out on a limb and say the truth is you desperately wanted to be loved. The child or children were the consequence of your selfish action. If you *willingly* went into that relationship, that man is not solely responsible for your pregnancy. You are also responsible. What is your truth?

I just gave you the brutal truth about my heart condition in a few paragraphs. The realization of that truth was not an event. I could never have handled all that truth at once. Discovering the truth was a journey across the invisible bridge of Faith with Jesus. It is important to let Jesus lead you to the truth because you cannot do this alone. The truth is at the core of your painful wound and Jesus knows your condition. Without Jesus I never would have chosen to look at the truth about my responsibility in the death of the relationship. And I never would have been able to handle that truth without Jesus because he does something absolutely amazing as he reveals the truth. Never does Jesus reveal the truth without hope and love. Jesus always reveals truth surrounded by the hope of forgiveness.

The Hope

I never could have embraced forgiveness without Jesus. The truth without hope is a cold, dark lonely place. Have you ever had anyone hit you with some truth and then walk away from you? I have experienced that interaction especially as related to my failed marriage. I got hit with the passage, "I hate divorce, says the Lord God of Israel" (Malachi 3:16). When those words were taken out of context and thrown at me, I felt hopeless. I felt alone. (By the way that passage says that God hates divorce, not you). Jesus will never clobber you with the truth and walk away. Jesus will show you the truth about your responsibility in the death of the relationship with the hope of forgiveness that leads you to the love to embrace forgiveness.

The journey to embracing forgiveness requires the invisible bridge walk over the Chasm of the destroyed relationship and your responsibility. It requires a walk through pain and fear, and we need all our self-care instructions from our spiritual margin for this faith walk. We need Jesus, the Bible, and prayer.

Before I share my forgiveness experience with you, I want to tell you a story. It is a biblical story that many of you may have read. It is a story of forgiveness and wholeness. It is a "Jesus" story that has brought me great healing and love. So I want to share with you what I have learned from reading and praying about this story. Keep in mind that embracing forgiveness is an internal journey.

John 4:4–42 Jesus Talks with a Samaritan Woman

The Pharisees heard that Jesus was gaining and baptizing more disciples than John, although it was not Jesus who baptized, but his disciples. When the

Lord learned of this, he left Judea and went back once more to Galilee. Now he had to go through Samaria. So he came to a town in Samaria called Sycar, near a plot of ground Jacob had given to his son Joseph. Jacob's well was there, and Jesus, tired as he was from the journey, sat down by the well. It was about the sixth hour. (vs.4–6)

Remember I said that love is everything. Well, this story begins with love, is covered in love and ends in love. Now don't reread these passages. You did not miss the word "love." The word is not there, but let me show you Jesus' love hidden between the lines in these verses. Let me show you how Jesus has made a deliberate, selfless, sacrificial choice to love someone. Here are the clues that reveal that choice.

Look at the words "he left Judea and went back once more to Galilee. Now he had to go through Samaria". No, to get to Galilee, Jesus did not have to go through Samaria. In fact, Jews would often avoid traveling through Samaria to get to Galilee. The Samaritans were considered unclean (unlovable). Yet, it clearly states that Jesus had to travel through Samaria. He had to take this road because Jesus had made a deliberate choice to love someone in Samaria.

Then the passage says he deliberately stopped in Sycar at Jacob's well because he was tired. There is no doubt that Jesus was tired, but I do not believe that was the reason he stopped at this town and this well. Throughout his ministry, Jesus would choose to stay up all night praying and then teach, preach, and heal people the next day. I believe Jesus could have walked through Samaria to Galilee. I believe the reason he stopped in Sycar was because he had made a deliberate, selfless choice to love someone in Sycar.

Also, he sat down at the well at noon, the sixth hour. If Jesus wanted someone to draw water from the well, he had made a strange choice. No one came to the well at noon. The women, normally, drew water from the well in the cool of the evening. But we will learn Jesus did not really sit down for a cup of water but rather to give a cup of water. He had a divine appointment with someone at this well. All of his actions were a deliberate choice to be in this particular town, at this particular well at noon. He had made a deliberate, selfless, sacrificial choice to love someone, but who?

When a Samaritan woman came to draw water, Jesus said to her, "Will you give me a drink?" (His disciples had gone into the town to buy food.)
The Samaritan woman said to him, "You are a Jew and I am a Samaritan woman. How can you ask me for a drink?" (For Jews did not associate with Samaritans) Jesus answered her, "If you knew the gift of God and who it is

that asks you for a drink, you would have asked him and he would have given you living water." (vs.7–10)

Here is the divine personal appointment. Jesus had gone through Samaria, stopped in Sycar, and sat down at this well to meet this woman. She was the reason for Jesus' presence in Sycar. This Samaritan woman was his divine appointment. He had made a deliberate, selfless, sacrificial choice to love her.

Jesus begins the journey with this woman toward embracing forgiveness. Wait, forgiveness has not been mentioned in the story. In fact, forgiveness is not mentioned anywhere in this story. That is true, but forgiveness is found in every word Jesus says to her heart. Embracing forgiveness is an internal journey. The words in this story are clues to the true encounter between Jesus and this woman. Jesus has chosen to travel with this woman to embrace forgiveness. So let's look beyond the words and take this internal journey.

Jesus does not clobber the woman over the head with the truth about her internal world, her painful wound. Yes, this woman has a wound; which is the reason for Jesus' presence. He knows the truth about her internal condition. And we will watch Jesus lead her to the truth through hope.

Jesus draws her to him by doing something absolutely outrageous. He asks her for a drink. Jesus is a Jew and she is an unclean Samaritan. Never would a Jew soil himself by drinking from a Samaritan's cup. Therefore, this woman is shocked by his request and asks him how he can make such an outrageous request. She understands the difference between them. Jesus ignores the "external" question and answers her question with "internal" hope. Actually, he gives her what she needs and answers her unasked question. She may physically need water, but her soul needs this living water. This living water refers to eternal life. Why if Jesus knows the truth about this woman would he offer her such a lavish gift as eternal life? Because Jesus loves us and knows the truth can only be accepted with hope. Just like us, he knows this woman will need this hope in order to come face to face with the truth.

Even at this point, she wants to focus on her external world, but Jesus draws her into the truth of her internal world. Jesus wants a "heart conversation" with this woman.

> "Sir," the woman said, "you have nothing to draw with and the well is deep. Where can you get this living water? Are you greater than our father Jacob, who gave us this well and drank from it himself, as did also his sons and his flocks and herds?"

> Jesus answered, "Everyone who drinks this water will be thirsty again, but whoever drinks the water I give him will become in him a spring of water welling up to eternal life."
>
> The woman said to him, "Sir, give me this water so that I won't get thirsty and have to keep coming here to draw water." (vs.11–15)

Notice how this woman tries to hang on to the external world. She wants to believe the hope of the living water, but she is looking at the Chasm of the well. She questions Jesus' ability to retrieve this water. Yet again, Jesus does not answer her external questions. Instead, he clearly and deliberately speaks of the hope of "a spring of water welling up to eternal life." Look beyond the words to the heart conversation; Jesus is calling her to take a faith walk across the invisible bridge. He is telling her that even though she cannot understand how he will give her this living water, she must believe he will deliver what he promises. So this woman believes and asks for this water.

Her deep soul thirst compels her to ask for this living water. When she asks, some of the truth of our internal world is revealed. She wants the living water so she does not "have to keep coming here to draw water." Remember, she was alone and went to the well in the heat of the day. Obviously, there was a reason for this. Could this daily noonday trip be a constant reminder about some truth, some sin? Could there be a painful wound in her internal world? Did her aloneness at the well only rub salt in an internal wound? Jesus knows the answer to these questions, and he has prepared her with hope to reveal the truth, her sin.

> He told her, "Go, call your husband and come back."
>
> "I have no husband," she replied.
>
> Jesus said to her, "You are right when you say you have no husband. The fact is, you have had five husbands, and the man you now have is not your husband. What you say is quite true." (vs.16–18)

Jesus has saturated this woman in hope. He has given her the hope of living waters. He has given her the hope of eternal life and now he leads her to the truth. Even now, he does not blast her with it. Instead, he instructs her to go and get her husband. Notice he does not ask her where her husband is, but rather he leaves it to her to answer the unasked question. This is the moment of truth. Jesus knows this woman's heart and she has a choice to make. She can lie to Jesus about her husband. Jesus does not live in Sycar, and she has no reason to think he would know the truth about her marital status. Or she can verbalize her truth. She can choose to take a step of faith towards Jesus. She can choose to trust him.

She chooses to face the truth slowly. Her desire for the hope of "living water" drives her to admit she does not have a husband. Then Jesus shows her that he knows everything.

Take a close look at this part of the conversation. She made a small choice to say the truth. Then and only then does Jesus reveal he knows the Whole Truth about her. She has not been divorced once or twice but five times and she was now living with a man. (Isn't it interesting that this woman represents both relationships divorced and unmarried.) This woman was so unclean that even the Samaritans had isolated her from society. She was an outcast, and that is why she came to well alone at noon. She could not go to the well with the other women in the evening. She had committed "unforgivable" sins. Yet, in Jesus' eyes, she had not committed unforgivable sins. He chose to deliberately, selflessly, and sacrificially love this seemingly unlovable woman.

> "Sir," the woman said, "I can see that you are a prophet. Our fathers worshipped on this mountain, but you Jews claim that the place where we must worship is in Jerusalem."
> Jesus declared, "Believe me, woman, a time is coming when you will worship the Father neither on this mountain nor in Jerusalem. You Samaritans worship what you do not know; we worship what we do know, for salvation is from the Jews.
> Yet a time is coming and has now come when the true worshipers will worship the Father in spirit and truth, for they are the kind of worshipers the Father seeks, God is spirit, and his worshipers must worship in Spirit and in truth."
> The woman said, "I know that Messiah (called Christ) is coming. When he comes, he will explain everything to us."
> Then Jesus declared, "I who speak to you am he." (vs.19–26)

Now there are probably other interpretations of these passages, but here is what I think happened. This woman had been exposed. In her mind, this man was a prophet who had seen into her internal world and spoken the truth. Now she is concerned and beginning to realize that this prophet, like the rest of society might reject her. She wants the living water, but she is an unclean, very unclean, Samaritan woman. How could she possibly be given eternal life? She doesn't even worship in the right place? Will he reject her?

Then Jesus point blank tells her that the internal world is more important than the external world. "God is spirit, and his worshipers must worship in Spirit and truth." Now she thinks maybe there is some hope for her. She tells this prophet she longs for the Messiah and the truth.

Then Jesus does something absolutely amazing. Jesus tells her that he is the Messiah. Please understand the power of his words. Nowhere else during Jesus' ministry does he actually tell anyone he is the Messiah. He does not tell any of the disciples who follow him. He does not tell the religious leaders of his day. He does not tell the people that he physically heals. No one is told he is the Messiah except this one outcast, unclean Samaritan woman, who had committed unforgivable sins. What an incredible special gift for us. Yes, the gift is for us because this woman had no way of knowing the power of his statement. But we know.

This woman had not committed unforgivable sins. Jesus looked past the wreckage of her life and saw her painful soul wound. He saw her longing to be healed. Yet, she did not know who this man was. Can you imagine the courage it took for her to share the truth with this man, to take a step of faith? Jesus honored that step of faith with the amazing revelation of who he was. She was speechless.

> Just then his disciples returned and were surprised to find him talking with a woman. But no one asked, "What do you want?" or "Why are you talking with her?" Then leaving her water jar, the woman went back to the town and said to the people, "Come see a man who told me everything I ever did. Could this be the Christ?" They came out of the town and made their way toward him. (vs.27–30)

Forget the words and look at the picture here. Jesus has just told this woman that he is the Messiah. It says that just then the disciples arrived. Maybe they saw or heard Jesus' final few words. They had no idea what was going on, but my guess is they could see the "heart" communication all over this woman's face. Notice that for the first time in this story there are no words exchanged between Jesus and this woman. I am convinced that a life-changing heart conversation was occurring between Jesus and this woman at that moment. Personally, I think Jesus was leading her to fully embrace forgiveness. She now knew the fullness of Jesus' deliberate, selfless, and sacrificial act of forgiveness. She knew love and became open to flow of that love. In those last "heart" conversations beyond our ears, Jesus transformed this woman. How do I know all that? Because she leaves her water jug (her external world) and does the unthinkable. She forgets she is an outcast and runs into town to tell people the "good news." She exclaims that a man told her everything she did. Then she says, "Is this person the Christ?" My personal interpretation of that question is not that she doubted Jesus, but rather that she was drawing these people to their own encounter with Jesus. She was extending hope to them. And it worked.

They said to the woman, "We no longer believe just because of what you said; now we have heard for ourselves, and we know that this man really is the Savior of the World." (vs.42)

Look at this internal journey to embracing forgiveness. Jesus attracts this woman to him by extending hope. He envelops her truth in the hope of living waters. He leads her to accept the truth through hope and embraces her in forgiveness and salvation through love. Then he uses this unclean, outcast woman to bring salvation to a whole town.

I love this forgiveness story. Just like this woman at the well thousands of years ago, we cannot hide the truth from Jesus. He sees our hearts. He knows us. Just as Jesus extended hope to this woman knowing all the time who and what she was, he does the same for us. There is no unforgivable sin in Jesus' eyes. It does not matter how unclean, outcast, unforgivable you feel. If Jesus can forgive a woman married five times and living with a man, he will forgive us. No sin is greater than another. Sin is just sin in God's eyes.

Jesus sees us as wounded women who need to accept the self-truth about our responsibility in the death of our relationship surrounded in hope and who need to embrace forgiveness in love.

The Love

Forgiving Your Ex-partner

I accepted the truth concerning my responsibility in the death of the relationship, my marriage, and I asked Jesus to forgive me. I asked over and over again to be forgiven. I wanted to "feel" forgiven. I did not "feel" forgiven. If I had not committed the unforgivable sin, why did I not "feel" like Jesus had forgiven me? Why was I still in pain? Why did I feel so distant from God? Why did I feel like he did not love me? Obviously, I was a tad confused. *Forgiveness is not a feeling.* All together now, "Forgiveness is not a feeling; it is a choice." I had made the choice to look at the truth about my internal world and I had accepted the hope of forgiveness, but I had missed the love part.

Look again at the end of the story of the Samaritan woman. When this woman ran into the town, she did not forget she was an outcast. In her encounter with Jesus, she had fully embraced forgiveness and had forgiven the people who had made her an outcast. I know the story does not explain that fact, but her actions demonstrate it. She made a deliberate, selfless, sacrificial choice to share her marvelous encounter with Jesus with others. She freely let go of herself and decided to meet their need for "living water". Therefore, we cannot embrace forgiveness without love.

I realized I needed to forgive my ex-husband. In fact, I had to forgive my husband even if he did not want to be forgiven. Ouch! Let's just pour salt in the wound. With this realization, I pretty much sat down in the middle of the road and refused to move again. I was in no way going to forgive that (expletive deleted) man. He did not ask for forgiveness. He was not sorry for his actions. He did not think he had done anything wrong. No, I was not going to forgive him.

Did I *really have* to forgive my ex-husband? Yes I did. If I chose to accept forgiveness from Jesus, then I must be willing to forgive others. Now if you are still looking for loopholes and are convinced that the story above does not clearly state we need to forgive, you will find the answer clearly stated in the book of Matthew.

Do you know the Lord's Prayer? Well, let's look at this prayer from the biblical perspective. There is a section in the prayer that says, *"Forgive us the wrongs we have done, as we forgive the wrongs that others have done to us"* (Matthew 6:12—Good News Translation). Many of us may skip lightly over this passage. I certainly did. Jesus knows we like to skip or jump over spiritual truths that we do not like or accept. So he spelled it out clearly. Have you read the passage after the Lord's Prayer?

> *Matthew 6:14, "For if you forgive men when they sin against you, your heavenly father will also forgive you. But if you do not forgive men their sins, your father will not forgive your sins."*

There are no loopholes for embracing forgiveness. Forgiveness is not a selfish choice, something to make myself feel better. Forgiveness also does not mean I only forgive those people who know they need forgiveness. No, in order for us to fully embrace forgiveness, we must choose to deliberately, selflessly, and sacrificially forgive others. We cannot selectively choose to forgive some people and not others. When Jesus forgave the Samaritan woman, she gave away the forgiveness she had been given. Did the people in the town know she had forgiven them? Did these people even think they needed to be forgiven? Did they think they were justified in classifying this woman as an outcast? This woman's actions had nothing to do with other people's actions. Her actions had nothing to do with her external world and everything to do with her internal world. She made an "internal" deliberate, selfless, sacrificial choice to embrace forgiveness.

It took me years to accept that truth. If I had not committed the unforgivable sin, then my husband had not committed the unforgivable sin. I could not completely travel the journey to wholeness without fully embracing forgiveness. I remained in pain for a long time because of my stubborn pride.

My pride created a spiritual Chasm I did not anticipate. This dark hole opened up in front of me as soon as I sat down on the road and refused to move forward to embrace forgiveness in love. As a Christian, I read about forgiveness in the Bible, heard it in sermons, and heard it from friends, but I refused to move forward. I ignored Jesus' promptings through the Holy Spirit and I was miserable.

I truly do not remember how long I struggled with this issue of forgiving my husband, but it was several years. Jesus was relentless in my prayer times to get through to me. At some point, I began to visualize my situation, and the picture was disturbing. I had chained myself to my husband and my past by refusing to forgive him. I left my husband to be free from the tyranny, and my inability to forgive him had kept me a prisoner of that tyranny. At first, I may have stubbornly sat down on the road, but now I was stuck. When I had had enough of my own self-induced pain, I chose to trust Jesus and move towards embracing forgiveness. So I took one small step of faith and made a decision that I needed to forgive my husband.

In the beginning, I did not clearly understand my own forgiveness was linked to the forgiveness I extended to my husband. I was just in so much pain I made a last-resort decision to forgive my husband. So I surrendered my need to be right, my need to be the victim, my desire for revenge, my desire to want to hate him, my desire to revisit all the pain and hurt, and my desire to tell Jesus that my husband did not deserve forgiveness. It is this last selfish desire that still stops me in my tracks. Who was I to say that my husband did not deserve forgiveness? If Jesus had taken this perspective with me, I did not deserve to be forgiven. From Jesus' holy position, I deserved nothing. In his grace, he daily forgives me even though I have done nothing to deserve that grace.

I began a journey toward forgiving my husband. For me, embracing forgiveness was not an event. I had so many years of emotional turmoil inside that my journey was slow. But once I made the decision to forgive, I kept moving forward.

By now you can probably understand I needed all the self-care instructions from the Spiritual Margin of Faith empowered by love to cross this Chasm. If you are squirming in your chair right now at the thought of forgiving your ex, I will tell you a secret to help move you towards this decision. I wish I had known it standing on the edge of my Chasm. *Forgiving your ex will break the chains that bind you to pain and fear.*

When I made the forgiveness decision, my husband was not physically around. In fact, I had not seen him in many, many years. Believe it or not, forgiveness does not have much to do with the physical presence of that person or your external world. Forgiveness is an internal decision to surrender your thoughts and emotions. For me, I became aware on a daily basis that my husband negatively impacted my life and he was not physically even there. If I struggled to pay the rent, or buy food, I would blame it on him. It, whatever the situation, was always his fault. I would gladly tell anyone who would listen to all the gory details of the last months of my marriage. Yes, you need to get this inner turmoil out, but I was still talking about it two to three years after the fact. I had chained myself to him. I chained myself to my pain and fear. I was actually fueling that pain and fear all by myself.

So I moved toward embracing forgiveness. Each time I found myself thinking or spewing this venom about my husband (it did get poisonous), I would try to pray for forgiveness and be open to forgiving him. This journey took me a long time. It was one faltering step at a time. I remember when the final link in the chain was broken and I released my husband in forgiveness.

Over the years, I had trouble collecting any child support from my husband. Can any of you relate to that fact? For many of you unwed mothers, I am sure that trouble is not an appropriate description. As an unwed mother, you find the task of obtaining any financial support from your ex-partner to be an impossible task. I can relate to that feeling. Some fifteen to twenty years ago, the courts did not have the infrastructure in place to deal with the volume of uncollected child support payments. I was caught in that situation and jumped through so many government hoops that I got frustrated. That frustration only fueled the pain from my wound and my anger towards my husband.

One day in prayer, I saw forgiving my husband's debt to me would release us both from the chains of unforgiveness. He clearly did not think he should pay me child support, and he was going to continue to fight paying me this money. We were not in physical contact with each other, but we were clearly in a tug of war over these child support payments. I cannot explain it, but I had the sense that this issue was the last link keeping me chained to my past and my husband. On my knees, I forgave my husband for any "debt" the court had decreed he owed me. I told Jesus I would not pursue any further legal action, and I have kept that commitment. I took a step onto the invisible bridge to trust Jesus would supply the financial resources. I made a choice to love my husband and allow Jesus' kindness and grace to flow through me to my husband. Yes, choosing to forgive him was an act of love. I chose to surrender the need to be right and broke the chains that had trapped both my husband and I. He was free as well as I.

Now I caution you that your journey to embracing forgiveness may not include forgiving child support payments. Do not focus on my tangible act but the intangible choice. Make a deliberate, selfless, sacrificial decision to extend forgiveness to your ex-partner. Take small steps on this invisible bridge. In prayer with Jesus, find the chains that bind you to your ex-partner in pain and fear. What are you hanging onto that is creating a self-induced Chasm on your journey to wholeness?

I was free. The minute I got up from that prayer, I knew I had forgiven my husband. I can still recall the sweet joy of freedom that came from my decision to take one more step on the invisible bridge towards embracing forgiveness. I embraced forgiveness with a passion, which surprised me. I made choices that could only have come from Jesus.

For the first time, I truly saw my husband's pain and fear. I began to pray for him not because Jesus told me to but because I chose to pray for him. Unbelievable! I prayed for my husband's healing and his salvation. Can you imagine the power of those prayers? Here was a man who hurt me deeply emotionally, physically, and mentally. Yet, through the miraculous, transforming love of Jesus, I was able to sincerely pray and weep for my husband's soul. That my friends is sweet freedom.

Another unbelievable by-product of embracing forgiveness was the realization of my need to ask my husband for forgiveness. It takes two people to build a relationship and it takes two people to destroy a relationship. Even more unbelievable was my willingness, even eagerness, to ask for that forgiveness. Unfortunately, for several years, I did not have a clear indication of my husband's location. One day, I got a letter, actually, a hateful letter. I wrote him back a "forgiveness" letter. I still have a copy of that letter. As I reread it, I am amazed how Jesus transformed me to be able to write that letter. It was honest and not hateful. Most important is I shared the salvation message with my husband in it. Jesus gave me the words and the scripture verses. I do not know to this day whether my husband has forgiven me for my part in the destruction of our marriage. I am only responsible for the condition of my internal world. I have no control over my husband's internal world. But I am free.

What incredible joy lies in embracing forgiveness. I no longer want to "feel forgiven." I know I am forgiven. My personal journey to embracing forgiveness was just that—personal. Your journey is your choice. Just as Jesus led me on the invisible bridge across the Chasm of a destroyed marriage, he will lead you. Just as he was patient, kind, and faithful with me every step of the way, he will do the same for you. It was not an easy crossing, but it was an incredible experience that changed me forever.

Embracing Forgiveness

Embracing forgiveness is a very rough spot on the road to wholeness and a difficult place to begin this journey. However, it is the only place to begin this inside out trip. More importantly, if you want the painful wound to heal and the Nightmare Fear to go away, you must check into the intensive care unit of embracing forgiveness. If you follow the self-care instructions for the Spiritual Margin of Faith, you can be free from the pain and fear. If you take one step at a time with Jesus across the invisible bridge of Faith, you can accept the truth about your responsibility in the death of your relationship. Jesus will envelop this truth in the hope of forgiveness. He will forgive you and lead you to forgive your partner. He will lead you to embrace forgiveness in love. Jesus, the Bible, and prayer will never fail you.

But embracing forgiveness is a journey. It will be a dirty personal journey. You may have a desire to sit down in the middle of the road and throw mud pies. You may want to continue to spit venom at your unforgivable, unlovable ex-partner. You may choose to escape into your misery and dig a hole in the road. That hole may become a Chasm. I have been there. Just remember, Jesus is always waiting to lead you to embrace forgiveness, but you must choose to get up and take a step towards him. He will lead you into wholeness. The choice is yours.

(I must share a very personal note with you about embracing forgiveness and forgiving my husband. Did you notice that when I wrote about my personal journey to forgiving this man, I began to refer to him as my husband not my ex-husband. I did not even realize I had done this until I started to edit this chapter. If you want to see the external result of an internal journey, you only need to grasp this fact. I no longer have to put something between this man and me like the word *ex*. In God's eyes, he is my husband. I chose to tear the relationship apart. This man is and will always be my husband. That may twist your brain. But when you choose to embrace forgiveness, Jesus will give you his perspective.)

CHEAT SHEET

Embracing Forgiveness

The Truth

1. Forgiveness is the intensive care unit for our painful wound and our vulnerability to Nightmare Fear.

2. We need forgiveness for our responsibility in the death of the relationship.

The Hope

1. The Spiritual Margin of Faith is required to cross the Chasm of unforgiveness.

2. The hope of forgiveness is found in John 4:4–42

The Love

1. Love to forgive our partner

2. Love to ask for forgiveness

9

Guiding Our Children to Embrace Forgiveness

When I was sitting in the middle of the road refusing to move forward in forgiveness, guess who was sitting next to me? When I was kicking up dirt and digging holes, guess who was getting dirty with me? When I was making mud pies, guess who helped me throw them? The answer is my son. He saw my depression, my fits of anger, my pain and my tears. He heard my venom spewing at his father. He witnessed my fitful steps toward forgiveness and he saw me embrace it.

As mothers in the Half Family, our parenting includes guiding our children to embrace forgiveness. Their journey to wholeness also begins at the core of their internal world, their painful wound, and vulnerability to Nightmare Fear. They are no different from us. Forgiveness is also the intensive care unit for their wound. It will never heal and their vulnerability to Nightmare Fear will never leave them until they embrace forgiveness. The truth is it is necessary step for them to be whole.

Right now I may not be your favorite person. As much as you did not want to begin this Half Family journey by embracing forgiveness, you probably most certainly do not want to guide your children to do it. Instead, we want to focus on the external symptoms of our children's painful wound and vulnerability to Nightmare Fear. That approach is only putting Band-Aids on their wound. It did not work for me and I doubt that approach will work for you.

But there is another reason for our hesitation. We may not want to stop at this spot in the road because we have not embraced forgiveness. And here lies the difficulty.

Lovingly guiding my son to embrace forgiveness has been difficult for me. Much of the time, I was in the intensive care unit for my own wound, and at the same time I was trying to deal with his wound. I was overwhelmed by my own need for forgiveness let alone my son's need to take this forgiveness journey. I wanted to get through my own pain and fear and then help my son. Unfortunately, just as the emotional turmoil from my internal world spilled out our Half Family, so did his. Whether I liked it or not, I would have to deal with his pain and fear. Therefore, guiding my son to embrace forgiveness was filled with many faltering steps on my part. Those faltering steps, my failures, have taught me a great deal about this part of the road. It was a messy journey, but I have learned the truth about what it means to be my son's guide. I have accessed the hope to guide him and love to show him how to embrace forgiveness.

This part of the journey may seem overwhelming to you or even impossible. I can certainly understand that feeling, but we cannot ignore our children's need to take the forgiveness journey. The good news is we have the truth, hope, and love to show us the way.

The Truth

We Are the Guides

Parenting is not an event; it is a journey. We are the guides for our children. Whether we realize it or not, our children are following our lead. They are learning from us how to handle the rough spots on the road. Our children are learning from our example.

Oh how I wish that meant they would just follow our example and embrace forgiveness. I wish it were that easy. My son may have seen my example, but like me, he did not want anything to do with forgiveness. So he dug his own holes, threw his own dirt, and was much better at making mud pies than I. He needed more than my example in order to embrace forgiveness. My son needed me to guide him.

If this journey was difficult for me, it was difficult for him. If I could not travel toward forgiveness alone, my son certainly could not travel this road alone. But I also could not guide him alone.

Remember, we are not the leader of our Half Families. Jesus is the leader and we are the guides for our children. We need to follow Jesus' lead and guide our children towards forgiveness. Sounds pretty simple. It is if you know the truth about guidance. Like so many aspects of parenting, I had to be educated. After many failed attempts, I learned three truths: 1.) guidance is not control, 2.) forgiveness is a choice, and 3.) entrust the results to Jesus.

Guidance Is Not Control. I had a distorted view of my role in guiding my son towards embracing forgiveness. I wanted control. Though I never verbalized that definition and in fact would have denied that description of my behavior, it was true. Desire for control was one of the reasons for my love of gimmicks and techniques. They gave me the illusion of control, that I could fix my son. But my son was not broken. Your children are not broken. They are wounded and Jesus possesses the healing touch. Yet even when I knew my son was wounded and I let go of the gimmicks, I was still trying to control.

I wanted to make my son embrace forgiveness. So I talked *at* him not *to* him. I would give him all *my* words. Actually, I would throw words at him about forgiveness, hoping that some of them would stick. My son is strong willed, so you can imagine how ineffective I was with word throwing. Trust me, control is an illusion. We control nothing. We can never control our children.

Your control may be different from mine. Do you use guilt, anger, or bribes, to get your son or daughter to do what you want? Some mothers may think of themselves as passive and they would deny they control their children. Is that true? Our children are in pain and fear. At some point, just like us, their pain and fear are going to come out. It may emerge from their internal world in the form of hurtful words or inappropriate behavior. What do we do in that situation? Will we scold them for the hurtful words or inappropriate behavior and walk away from them? Certainly, we should not accept this type of behavior from our children. However, if we only scold them and try to control the external symptoms, how will our children ever be free from their internal pain and fear?

Guidance is not control. Trying to exert control over a child to embrace forgiveness will only drive that child further away from forgiveness.

Forgiveness Is a Choice. The reason that control will not work is because I cannot make my son embrace forgiveness. It is a personal choice. Look again at the story of the Samaritan woman. Did Jesus make this woman ask for forgiveness? No. If Jesus would not make this woman ask for forgiveness, Jesus will not make our children ask for it?

If Jesus will not make our children forgive, we cannot make our children forgive. If Jesus would not make me forgive my husband, Jesus will not make my son forgive his father. If I cannot make my husband forgive me, I cannot make my son forgive me. Forgiveness is a personal choice. Our children must choose to understand and accept the truth about their own internal worlds. They will have to walk across their own Chasm on their own invisible bridge to embrace forgiveness. They will have to exercise their own faith and walk through their pain and fear. It is their choice. We can lovingly walk with them and guide them, but our children must choose forgiveness through Jesus. If we cannot embrace forgiveness without Jesus, our children cannot embrace forgiveness without Jesus.

This truth brings us to an important point. Like us, our children must experience the birth of faith and accept Jesus as their Savior. It took me time to grasp this fact. If I am only the loving guide and forgiveness is a personal choice, then my son must make the choice. I can lead him to Jesus, but he must choose. Do not assume that just because you believe in Jesus and go to church on Sunday that your children have the same belief as you. Our children must have a personal relationship with Jesus in order to embrace forgiveness.

For those women who do not have a relationship with Jesus, guiding your children into forgiveness cannot be manufactured. It is not a technique. Embracing forgiveness for your child or yourself cannot occur without Jesus. Everyone must make a personal choice to accept Jesus. We cannot save our children.

This truth is hard for us to accept as mothers. What if your child is a mere infant or toddler, how can they have an encounter with Jesus? What if your adolescent or teenager just digs a fox hole in the middle of the road? Let me surround this cold truth with some hope. Jesus loves our children far beyond what we could ever imagine. Our love for our children is flawed, but Jesus' love for our children is perfect. He can see deep into their wounded souls and knows exactly how to reach them. He will lovingly lead them on their own personal, internal journey towards forgiveness. It is their faith walk. Therefore, we must have faith that if Jesus has a forgiveness journey for us, he has one for our children. It is their choice.

Entrust the Results to Jesus. We are to guide our children to Jesus, allow them to choose forgiveness, and leave the results to him. It was difficult for me to take my hands off my son. When I finally realized forgiveness was the healing touch for his wound, I wanted to push my son into forgiveness. I wanted to take away his pain and fear. I wanted the end result: a whole child.

We all want to take away our children's pain and fear. We want them to be happy, healthy, and whole. As a mother, I can bear my pain, but when my son hurts, it is unbearable. I hurt for many of you who are experiencing that pain and are feeling overwhelmed right now. I truly understand those emotions, but we must be willing to guide and walk with our children to forgiveness and entrust the results to Jesus.

The result, forgiveness, is based on Jesus' time schedule. For those women with older children, they may stubbornly refuse to go beyond the truth to embrace forgiveness.

For those women with infants or toddlers, your children's forgiveness journey may require years. When I left my husband, my son was almost four. My son did not grasp the truth about his internal world until he was nine or ten. Trusting Jesus with my son was excruciating for me. In the beginning, I barely had enough faith to trust Jesus with me let alone my son. I wanted to see the result. I wanted my son healed and free from pain and fear. I had to accept that my son's healing was not my journey; it was his journey.

We are the guides for our children. I know it is difficult, but we need to accept the truth about that guidance. It is not control. We cannot control our children and guide them to embrace forgiveness at the same time. It will not work because forgiveness is a personal choice. And our children must make that choice. We must leave the results to Jesus. As a mother I know that this last sentence is difficult to accept. We need hope to be this type of guide.

The Hope

The hope that I want to share with you is not what I have learned from my success in guiding my son to forgiveness, it is what I have learned from my failures. That's right, this hope was born in my failure. I have failed in my role as a guide for my son. For too many years, I failed to recognize that my son must also begin to embrace forgiveness in his internal world. I was so focused on controlling the symptoms of his pain and fear that I did not guide him to the truth. I failed to accept forgiveness was his choice. I failed to trust Jesus with the results.

Therefore, the fact my son loves me and has forgiven me is absolutely amazing. It took me a long time to realize that even in my mistakes, my son found hope. I was his hope.

Our Children Need a Loving Confidante.

Our children are no different from us. If we need to talk to someone, our children need to talk to someone. They need a confidante. We need to learn from Jesus and become a loving confidante for our children. We can be a safe place for them to release their pain and fear and find hope.

For me, becoming my son's confidante meant I needed to learn a new way of guidance: 1.) I must be emotionally available for my son in kindness, 2.) I must choose patience to be a loving confidante and 3.) I must accept the role of confidante.

Emotionally Available for Our Children in Kindness. We must make a conscious decision to be available for our children. That means when they talk we listen. Did you ever get home from work and have a child that wanted to talk to you? You are exhausted and needed to prepare dinner. It is not convenient for you to listen to this annoying child. However, something could have happened at school that triggered his or her desire to talk to you. We need to be willing to walk away from our agenda and be open to listening to our children. We need to extend kindness to them and give them our full attention. We need to be emotionally available for them. This availability is messy and inconvenient. Clearly, there will be times when we cannot be available for our children, which should be the exception, not the rule.

Think about our emotional margins from the Hope Roadmap. Can you see the value of those margins in this situation? We need to create and use our emotional margins to ensure that we have an "extra amount" left for our children. We need to use our confidantes (other women) and Jesus to release our own pain and fear. We need to play to release stress. If we use up our emotional availability somewhere else, we will not be emotionally available for our children.

Actually, whether we are prepared or not, our children's emotions from pain and fear will spill out in the Half Family. Also, do not assume if your child is an infant there is no painful wound or Nightmare Fear. This child simply cannot verbally express their emotions yet. Therefore, it is not a question of if a child's pain and fear will emerge, but rather a question of when? Will we be emotionally available for our children in kindness? Becoming a confidante for our children will not just happen. We must choose to become emotionally available.

Patiently Enduring Our Children's Pain. The most difficult aspect in being our children's confidante is found in the truth about their condition. They are wounded from the death of the relationship, and they are vulnerable to the Nightmare Fear of abandonment. And *they are angry with us*. Yes, they are angry with both parents. They are in pain that they cannot understand. They have lost one parent and are afraid of losing their mother. Their emotions are confusing and volatile. Given their "intensive care" condition, we need to exercise patience as their confidante.

This patience is a choice and will take practice. For a long time, I saw myself as a victim of divorce. My son saw me as partly responsible for it. He could not verbalize that fact, but his emotional venting certainly said, "You are responsible." Our children are angry with us and they may have little control over the content of their words. Once they decide to share their internal pain and fear, you will get a flood of emotions. Some of this communication can be raw, ugly, and hurtful.

This is a tough position for any mother. We are wounded and afraid and our children's exposed wound and fear can fuel our internal emotions. Without Jesus' guidance, this raw communication can be deadly for a Half Family.

If I reacted to my son's raw emotion with tears or defensive words, I could fuel my son's fear of abandonment. He might be afraid if he hurt me and made me angry enough I would leave him. Can you see the downward spiral in this conversation? Can you see how we could get to the edge of a Chasm? Can you see how one or both of us may choose escape over forgiveness? Therefore, there is no way that we can handle our role as a confidante to our children without choosing patience. We have a choice to make about our role in this interaction. We need to be willing to love our children by being self-controlled and willing to listen and endure pain and trouble. I guarantee that you cannot exercise patience in this situation without Jesus' assistance.

If you have not guessed by now, let me share something with you. Becoming a confidante for your wounded child is going to create some pain for you. Because extending hope to our children will mean we focus on them and not us. Therefore, we need to make a decision.

Accepting Our Role as a Loving Confidante. This parenting journey of guiding your children to embrace forgiveness will hurt. (But it will also result in great joy.) Therefore, we must make a decision to accept this role of confidante. Prayerfully make this decision.

If, after prayer, you decide you cannot allow your child to verbally vent with you, you need to find a safe place for them to talk about their inner turmoil. If the pain from the wound and the vulnerability to Nightmare Fear are not faced, children will jump into their own Chasm of unhealthy escape. They will stop eating, overeat, disrupt school classes, get in trouble inside the home and outside the home, or heaven forbid, commit suicide. I certainly understand the need for a professional counselor. Only you, as the mother, can make that decision to seek professional help. If you think this help is the best method, then follow through with that decision.

But sometimes we are too quick to use a counselor and it becomes a gimmick to "fix" a child. I encourage you to carefully consider this decision. Instead, try being a loving confidante to your child. In reality, that is really what our children want from us. They want us to listen to them. They long for our patience and the warmth of our kindness.

If you choose to be a loving confidante, you will need to be emotionally available for your children in kindness and patiently listen to their pain. You can be hope for your children, but you must use love to actually guide them to embrace forgiveness.

The Love

Each child in a Half Family is unique and precious. Therefore, for us, as confidantes, there is no "forgiveness" guide that is a one-size-fits-all approach. Forgiveness is personal for each child, and I do not have all the answers for your specific situations. I do have some recommendations for lovingly guiding your children.

Listen to Our Children's Pain and Fear

When your child starts to vent the pain and fear from their internal world, listen. Do not open your mouth. Be still and calm until they stop. Body language speaks volumes. Do not roll your eyes, cross your arms, or take deep sighs. Remember, this communication is about our children not us.

My experience has shown me that when a child is ready to vent their emotions, they will come pouring out. My son tends to get verbal in the evening: sometimes late at night. When you encounter these emotions spewing out, you need to stop what you are doing and listen. Get out of bed, delay bedtime, pull the car over, or hang up the phone. Do whatever it takes to listen. Do not interrupt the flow.

Stop here for a minute and think about your own emotional venting to your unfailing, perfect confidante, Jesus. As I struggled through forgiveness, my venting to Jesus came at all times of the day or night. He was always there for me. We need to be there for our children. Clearly, there may be times we simply cannot listen to our children, but those times should be the exception, not the rule. If you cannot listen to them, encourage them to talk to Jesus. Direct them to the perfect, unfailing confidante.

Speak Love.

Do you notice that talking to a child comes after you listen? I don't know about you, but I tend to open my mouth first. Only when we have patiently and kindly listened to our children are we in a position to say anything.

The first words out of our mouths should be encouraging. If a child has poured out pain and fear, he or she needs some encouragement that there is a life beyond this "black monster." We need to tell them that we too have had similar emotions. Do not spill *your* emotions just affirm *your child's* emotions. Let them know anyone else in their situation would be in pain and fear. The purpose is to give them hope they are not alone. Now you need to do something important.

Tell them nothing they say to you would ever stop you from loving them. Do not assume they know this fact. They need to hear those words, and those words need to be backed up with actions. Do not punish them for their venting or words. It is their pain talking. That does not mean we should ignore hurtful words or inappropriate behavior. Rather than punish, we need to lovingly teach our children. We need to help our children to express themselves in constructive ways. Punishment addresses the external symptoms but lovingly teaching our children addresses the pain and fear in their internal world.

For example, while my venting normally included crying or yelling, my son's emotional venting normally included some physical behavior. While my anger would manifest in tears, my son would get angry and hit walls. I needed to help him manage that anger. One year, my son got a six-foot basketball hoop and Nerf ball from his grandfather. I put it in the corner of his bedroom. When he got angry, he would take out his aggression on the basketball hoop, not walls. If he wanted to verbally let his anger out, he could do that. When he was finished with the basketball, we would talk. He beat that basketball hoop to death. After his outbursts, we had some good conversations. Here is the key. We had to get all the emotions out of the way so we could deal with truth at the core of his internal world: his painful wound and vulnerability to Nightmare Fear.

Release Them to Jesus and Their Own Encounter with Forgiveness.

Releasing our children to Jesus and forgiveness is difficult. Many times after my son vented his anger and wanted to talk, he could see he was angry with his father. He could even admit his emotional outburst was a result of that anger, but forgiving his father was another story. He could not and would not forgive this man. Does that sound familiar?

In order to guide our children to Jesus and forgiveness, we need to give them the appropriate scripture a spoonful at a time and cover everything in prayer. Keep your Bible close by and use the *meet my need* approach for your children. Let them see you search the concordance for the right scripture for their needs. Share small pieces of God's Word. You can start with the Lord's Prayer. In particular, share Matthew 6:12–15 with your child and pray.

While I do not have access to my son's heart, I have glimpsed parts of his internal journey towards embracing forgiveness. I can see the impact of scripture and prayer. In the beginning, my son simply would not acknowledge his father existed because he was so angry with him. I remember one night we were praying and I started to pray for my son's father. My son interrupted and said, "God, excuse me from this part of the prayer." At that point in his life, he referred to his father as "the bum." Then, he moved to calling his father by his first name. Slowly, my son began to refer to him as "my father." I watched how small doses of God's word and prayer were moving my son toward forgiveness. This journey was and is still difficult for my son.

But there was another person my son needed to forgive, me. Expressing anger towards his father was safe for him to tell me. His father was not physically around. However, anger at me was another story. I was present. Letting out his emotions towards me was risky. He needed his mother.

Eventually that anger towards me came out. Actually, the anger at me sometimes came out in the form of a question. My son would say, "Why did you ever marry this guy?" I learned over time he really did not want an answer. He just wanted to say, "I am angry with you." When I got further down my own forgiveness road and he would ask this question, I would say, "I was brain-dead at the moment, I guess." He always suspected the answer. He just wanted me to admit it. I did not try to defend myself. I did not say I was sorry. His question was not about me. It was about him. I had to extend love to my son and make it easier for him to walk the invisible bridge of Faith with Jesus and forgive me.

Asking Your Child for Forgiveness

We are responsible for part of our children's pain and fear, and we will need to ask them for forgiveness. There is an important point that I want to make here. If you are in the middle of a discussion with your child that is focusing on their forgiveness, do not say the words "I am sorry." I have made this mistake many, many times. When my son would say, "Why did you marry this guy?" I used to say, "I am sorry." Immediately, my son would get defensive. This communication was not about me; it was about him.

We need to seek our children's forgiveness, but that interaction cannot be a flippant "I am sorry." We need to set aside time to tell them the truth about our responsibility in the death of the relationship. We need to tell them it was not their fault and we are deeply and sincerely sorry. Then we need to ask for their forgiveness. This example will go a long way in helping them on their own journey to embracing forgiveness.

It is a Journey

When we became mothers, our parenting roadmap did not have a rough spot in the road for embracing forgiveness. Unfortunately, after the death of our relationships, our parenting roadmaps changed. If you are in deep pain and fear right now, this stop on the journey may be overwhelming to you. If you have been the mother in a Half Family for a while and have ignored your children's pain and fear, you may be feeling guilty right now. It does not matter where you are at this moment. It matters what you do in the next moment. We are on a Half Family journey with our children. We begin, travel, and end this journey together one step at a time. When we step forward in faith into Jesus' love to guide our children towards embracing forgiveness, he will honor that one step of faith.

My experience has shown me the amazing power of love that is available for all mothers in the Half Family. If our children can talk to us, they will discover they have the same wound. They are not alone. They can ask us questions about the death of the relationship. As strange as it sounds, the wound can bring a mother and child closer together. If our children can spill all their raw emotion on us and we do not react, we will help dissipate their fear of abandonment. They do not talk to us because our children are afraid they will hurt us and we will leave them. If that fear is not reality, our children will move one step closer to healing. Plus you create a bond that will never be broken. My son and I have an incredible relationship. That relationship did not just happen; it was a journey of one step at a time. It was a miraculous journey into Jesus' love. And my joy from the pain of the forgiveness journey with my son is this: the love that flowed through me came back to me.

CHEAT SHEET

Guiding Our Children to Embrace Forgiveness

The Truth

1. We are the guides for our children.

2. Guidance is not control.

3. Forgiveness is a choice.

4. Entrust the results to Jesus.

The Hope

1. Our children need a loving confidante.

2. Be emotionally available in kindness.

3. Patiently endure our children's pain.

4. Accept our role as a loving confidante.

The Love

1. Listen to our children's pain and fear.

2. Speak love.

3. Release them to Jesus and their own encounter with forgiveness.

4. Ask your children for forgiveness.

10

Learning How to Wrap Relationships

The next stop on our journey through our internal world is relationships. That's right, relationships reside in our internal world. I used to think of relationships in terms of a physical touch or a spoken word and therefore, part of my external world. Even though I had internal feelings about the people around me, I thought of relationships as the physical presence of family and friends. That understanding was not correct. I have come to realize that relationships reside in my internal world.

When I reflect on my relationship with my son, I think about his sweet spirit, his sense of humor and quick wit, his loyalty to me, his laughter, his keen business sense, his unspoken love for Jesus, and his patience with me and trust of me. None of those reflections came from my external world. I did not mention that my son is handsome and athletic because our relationship is not built on his physical presence. My relationship with my son is built on our ongoing internal journey. My son is wrapped around my heart. We all have people wrapped around our hearts. You may never have expressed this concept, but I bet you have someone living in your internal world. Who is wrapped around your heart? What are your reflections about that person? I am not talking about an acquaintance but someone who has access to your internal world.

I am sure you can reflect on relationships that are wrapped in warmth around your heart and bring you joy. Your journey together may have its potholes, but you always get around any difficulty. Cherish those relationships because they are priceless. But it is not these relationships that we will encounter at this stop on our journey to wholeness; it is the difficult relationships. Therefore I want to ask you this question: Is there a difficult person wrapped around your heart? Who drains your energy? Who pushes your pain or fear buttons? Certainly, relationships are not black and white. All relationships have moments of pain and joy, but difficult relationships tend to have more pain than joy and require a lot of work.

Because we have gone through the death of a relationship, there may be several difficult people in our lives. They can make us stumble on this road, but it is not the occasional misstep that can stop us from reaching our wholeness destination. No, it is those difficult people who are wrapped so tightly around our heart that we feel like we are being squeezed to death. You know that feeling because we all have two difficult relationships in common: our ex-partners and new male relationships. Quite frankly, if we can learn to manage these "difficult" relationships, we can manage any relationship.

You can probably accept you have a difficult relationship with your ex-partner, but you may not agree that a new man can represent one. I used to think that way, but I was wrong. Here is my experience with these two relationships.

In the beginning of my journey, I did not understand the reality of relationships. Even though I was divorced and my husband was physically gone, the relationship still lived in my internal world. My husband was wrapped around my heart and I was in pain and fear. I determined that the pain and fear were the result of the "external" void in my life. My husband was gone. There was no man physically present in my daily existence. I thought if I filled that "external" void with another man, the pain and fear would go away. But filling the void with another man was only a Band-Aid for an external symptom. The pain and fear were not the result of an external void but rather the result of a painful wound. My husband was already wrapped around my heart in pain and fear, and I tried to wrap another man on top of it. Guess what happened? All the pain and fear from my last relationship seeped into the new one. Therefore, this new man may have filled the external void in my life but he did not take away any pain and fear. In fact, it spilled into this new relationship, and this new man became another difficult relationship.

This new relationship mistake was an escape jump for me. My pain and fear had pushed me to the edge of the Chasm. I wanted relief. So instead of facing the pain and fear, I chose the escape of another man. This escape jump is all too common among women in this situation.

I truly believe new male relationships can bring great joy for a "whole" mother in the Half Family, but we must be ready for them. Remember, our ultimate destination is wholeness. We need to heal. We need to unwrap the old relationship from our heart before we allow a new relationship to have access to our internal world.

So how do we unwrap that ex-partner from our heart? And how do we wrap a new relationship around our healed heart? In order to answer those questions, we need to travel through the truth first and decide which self-care instructions from the Hope Roadmap will help us maneuver this area of our internal world.

The Truth

Our Ex-partners Push our "History" Buttons.

At one point in my illustrious career of working to make ends meet, I was a salesperson. Those years taught me a lot about relationships, about difficult business relationships. I once worked for a sales manager who had a favorite saying. If I came into the office after a particularly difficult day, he would say, "Who's wrong with you today," not "What's wrong with you today." That statement hit home. Who did I let into my internal world to totally disrupt my day? More often than not, my difficult day was the result of a difficult person. The best lesson I learned from my sales experience is that the only person I can control in a relationship is "I."

If I could let a difficult person who I did not really know upset me, can you imagine the intensity and frequency of emotions generated by my husband? We have an "internal" history with our ex-partner; it could be nine months or twenty years. Time is not the issue. The issue is that our ex-partners are wrapped around our hearts and we have a history with them. That history is the good, the bad, and the ugly, and it drives how we communicate with our ex-partners. Unfortunately, if we have a painful wound and are vulnerable to Nightmare Fear as a result of death of that relationship, we tend to focus only on the bad and ugly history. Our ex-partners have similar pain, fear, and history. They tend to focus on the bad and ugly history. Our ex-partners push those history buttons. The words or actions from our ex-partners that emerge from that bad and ugly history can push our buttons. Their words can squeeze our hearts until we throb in pain. Their actions can stir up fear inside our internal world. We have a history with our ex-partners and they know all the buttons to push to make us react. If someone deliberately pushes on a wound that we have, we will react. If someone deliberately does something to frighten us, we will react. How do we react when our ex-partner pushes our buttons?

We react by pushing our ex-partners' buttons. He says something bad to you so you say something bad to him. Therefore, he responds with some ugly words and you throw some ugly words back at him. This type of communication never allows you to unwrap your ex-partner from your heart. This type of communication never leads to healing and wholeness. In fact, this button-pushing behavior is not communication; it is target practice with missiles aimed squarely at the other person's wound and vulnerability. As long as we react to the history buttons, we will never be able to unwrap our ex-partners from our hearts.

We Need to Disable the Buttons.

If we want to unwrap this painful, fearful relationship from our heart, we must choose to disable our history buttons by not reacting to our ex-partner. That means when your ex-partner pushes your buttons, you do not react by pushing their buttons. I am sure many of you would rather do open heart surgery on your ex-partner without anesthesia and cut out that bad and ugly history that causes them to push your buttons. Ladies, it won't work. We do not have control over our ex-partner's internal worlds. We only have control over our internal worlds. We must make a choice to disable the buttons from our history with our ex-partners that fuel our pain and fear.

This choice is difficult but not impossible. Let me give you some hope around this truth. When I embraced forgiveness, I traveled most of the way to disabling the buttons. I mentioned that part of my journey to forgiveness was asking for it every time something venomous came out of my mouth. That venom spewing erupted in my heart before it ever came out of my mouth. In my heart, I would travel through the bad and ugly history and revisit every word, action, and behavior of my husband. That journey would fuel my pain and fear. It took me a long time to realize I was actually pushing my buttons all by myself. How many of you push your own buttons by constantly reliving the past? Once I embraced forgiveness, I stopped this self-destructive behavior. Unfortunately, my husband did not stop his attacks on my heart. Therefore, I needed to guard my heart from any outside venomous attacks by completely disabling the buttons.

Be assured, once you have embraced forgiveness, it is so much easier to avoid reacting to attacks. Those attacks that used to look like missiles, over time, became annoying spitballs. The missile attacks will only stop when we make a choice to disable the buttons. But disabling history buttons will only get us halfway down the road to unwrapping our ex-partners from our hearts.

Our Partner Is the Father of Our Children.

This next truth may make you squirm. Even if we disable our history buttons with our ex-partner, this man will not magically disappear from our internal world. We can embrace forgiveness and stop the missile attacks, but we will still need to have a relationship with him, because he will always be the father of our children. We cannot change that fact. They will always live in our internal world whether we want them there or not. However, we can make a choice as to where this man lives in our internal world. Will we allow him to stay wrapped around our heart as our ex-partner or will we choose to release him and accept him as the father of our children? We may not want a partner anymore, but we need to accept this man as the father of our children. He may not be a good father in your estimation, but he is the father of your child or children.

The reality is we are already communicating with our partner as the father of our children. If the pain and fear from our history with this man is still wrapped around our heart, these emotions get in the way of any communication concerning the children. If you are reacting to button pushing, it is difficult to separate the pain long enough to have a parenting discussion with your ex-partner. In this internal battleground, parenting discussions tend to end with a lot of yelling and finger-pointing. If your buttons have not been disabled, you will not be able to discern between valid parenting issues and the painful wound and the vulnerability to Nightmare Fear from the death of the relationship.

Also, do not assume that if your ex-partner is not present in your external world that he is not the father of your children. While I have not had to deal with daily or weekly interaction with my husband, I have still had to accept him as the father of my son. This acceptance had nothing to do with my external world; it was an internal choice.

One last item before we move into hope, just because you choose to disable history buttons and build a new relationship does not mean that your ex-partner will choose to take this journey with you. He may like button pushing and no matter how destructive, he may still want this type of relationship. You cannot change his heart but he will be challenged to communicate differently with you. If you do not react to the buttons, he will become confused. If your communication with him centers on the children, he will have no option but to respond appropriately. Despite the condition of your ex-partner's internal world, you can change the dynamics of your communication with him.

The Hope

The good news is you can unwrap your ex-partner from your heart. You can disable those history buttons and create a different relationship. The first thing we are going to do is drop the "ex" from partner. From now on, we will refer to this man as partner. It may seem like a simple change, but it is a big step towards disabling that history. I want you to do something for me. Stand in front of a mirror and say ex-partner and then say partner. Does your facial expression change? Does one word churn up emotions inside? Listen to yourself, and make a choice to view this man differently. Remember, it is an inside out trip and what is in your brain comes out of your mouth.

Mental Margins

When I embraced forgiveness, I was free. I no longer pushed the history buttons from my marriage by myself, which I did when I lived in unforgiveness. However, my forgiveness did not mean my husband was gone from the face of the earth or that his behavior changed. I had changed. If that statement was true, then I needed to communicate differently with this man. It was not easy.

I don't know about you, but difficult people tend to rattle around in my head sometimes. I can rewind and play conversations. I can think up responses I wished I had said to them. I can let that kind of mental gymnastics travel from my head to my heart and squeeze it with anger, resentment, and revenge. In the early days of this relationship transformation with my husband, it was a very short trip from my head to my heart. So for me it was very important to not allow this junk into my head. Remember the self-care instructions for our mental margins: Positive Input for Positive Thoughts and The MHD (Mental Health Day). I have used this mental margin to help me disable the history buttons from my marriage.

Positive Input for Positive Thoughts. While we can choose to walk away from negative people in our lives, most of us cannot walk away from the father of our children. Chances are good we will need to have some communication with this man concerning our children, and we do have a choice about how we communicate with him. We can make a choice about the words or actions that travel into our brains.

I have strong feelings about this subject because I was verbally abused for many years. So I made a choice not to be abused anymore, which meant a drastic change in my behavior.

After the divorce and from a distance, my husband launched missiles aimed at my heart. He used to write me hateful letters, which of course, I read, reread, and saved. I allowed him to enter my head and travel to my heart. Now I cannot stress enough that when I embraced forgiveness, many, many head to heart attacks missed the target. But there were some attacks that hit their target. So I needed to change my behavior and my reactions. I made a choice not to let this hate enter my head and travel to my heart. Therefore, when my husband would write me a letter, I would read the first few lines. If the letter started out hateful, I would not read the rest of it. Over time, I threw away all the letters and the history buttons do not work anymore.

I truly sympathize if you are in a situation where you cannot do the same. If you must have physical contact with your partner, learn to stop the missiles before they reach your heart. I know it is difficult. This process requires one step at a time, one word at a time, one conversation at a time. Remember, relationships live in our internal worlds. So here are some suggestions to help you on this bumpy road.

1. *When some word or action from your partner is headed like a missile towards your heart and focused squarely at a button, do not react.* Take the hit. Ouch. Not exactly the counsel that you were looking for? Look, it takes two people to build a relationship and two people to destroy a relationship. And it takes two people to keep history buttons fully armed with missiles. Our normal reaction to button pushing is to push the other person's button. That reaction only keeps the history alive and well and ready for more missile attacks. The best way to disable a button is not to react. Trust me, if you do not react, the history with your partner will become just that, history. If he cannot get a reaction, his missile attacks will subside and stop. But here is the real hope: you will change. I would like to take credit for this idea of taking the hit, but the Bible is the source. Matthew 5:39: "But I tell you, do not resist an evil person. If someone strikes you on the cheek, turn to him the other also." Romans 12:17: "Do not repay anyone evil for evil." Romans 12:21: "Do not be overcome by evil, but overcome evil with good." Even if this recommendation makes no sense to you at this moment, what have you got to loose? Try this suggestion and see what happens. Again, here is the hope: *you will change.*

2. *Tell your partner you are not willing to communicate in a negative manner.* Turning the other cheek does not mean we become a doormat. It means we refuse to communicate with missiles. When a button is pushed, tell your partner you no longer want to communicate in a negative manner. If he is spewing venom, walk away and tell him you will not communicate until he calms down.

   To women who have been abused, do not enable your partner. Do not react with button pushing, but also do not accept this behavior. It is dangerous to react to an abuser's buttons. You must make the choice to change your behavior. I view abuse as a roller coaster. My husband would abuse me and then maybe ask for forgiveness but normally he would just be nice to me again. We would go up and down on this roller coaster from the heights to the depths of our relationship. At some point, I had to choose to get off the roller coaster. You cannot change an abusive person, but you can change yourself. You can choose to stop the verbal abuse from entering your mind, and you can protect your Half Family from the physical abuse. Therefore, seek counseling and use whatever legal means necessary to stop the verbal and/or physical abuse. If you are in this position, I cannot stress enough the need for assistance with this unacceptable behavior of your partner.

3. *Do not assume that every word that comes out of your partner's mouth is negative.* Listen for the parts of conversations that reflect valid concerns, questions, hopes and dreams about and for the children. It is amazing how much you will hear once you stop reacting to the buttons. We have talked about our partners not changing. Guess what? They have a painful wound and vulnerability to Nightmare Fear. They want to be free from pain and fear. And they may choose to journey towards healing. Do not prejudge that this man will never change. He has the same opportunity as you to heal. So be open to those positive words that come out of his mouth.

A MHD (Mental Health Day). This is a great vehicle for getting perspective. If you have had a stressful, emotional day in divorce court, take a MHD. If you are sick and tired of taking the missile hits from your partner's button pushing, take a MHD. If you and your partner cannot seem to talk to each other with out yelling or harsh words, take a MHD. Get away from the situation. Use the MHD to run away and get perspective. Run away and relax. And just before you come back, here are some questions you can ask yourself.

1. If your partner is pushing your buttons, are you reacting? Renew your commitment to not react to the past history and launch missiles.

2. Am I pushing his buttons? Do I need to apologize? Yes, if you have pushed his buttons, you need to apologize and ask for forgiveness. Even if he does not apologize for his role in button pushing, you need to ask for forgiveness.

3. Were you reacting to button pushing or did you have some valid concerns about your child or children? Here is what I mean by that question.Let's assume your partner is supposed to pick up the children for the weekend at 7:00 p.m. on Friday night. He does not arrive until 8:00 p.m. and gives you a lame excuse. You respond by giving him a piece of your mind about his responsibility to the children. Now did you react to a history of his always being late and expecting you to accept this behavior, or were you truly concerned about the children? If your partner is always late, your children probably expect this behavior. Let it go. Focus on the important issues concerning the children like their safety, their health, and their spiritual growth. Clearly, there may be some critical issues concerning your children that need to be discussed with their father. Do not waste your precious time and energy on button pushing disguised as a valid concern for the children.

4. What can I do differently to change the pattern of communication between my partner and I? The key focus here is "I". Relationships are a personal, internal journey. I can only change me. You can only change you. Reflect on what you have allowed in your brain. Reflect on what you say and do. Don't beat yourself up or justify your behavior, but rather learn from past communication. Use that learning to move forward.

These margins have assisted me in disabling buttons from my history with my husband. But changing our behavior will only get us halfway to our destination. We need to develop and nurture a different relationship with our partner in order to fully unwrap him from our heart.

I need to stop here for a moment. As I think about this relationship journey, I understand you may think this part of the journey is impossible. Maybe you are willing to forgive your partner, but you are not willing to accept him as the father of your children. You are willing for the sake of the children to be civil to him through clenched teeth. You want to say to me if I only understood what this man had done to you and your children, I would understand your reluctance to accept him as a father. Obviously, I do not know your situation, but I understand the emotions. I wanted my husband to be wiped from my memory, but he was the father of my son. In fact, every time I looked at my son, I saw a mannerism or look that reminded me of his father. Personally, in and of myself, I never would have been able to accept my husband as the father of my son. The only way I was able to take this journey was by taking one step at time in love on the invisible bridge of Faith across this relationship Chasm.

The Love

Building a Different Relationship

I had to make a choice to accept my husband as the father of my son. I had to make a choice to become *the mother, not the wife.* If I wanted this man unwrapped from my heart, I had to accept him as the father of my son. Oh, that the transformation could be accomplished in two or three sentences! In fact, it was a messy journey of unwrapping this man from my heart and accepting him as the father of my son.

This transformation from partner relationship to parenting relationship truly occurs one step at a time. Ultimately, we can only completely unwrap our partners from our hearts and accept them as the father of our children by accessing the power of love.

> Love is kind, it does not envy, it does not boast, it is not proud. It is not rude, it is not self-seeking, it is not easily angered, it keeps no record of wrongs. (1 Corinthians 13:4–5)

The words "envy, boast, proud, rude, self-seeking, easily angered, record of wrongs," cover most of the reactions that encompass button pushing. Yet, those are all the things that we should not do. We need to replace those reactions with kindness. We can dramatically change our relationship with our partners by filling our hearts with kindness.

Kindness means that no matter how many times our buttons are pushed, we do not react. Taking a hit can be extremely painful. When I came to realize I could not react to missile attacks from my husband, I did not just turn off my internal emotions. No, when he hit a button, it hurt and I wanted to retaliate. So, I would go into my bedroom, shut the door, and lay on the floor screaming and yelling in agony...in prayer to Jesus. Jesus never failed to honor my steps of faith towards love rather than hate. Button pushing is hateful. The sole purpose of hateful button pushing is to destroy the other person's heart. Taking the hit is a step of love. The result of this step of faith is not more wounding but healing. Believe me, there is less pain from taking the hit than from an all out internal battle from button pushing. Button pushing only maintains an open, raw wound. Taking a hit will heal a wound over time.

The kindness you extend will result in Jesus' kindness to heal your wounded heart. This kindness goes beyond just gritting your teeth, crossing your arms, and taking a hit. This kindness means you forget about yourself and see the wound and vulnerability of your partner. You choose to meet their need. If you do not react but speak kind words, can you imagine the impact on your partner? Can you imagine the reaction if you said, "Why don't we pray about this situation?" Learn about kindness from Jesus.

Love does not delight in evil but rejoices with the truth. (1Corinthians 13:6)

Rather than reacting to an intended heart missile, guide all your conversations to parenting your children. Unfortunately, there may be some buttons here as well. Remember our children have a history in this Half Family. Therefore, both your partner and you will probably have missiles that can be launched concerning parenting. Unless your partner's parenting is going to harm a child physically, emotionally, mentally, or spiritually, you might want to consider taking the hit. Remember, we are striving to build a different relationship with our partner. So I would recommend clearly defining for yourself what is considered harmful and then communicate that information to your partner. Search your heart for the truth, not the evil.

Remember at the end of chapter 7, I mentioned I no longer needed to put an "ex" in front of my husband. I have forgiven my husband and God has forgiven me. I have chosen to accept my husband as the father of my son, and the buttons from our history are gone. My husband is no longer wrapped around my heart. Therefore, I am no longer "delighted" in the evil by spewing venom or reacting to button pushing. I delight in the truth that I am forgiven. I delight in the truth that our relationship is a parenting partnership, which exists in my internal world. I delight that I can change even if my husband does not. I delight in the freedom to accept that the father of my son was my husband.

It always protects, always trusts, always hopes, always perseveres.
(1Corinthians 13:7)

Jesus and faith bridge walking in love was the key to the relationship transformation that took place in my internal world. This transformation really stretched me in choosing to love someone. This relationship transformation was not about me; it was about my husband and my son. I did not understand that fact for many years. Actually, only now as I write do I begin to see the whole picture. Whether my husband realizes it or not, I have given him freedom. By not reacting to his button pushing, I have freed him from part of our history. Just like me, he may be inflicting his own pain by pushing his buttons, but I am not contributing to that pain. My son clearly knows I view my husband as his father. The old history does not get in the way. Without my knowledge, Jesus' love has flowed through me to my husband and son. When we step forward in faith and choose to love, Jesus' love will always protect, always trust, always hope, and always persevere.

New Relationships—Are We Ready?

Unless we unwrap our previous partner from our hearts, we will never be able to successfully wrap another man around our hearts. We will repeat our past history. If we do not disable the history buttons and develop a different relationship with our partners, we will simply put a new male relationship in the middle of our internal battlefield. Statistics show that 49 percent of remarriages end in divorce[1], and 48 percent of unwed mothers[2] are likely to have another baby outside of marriage. In other words, a new relationship too soon after the death of the last relationship will give you about a 50/50 chance of success: not very good odds. So how do you know if you are ready for a new relationship? Here are some questions that you can ask yourself to determine your heart condition.

1. *Have I forgiven my partner?* Do you have a sense of freedom or are you still chained to your partner? If you are still spewing venom about him, you have not forgiven him. If you have not accepted your responsibility in the relationship, you have not forgiven him.

2. *Have I healed?* I cannot give you a time frame on healing, but I can give you some insight on being healed. At one point, I thought I was ready for another relationship. When I look back, I was repeating my history. I was abused in my marriage. Therefore, I simply replaced one abusive relationship for another. If you are simply wrapping the same man with a different face around your heart, you have not healed.

   But there is another indication of healing. Have you accepted forgiveness? When we talked about forgiveness, I mentioned I asked for it over and over again, but I did not feel forgiven. You have heard the phrase "you need to forgive yourself." Well, I prefer to view it as "have you accepted God's forgiveness?" Have you made the choice, actually taken a step of faith, to accept forgiveness from God?

3. *Have you disabled the history buttons and developed a new relationship with your partner?* Really search your heart and pray about this fact. If you have not disabled the buttons, you will react to your new partner in inappropriate ways.

4. *What is your motivation?* If we are honest with ourselves, this question can stop us in our tracks. Do I want a partner because I am afraid or lonely, for financial stability, to be a father to my children or to be accepted in social circles? Notice how the question begins with "I want". I recommend you spend time with Jesus to search your heart on this question. He will reveal the right motivation.

New Relationships—When We Are Ready?

It is this last question about motivation that we need to explore further. Maybe you are ready, but how do you build a new relationship? How do we increase the odds in our favor? I think that there are few things we do that are backwards and may contribute to the odds being against us. There are two major things I did wrong in looking for a new relationship.

1. When considering a new relationship, I focused on the man's physical appearance and age, his occupation, his financial status, color, race, and nationality. In other words, I gave the external world priority over the internal world. Clearly, I also wanted a man who was kind, considerate, loving, and caring. Sadly, I was focused on the external world and missed the truth. The truth is relationships begin in our internal world with the external world only a physical manifestation of the heart. For example, I wanted a man with a good occupation and a stable income. There is actually nothing wrong with that desire, but it cannot be the basis for a relationship. What if fear motivates a man's work ethic? What if this man only sees his worth in what he does? What if he is a workaholic? Do I really want this man wrapped around my heart? What is on your criteria list for a new relationship? Are you motivated by the external world or your internal world? Be honest with yourself. If you could have only one criterion for choosing a new partner, would you choose based on the external or the internal world?

2.   When considering a new relationship, I went on the hunt. Have you ever met a woman whose sole motivation is to be married? She talks about it and her actions scream, "Marry me." I hope I was subtler than that, but I was on the hunt. If your heart says I want a man, I want, I want, I want, you are on the hunt. This motivation can cloud your internal vision. I mentioned I wanted a man with a good occupation and a good income. Can you guess what motivated that desire: the Cold Hard Facts. The Cold Hard Facts of our lives can be so brutal that we determine a new partner must be found. Money can be a strong motivation to find a man. On the surface, we can view the external occupation and income of a man as the answer to all our problems. It is the wrong view. Relationships live in our internal world. The truth is if we are on the hunt for a new partner, we are motivated by the wrong desires.

New Relationships Built on Love. My only motivation for a new relationship should be love. I hate to sound like a broken record, but new relationships need to be built on love: not romantic love but biblical love. Romantic love is based on our external world. As we have seen in our travels so far, God's love is not born in our external world; it is born in our internal world. God's love grows in our internal world and then blooms in our external world. Love is an internal transformation in our heart, and only this seed of love can grow a new relationship. We need to give birth to love in our hearts before we go on the hunt for a new partner. Again, love is not about what I want; love is about what another person needs. Here is what will happen when you open yourself to God's definition of love; you will have no desire to go on a hunt for a new partner. Clearly, you may have a desire for a new partner. But you will look to God's timing rather than your own for finding a new partner. That statement is a walk on the invisible bridge of Faith. We must entrust our heart's desires to Jesus' loving care. This approach to finding a new partner may seem upside down. It is the complete reverse of the world's approach to relationship.

Romantic Love	*God's Love*
Focused on the external world	Focused on the internal world
I need to be loved	I love to meet a need
Go on the hunt to satisfy my desire	Trust God to find the desire of my heart

God's love means our focus is on the other person in the relationship. We need to be willing to accept a new partner's strengths and weaknesses. We need to rejoice in his strengths and patiently encourage him to grow beyond his weaknesses. We need to be willing to lovingly hold a partner's strengths to the path of humility and never use a weakness against them. I believe we are to love their hearts enough to speak the truth surrounded by hope and rejoice in their diversity of soul and spirit. We are to always protect, always trust, always hope, and always persevere.

I know that my next thought will really fly in the face of conventional wisdom. We need to be surrendered to love, not go on the hunt for it. We are not in charge of finding a new relationship; God is in charge of finding a new relationship for us. Our job is not to go on the hunt for a new man; our job is to be surrendered in our internal world to love. We are to focus on being a channel of Jesus' love. It is a faith walk.

I want to end this stop on our journey with a very personal story. I debated about sharing this information, but it may be helpful to you.

When I began this journey to healing in male relationships, I was an extremely needy woman. I sought relationships with only one thought in mind: I need a man. I wanted to be married. Although my marriage failed, I was in love with being married. As I traveled the journey of healing, I was filled with a sense of hope that eventually I would be married again.

Finally, I began to sense I was healed from my wound. I had embraced forgiveness and my heart was being transformed by love. I remember the joy and anticipation at the thought that maybe I was close to seeing my desire for marriage become a reality.

At the same time, Jesus was drawing me toward a different road. In his love, he began to reveal hundreds of hurting women around me. Women just like me; other mothers in Half Families who were courageously walking towards wholeness. I knew that Jesus wanted me to help these women, one at a time. I had come too far in love and I could not turn away. I became obedient to his call to meet a need.

And one day, I came to a fork in the road. I had to make a choice. I knew Jesus would give me the desire of my heart for marriage, but I also knew he was calling me to lead and walk with other women on this Half Family journey. He gave me a vision for this ministry that captured my heart completely. So I willingly did something I never thought I would do. I got on my knees and gave the desire of my heart, a new marriage, back to Jesus. And I chose to fully embrace this journey with other women in Half Families. I made that decision over fifteen years ago and I have never looked back. I have never regretted my decision. For you see, God really did give me the desire of my heart.

Never hold so tightly to the perceived desire of your heart that you miss the real desire from God. I know my experience is not the norm. For many of you, God may have a loving relationship waiting for you. Just be patient. Surrender your selfish motivations and desire to hunt for that relationship. Instead, surrender your heart to love and be transformed by its power. Become a loving person, and God will bless you in ways that you have never imagined possible.

CHEAT SHEET

Learning How to Wrap Relationships

The Truth

1. Our ex-partners push our history buttons and we react.

2. We need to disable those buttons.

3. Our partners are the fathers of our children.

The Hope

1. Use mental margins to disable the history buttons.

2. Use positive input for positive thoughts and a MHD.

The Love

1. Love will build a different relationship with your partner.

2. Are you ready for a new relationship?

3. New relationships are built on love.

11

Facing the Cold Hard Facts and the Income Gap

The Cold Hard Facts:

- **Income for Half Families**
  - **40 percent make below $40,000[1]**
  - **40 percent are below the poverty level (poverty is about $14,000 for family of 3)[2]**
  - **About 40 percent receive an average child support distribution of $2,400 annually[3]**
- **Expenses for Half Families**
  - **48 percent own a home with an average mortgage between $700–1499 per month[4]**
  - **52 percent rent housing with an average monthly rent between $500–749[5]**
  - **Average monthly cost of food for a family of four is $610[6]**
  - **Average food stamp distribution is about $200[7]**
  - **Average monthly cost for an automobile is $545[8]**
  - **Self-insured health insurance premium for a family as high as $757[9]**
  - **Average monthly cost for childcare is $258[10]**

We have finally reached the external part of our journey to wholeness. Some of you may be glad we are finished with the internal journey and have reached our external world. Don't be too quick to rejoice because this part of our journey to wholeness will be just as challenging.

Millions of mothers in Half Families across this country are daily facing a brutal external world filled with minimum income and maximum expenses. And there is no magic wand to make the Cold Hard Facts disappear. In fact, if we ever wanted a magic wand, it would be now. A winning lottery ticket would certainly solve our problems. I understand this fantasy, but the reality is we are faced with the daily challenge of maneuvering this brutal road on the way to wholeness.

And it is a brutal road. Unfortunately, like you, I have lived the reality of minimum income and maximum expenses. For many years, the Cold Hard Facts were huge boulders blocking my path. I would often get injured and bloody climbing over or around a boulder only to find another boulder in front of me. Day after day I faced one expense after another with little or no money. Daily I would negotiate with creditors asking for more time to pay a bill.

The boulders were challenging, but the road became almost impossible to maneuver as it started to rain. This cold hard rain made the boulders slippery, and the dirt on the road turned to mud. There were times early on when the pain and Nightmare Fear internally and the Real Fear in my external world felt like hard rain that pounded me to the point I felt paralyzed. Even when the storm inside me subsided and I healed internally, I still had to live in the "real" world.

Though it was not safe, I would sometimes curl up in a ball under a boulder just to avoid the pounding rain. I was weary from the pounding of daily financial challenges. So I tried to avoid creditors. There was no escape. Often I would have to make the slippery tough choices between food or electricity or rent. Those choices were always painful and only got me around one boulder. Often, I would find myself on the edge of a vast Chasm, the Income Gap. There were more expenses and no money and no way to cross this Income Gap. And I was in danger of sliding into this Chasm.

If you have felt this way about your own Cold Hard Facts and Income Gap, you are not alone. And those feelings are normal. Who would not find this road painful? Who would not be frightened by the Chasm? Who would not try to escape this day in and day out financial rain?

I cannot make your brutal world go away, but I can show you a way to maneuver the road and make it to the wholeness destination. The real challenge on this road is choosing to move forward one step at a time. It will take courage to avoid the temptation to run away—to try to escape. We may be in so much internal turmoil and facing the Real Fear externally that escape looks like the only option. Escape is never a solution. We must choose to step forward and walk through our fear.

Right about now, I know the Real Fear from the Cold Hard Facts may be overwhelming you. I have had the same feeling. That is why we will need to make several stops on this road with the Cold Hard Facts and the Income Gap. The only way to conquer this fear and learn to maneuver the road is one stop, one step at a time. At each stop on this journey through our external world, we will take a step forward toward managing the Cold Hard Facts and maneuvering this brutal road.

Therefore, we are going to make four stops in our external travels. At our first stop, we are going to face the Cold Hard Facts and the Income Gap. At our second stop, we will discover the facts that surround the Cold Hard Facts. At our third stop, we will create a management plan for the Cold Hard Facts and the Income Gap. Only then, at our fourth stop, will we be ready to manage the Cold Hard Facts and cross the Income Gap Chasm.

Remember, no skipping, running or jumping ahead allowed on our journey. Our first stop and beginning step is facing the Cold Hard Facts and the Income Gap.

The Truth

The Difference between the Facts and the Journey

Before we can face the Cold Hard Facts, we need to understand the truth about this part of the road. *The Cold Hard Facts are not personal but the journey is personal.*

Think about it this way. At our last stop, we talked about target practice in our past relationships. If your partner aims a missile at your heart, his intention is to hurt you and get a reaction. If your landlord gives you an eviction notice, chances are his intention is not to hurt you or get a reaction. You cannot pay your rent, and he is in the business of renting to tenants who can. It is just business to him. It is just a Cold Hard Fact. It is not personal. The Cold Hard Facts of boulders and pounding rain are not personal.

But how we deal with these facts is personal. The choices we make to maneuver the boulders and cope with the rain are personal. This journey is all about the choices we make to manage minimum income and maximum expenses and they *are* personal. You will not make the same choices as I. Your choices will be different because we are each unique and our families are unique.

I am going to go out on a limb here and tell you that no choice is wrong. If you learn not to take the Cold Hard Facts personally and make the best choice based on your situation, you made the right choice. If I choose to pay my rent instead of my electric bill and you choose to pay your electric bill rather than your rent, we both made the right choice based on our personal situation. The key word here is choice, not escape.

I want to stress the difference between the non-personal Cold Hard Facts and the personal journey. Because I am convinced there are millions of women in America today who are silently struggling daily with difficult financial challenges. Many are absolutely crushed by the burden of the Cold Hard Facts. Questions like "why is this happening to me" or "why me" torment them. They may feel isolated and, to one degree or another, guilty. Somehow they think that minimum income and maximum expenses are their punishment for the death of a relationship. It is true the death of a relationship may have resulted in a journey through the Cold Hard Facts. Minimum income and maximum expenses may be a consequence of our actions, but it is not a punishment. It is what it is.

It has taken me years to understand this truth at a deep gut level. For too many years, I did not see the difference between the non-personal Cold Hard Facts and my personal journey. So I used to take the Cold Hard Facts personally. My life became my personal Cold Hard Facts journey. Therefore, I focused all my energy on climbing over boulders. If I could just get over this financial challenge, I would be okay. The result of this exercise was I spent years personally reacting to the Cold Hard Facts rather than striving to manage minimum income and maximum expenses. Since I did not understand I had personal choices, I reacted to the Real Fear of the road. Only when I accepted the truth that the Cold Hard Facts are not personal did I start to make progress on the road.

Here lies the truth I want you to grasp. You have no control over the Cold Hard Facts. An expense is an expense. It is not personal. It is just a fact. But you do have control over how you handle that expense. You have a choice. You have choices at every step.

If you do not understand and accept the difference between the facts and the journey, you will take everything personally. You will not clearly see the road. Your fear of this external world will overpower you. In that condition, you will react to the Cold Hard Facts rather than manage them. And your journey will be filled with pounding cold hard rain and slippery boulders.

I know this truth is probably stopping you in your tracks. It makes sense. However, understanding the truth and stepping forward in this truth is something else. That is why we are only going to face the Cold Hard Facts at this stop. We are not ready to take the personal journey.

This truth that the Cold Hard Facts are not personal is unlike any other truth that we have encountered on this journey. It is different because these facts represent Real Fear. That boulder, that expense, in front of you can be intimidating.

In fact, those boulders still intimidate me. Cold Hard Facts represent Real Fear. Therefore, it will take enormous courage to accept that the boulder in front of you is not personal. So right now, I want you to take that first step in acceptance and choose to believe that the Cold Hard Facts are not personal. You will need to take this small step in order to face the next truth.

The Income Gap

This second truth may seem like a no-brainer. If the Cold Hard Facts represent minimum income and maximum expenses, we all face the Income Gap. We have a gap between our money and our bills. We need more money just to pay our basic daily, or monthly, expenses. Seems like a straightforward description of the Income Gap, but there is much more to this truth that we need to understand and accept.

The Income Gap is a vast Chasm that lies just beyond the Cold Hard Facts in front of us. If we are not careful, we can react to the Real Fear, climb over a boulder, and slide into this Chasm. Think about it, if you are spending all your time climbing over boulders in the rain, don't you run the risk of not seeing the Chasm in the road and sliding down into it? Yes, you do. If you are blindly climbing over boulders before you know what is on the other side, you will eventually slide into the Chasm.

I have slid down this slippery slope more than once. You have heard the saying the squeaky wheel gets the oil? That was how I reacted to the Cold Hard Facts. I only saw the boulder in front of me. If my car payment was late, I knew it was my *personal* responsibility to pay that bill. So I would react in fear of loosing my car and send all my money to the finance company. Right behind that boulder was my electric bill. I had no money to pay it and the electric company would not wait. So I would play hopscotch with my checking account, hoping that the check would not clear before I had money in my account. If the check bounced, I now had another expense, overdraft charges. And down I slid into the Income Gap Chasm.

I determined I would not slide into this Chasm again. And I took a reactive step. What did I do? This step is going to twist your brain because you are probably not prepared for this definition of reacting to minimum income and maximum expenses. Unfortunately, it is an all too common reaction that can easily cause us to slide down into the Income Gap Chasm. I reacted to the Cold Hard Facts by constructing a monthly budget. How can a budget be a reaction to the Cold Hard Facts? Have you not heard the budgeting message from many different sources? I thought if I could just budget away all those expenses, I would not face the Income Gap. This approach was a reaction to the Cold

Hard Facts. It is a reaction because a budget only focuses on our expenses, the Cold Hard Facts, and ignores the Income Gap.

A budget can help us contain expenses, but it will not generate income and get us across the Income Gap. It is not a magic wand. Unfortunately, we reactively try to swing the budget wand over the road and wait for some magic money. In this reactive state, we don't see the Chasm. Our vision is focused on that one boulder in front of us, that one bill, that one unexpected expense. And we don't see the danger just ahead on the road, the Income Gap.

We cannot budget our way through the Cold Hard Facts and across the Income Gap. It will not work. We are not two-parent families trying to manage our income more efficiently. We are mothers in Half Families who have minimum income and maximum expenses, and a budget will not magically change that situation. Often what looks good on paper, fails to work in the real world. We create a budget and still do not have enough money to cover our expenses. We try to climb over that boulder in front of us and end up sliding into the Income Gap Chasm. We wonder what happened. What did we do wrong? We reactively tried to use a budget as a magic wand. A budget can contain expenses, but it is only one tool for managing the Cold Hard Facts and the Income Gap.

What I want you to grasp about the Income Gap is simple. Any type of reactive step in an attempt to manage the Cold Hard Facts will result in a slide into the Income Gap Chasm. You will be so focused on the boulder in front of you that you will not see the slippery slope of the Income Gap until it is too late. Before we attempt any "management" steps, we need to clearly see the road. We need to face the non-personal Cold Hard Facts and the slippery Income Gap.

The Hope

We need to step back from that boulder in front of us and look at the whole road. That's right, we need to make the decision to look beyond that one Cold Hard Fact and look at *all* the Facts and the Income Gap Chasm. In other words, we need to see our whole financial picture. Doesn't it make sense that if we saw the entire road, we would be in a better position to take proactive steps around the boulders and across the Chasm? At least, we could avoid the surprise slide into the Chasm. We need to choose to look up and over the boulders and squarely face the non-personal Cold Hard Facts and the Income Gap.

Now squarely facing the Cold Hard Facts and the Income Gap Chasm may not be your idea of hope. Believe me, it truly is hope. It is the first proactive step that will lead you to a management plan and ultimately to managing the Cold Hard Facts.

If you have never viewed your whole financial picture, you may be feeling extremely uncomfortable with the idea. Most of us spend our days dealing with the massive boulders in front of us. And the thought of viewing all the boulders and the Chasm makes us curl up in an emotional ball. My guess is you need a big dose of hope that you can face this picture. Therefore, we are going to use one of our self-care instructions from our Hope Roadmap in a unique way; positive input for positive thoughts. If the Cold Hard Facts are not personal, we are not going to take them personally. So, I want you to pretend that the Cold Hard Facts of your life are not your life. That's right, for this part of the journey through the examination of the Cold Hard Facts, these facts are not your life.

In order to make this mental adjustment, this is what I want you to do. The Cold Hard Facts that were your life now represent a struggling business that you have been asked to manage. That's right, you are now the CEO (Chief Executive Officer) of Half Family, Inc. How is that for positive input? You have just been promoted. Do not worry if you have never managed a business. I will give you step by step coaching for your new position. Believe me, you are the most qualified person to run this business. From this point on, the Cold Hard Facts are not your life.

Half Family, Inc.

As the new CEO of Half Family, Inc. you have accepted the challenge of managing this struggling business. This business's financial performance is very poor. But before you can recommend a course of action to address this poor financial performance, you need to get a clear picture of the true condition of the business. Therefore, you determine that your first course of action is to review the financial statements for Half Family, Inc. Now, you could look at many different views of the company's financials. After careful consideration, you decide to examine the income statement: which reflects that Half Family, Inc. was at or near a net income loss for the year. In other words, the business has more bills than income on a yearly basis. In this condition, the business is struggling to survive. You decide to closely examine this income statement in order to identify any gaps in revenue (our income) as well as identify operating expenses (our expenses) that are draining the revenue stream. In order to determine the root cause of the poor financial performance, you will actually carefully examine each line item for both revenue (our income) and operating expenses (our expenses). This process will help you to identify any short-term and long-term strategies to move the business from the red to the black (negative income to positive income).

(For any financial types reading this book, I have taken some "huge" liberties with this statement of income. For one thing, a true statement of income from a company's annual report would be much more complex than the Half Family, Inc. statement. However, I think that this approach will help us see our financial picture from a non-personal perspective.)

Therefore, we are going to examine the income statement for Half Family, Inc. Proactive rather than reactive means that this examination will require work on your part. We are going to look at our sources of (minimum) income and (maximum) expenses and put those numbers down on paper. Do not try to skip over this exercise. You will not be able to go to the next stop until you complete your income statement. So take a piece of paper and create the following form to fill in.

Half Family, Inc. Statement of Income	
Revenue (Our Income)	
Net Income from Job	
Net Income from Government Assistance	
Income from Child Support	
Other Income	
Total Income	
Operating Expenses (Our Expenses)	
Housing	
Food	
Transportation	
Health Care	
Childcare	
Other Expenses	
Credit Card—Escape	
Credit Card—Fill the Gap	
Total Operating Expenses	
Total Net Income (Loss)	

Instructions for Creating the Income Statement

Revenue (Our Income)

The Job. Our main source of revenue (our income) for our business is generated from sales (our salary or wages). To really understand the true revenue of our business, we will only look at our net income. Now in most statements of income we would look at the gross revenue (our gross income) and deduct taxes at another point in the process. As the CEO of this struggling business, we have decided we need to have a clear picture of "net income" up front in the process. In other words, if your salary or wages are $20,000 a year, you do not get $1,666.66 on a monthly basis. You may see about $16,400 a year or $1,366.66 monthly. That $300 monthly difference between gross and net revenue (our income) could have a huge impact on our struggling business. Therefore, we need to correctly calculate this revenue (job income) for our business.

So look at your pay stub and calculate your net income for the year. You have no control over the federal, state, and local taxes, social security, and health care premiums. You only have control over the money that you get *in your hand* each day, each week, and each month. Since our goal is to get an annual picture of our income from the job, calculate that *in your hand* income for the year. So if you get paid once a week, multiply the *in your hand* income by 52 weeks. If you get paid once a month, multiply by 12, etc. Write down that number next to Net Income from Job.

Government Assistance: Welfare, Unemployment, Etc. This Half Family business may also receive additional sources of revenue (our income) from the government. We have discovered that many government programs have a limited time frame for receiving revenue and require tax deductions. For example, welfare payments may fluctuate during the year. Unemployment insurance may be limited to eight to nine months. Therefore, be careful to correctly calculate this annual net income from government assistance. In this case, since we are dealing with income that can fluctuate during the year, do not assume you can multiply your monthly income by 12. Look carefully at your monthly income from the government as well as anticipated income for the rest of the year. Be conservative about the monthly income that you can expect from government assistance. Then multiply that conservative monthly number by 12. Write down that number next to Net Income from Government Assistance.

Child Support. In any business, relying on an "unpredictable" source of revenue can negatively impact the company's cash flow and operating income. The statistics on child support payments clearly indicate that this revenue stream (our income) is unpredictable at best. Therefore, do not assume too much with this revenue stream (our yearly income). Make sure you calculate only the net income *in your hand* that was received, not promised. I do not like to say this, but unless wages are being garnished for child support, I would be careful with this income. Remember you are putting the business in a position to depend on this revenue (our income) to meet operating expenses (our expenses). Only calculate the net income (our income) that you are confident will come from child support payments. In fact, you may want to take the extra step and look at the historical revenue stream. In other words, what was the annual net income (our income) from child support payments last year or the year before? Calculate the net income carefully and write down that number next to Net Income from Child Support.

Other Revenue. If you have other sources of revenue (our income), you can write down those numbers. Be careful and ask yourself these questions? Is this net income (*in your hands* income) a stable and dependable source of revenue? Does the net income (*in your hands* income) fluctuate from month to month? Do you need to deduct taxes? Calculate net income from other revenue sources carefully and write down that number next to Other Income.

Now total all your revenue sources, write it down next to Total Income, and we will move to Operating Expenses (our expenses).

Operating Expenses

Housing. The location of our corporate offices may need to be evaluated for Half Family, Inc. So we need to determine the yearly operating expenses (our expenses) for this facility (our housing). In order to get a clear understanding of this expense, we, as CEOs, have decided to calculate all operating expenses (our expenses) associated with our corporate offices (our housing). In other words, we could just calculate the operating expenses (our expenses) for the mortgage or lease on this facility (our housing). But we want to ensure we do not miss any other operating expenses (our expenses) associated with our building (our housing).

Therefore, if you are renting an apartment or house, please include your utilities in this expense. Those utilities include phone, gas, electricity, water, sewer, and garbage expenses. Since these expenses can fluctuate during the year, make sure you calculate correctly. Now add your yearly utility expenses and your yearly rent payments. Write down that number next to Housing.

If you own a home, do the same process but make sure that you also calculate other expenses like taxes, insurance, association fees, etc. Then add together the yearly expenses for the mortgage, utilities, and other expenses. Write down that number next to Housing.

Food. In a business environment, I would relate this operating expense (food) to items like supplies, computers and accessories, wireless phone charges, etc. All these expenses are necessary to effectively manage and grow a business. Left unattended, these operating expenses can consume huge amounts of revenue (our income). Food is in the same category.

My experience has shown me that the food portion of our operating expenses can be an unseen contributor to the loss of net income. Therefore, the process of determining the actual annual operating expenses (our expenses) associated with food may take some work on your part as well as an educated guess. Make a choice to go through this process. Here is the hope. When you complete this exercise, you may clearly see some food expenses that can be cut. So when we get to the management of the Cold Hard Facts, you may already have one expense that can be reduced to improve the bottom line: your net income.

We will start with the food expense associated with the grocery store. Go through your bank statements or your checkbook and identify all those expenses. For this portion of the exercise, we are only interested in the paper trail. In other words, only use cancelled checks, bank statements, or receipts from the grocery store. Also, going forward, I encourage you to always write a check or use a debit card at the grocery store. Therefore, you will always have a record of expenses. That "unaccounted for" $5 or $10 that you spend at the grocery store can add up and eat your income. Calculate those expenses for the grocery store but do not write that number down yet.

Now calculate the food expense for eating out. If you are like me, this next calculation may take some time, but it will be a real eye opener. You will be amazed how much money is spent on this operating expense. If you do not think you are a victim of the "drive-through" and "eat out" food syndrome, do this simple test.

Do not change your behavior. For the next month, log the money you spend at the grocery store in one column and the money that you spend "eating out" in the other column. And it is not just fast food that can eat our income. Eating out for lunch every day, buying prepared food at the grocery store, takeout from our favorite restaurant, and snacks for a child's activities can eat our income. It is easy to slip into this behavior. Let's face it, we are all just plain tired and anything that makes our lives easier is appealing. That $5 or $10 here or there adds up quickly. Guess what? Businesses have the same issue. That $20–50 spent by several different employees on supplies can add up quickly. The combined wireless phone charges of $1,000 for one department added to the charges of other departments can be an unseen drain on revenue.

So add up these food expenses associated with eating out. Since many of us do sporadically spent $5–10 on eating out, you may have to estimate this expense. Just try to be honest with yourself and make an educated guess.

Now add up the grocery store expense and the eating out expense and write down that number next to Food.

Transportation. As the CEO of my own Half Family business, I truly wish I had a magic wand for this operating expense (my expense) as related to automobile ownership.

Aging automobiles have been a drain on my income more than once. In fact, my brother nicknamed me "Drive it and kill it, Frank" because of my history with repairs on one particular automobile. I remember one day walking into the mechanics bay where this particular car normally lived. As I entered I saw two mechanics and my brother standing over the engine of my car. I asked what they were doing, and my brother said, "We are considering exorcism." Actually, I do think that car was demon-possessed. It was hard for me not to take it all personal.

But that experience has given me a clearer picture of annual automobile expenses. It is imperative that when you calculate your annual automobile operating expense, you include all costs for gasoline, oil, *maintenance*, tires, insurance, financing, depreciation, license, registration, and taxes. It is imperative you save all those receipts for your automobile. If you are missing some expenses, make an educated guess. Add up all the operating expenses for your automobile and write down that number next to Transportation.

For women who use public transportation, this calculation should be fairly straightforward. However, like the operating expenses for the food budget, there may be some "unaccounted" cash that is spent on transportation. So don't forget to include the transportation expense for your children to get to school. Also, make an educated guess about the expense for the occasional taxi, train and bus ride. Total all those expenses and write down that number next to Transportation.

Health Care. What insurance plan can the business afford that will provide employees with adequate coverage for health care? This operating expense has caused me a great deal of turmoil in my life. Believe it or not, health care decisions for business owners can also create turmoil.

The Cold Hard Fact of paying for health care may look different for each of us. No matter which position you are in; take some time to add up all your expenses for health care.

If you do not have health insurance, make sure you total all expenses including money that is still owed to a doctor, clinic or hospital. Remember, we are looking at the picture for operating expenses, not just your monthly payment plan with a doctor or hospital. You may also be receiving some government assistance for medical expenses. Chances are good you still have some "out of pocket" expenses. Add up all your health care expenses and write down that number next to Health Care.

If you have health insurance through your employer, the premium is deducted from your gross income. So do not include this number in your calculation. But you do have a co-pay expense for doctor visits, a deductible expense, and pharmacy expenses that are not covered under the company plan. Add up these annual expenses and write down that number next to Health Care.

Childcare. As CEO, I know that the business's continued operations may require some employees to incur expenses from travel. These expenses are necessary and often nonnegotiable. In other words, the operating expenses for airlines, hotels, and car rentals may provide some discount pricing but are normally nonnegotiable.

Childcare is similar to travel expenses for a business. Childcare is necessary for the working mother and often is a nonnegotiable expense. For women with preschool children, you face a huge expense for childcare. For women with young children in school, you still face the expense for after-school programs. These expenses need to be captured.

But there are other childcare expenses that we need to include in this calculation. Don't forget the babysitter expenses during the weeknights or on the weekends. Just like our expenses for food, we have childcare expenses that are sometimes not captured. Again, it is $5 or $10 here and there that add up over the year. Add up these expenses and write down that number next to Childcare.

Other expenses. Businesses often have a difficult time containing credit card expenses. So let's take a moment to look at credit cards and the Half Family. In my experience, I have seen credit cards used primarily either as an escape (shop till you drop) or to cover the gap between revenue (our income) and operating expenses (our expense). If you are in either situation, you are not alone. Guess what, many, many CEOs across this country use their line of credit in the same way.

Now this exercise is going to take a little work, but it will be worth it in the long run. First, I want you to take out all your credit card bills for the last year and look at the line item charges for each month. Do not look at the balance; just look at each charge. I want you to add up only the charges that were "escape" shopping. If you are a little confused about what is and what is not escape shopping, ask yourself one question. What charges on my credit card were an impulse buy to make myself *feel good*, not to pay a bill or meet a need? Only you know which charges fit in this category. Only you know when you used a credit card to escape. Add up these charges and write down that number under operating expenses labeled Credit Card—Escape.

Now I want you to determine how many charges were "fill the gap" charges; in other words, grocery shopping, paying the electric bill, etc. If we put those charges down on our statement of income, we may be double counting expenses. For example, if you used a credit card to pay an electric bill, you have probably already included that operating expense under the Housing section. Also, if you used your credit card for eating out, you have probably already included that operating expense under the Food section. However, there was an expense generated by using a credit card to "fill the gap."

So I want you to do something different here. I want you to total the interest and finance fees you were charged on an annual basis. This total will actually include the interest and finance fees not only for the "fill the gap" charges but also the "escape" charges. That is okay. Just go ahead and add up these charges. The fees are found at the bottom of the credit card statement. If you need to you can make an educated guess. Write down the total for interest and finance fees under operating expenses labeled Credit Card—Fill the Gap.

Now that you are finished with operating expenses, you can total them. We have the annual revenue (our net income) and operating expenses (our expenses) from the Half Family business. Before you subtract the operating expenses from the revenue, I want you to remind yourself that you are the CEO of a struggling business. This is not your life. Subtract the operating expenses from the revenue. This is your net income.

Let me give you some counsel in interpreting the number for net income. If your net income is positive for the year, you may say "Hallelujah!!" But remember, we only looked at the five operating expenses that most of us have in common as CEOs in the Half Family. Clearly, there may be other expenses that are outside these five areas. Therefore, if your net income shows positive, but you are always short money every month, then you have other expenses that are draining your income. Those expenses, installment loans (other than a car), school loans, attorney's fees, etc. are negatively impacting the bottom line. I do recommend you add up all those additional expenses and write that number down at the bottom of the income statement.

If your net income is at a loss for the year, put a parenthesis around this number. I do not have a "magic" wand for your situation. Again, you are still the CEO of Half Family, Inc.

The Income Gap

As the CEO, you clearly see the Income Gap. The key word here is "see." The Income Gap is not lurking beyond a miscalculated revenue stream or operating expense. It is in front of you in black and white. Therefore, understand that this hope exercise was not an exercise in dollars and cents. It was about giving you a different perspective. It was about pulling you away from a narrow monthly "budget" focus. It was about awareness. It was about seeing the Chasm behind that boulder in front of you. It was about seeing the big picture. Remember, if you stand too close to a mosaic, you cannot see the picture.

For some of you this income statement confirms what you already knew, but were afraid to face. Others of you may have had some real eye openers as you reviewed your income statement. Maybe you learned you were depending too much on anticipated child support income, that food expenses were much larger than you thought, and the used automobile sitting in your driveway was not such a bargain after all. Maybe you already knew you were operating at a net income loss, and you now see the cause for the revenue drain.

No matter what you learned, you can now see the depth of the Income Gap Chasm. Know this: this picture is hope because when we can squarely face the Cold Hard Facts in a non-personal way and see the Chasm, there is hope that we can create a management plan to maneuver this difficult road. The picture is hope because when we choose to look at the yearly financial picture instead of monthly financial pieces of the picture, we have taken our first proactive step towards managing the Cold Hard Facts and crossing the Income Gap Chasm.

The Love

Walk into Jesus' Presence.

You have taken a courageous first step. Even though we have the hope of our income statement, we are not ready to move to the next stop. Why? We need to rest. This journey of creating an income statement was probably difficult at best for most of you. For many of you, this part of the journey was a struggle not to take the brutal facts personal. You may be newly separated from your partner and are tormented by pain and Nightmare Fear. Or you may be a veteran traveler through the Cold Hard Facts and are simply exhausted from the day in and day out struggle. Therefore, we need to rest before we move forward. We need to find a safe place on the side of the road and sit down. So make the proactive choice not to go to the next stop until you walk into Jesus' presence.

You see Jesus is not only concerned about the condition of our internal world, but he is passionately concerned about the harshness of our external world, the Cold Hard Facts and the Income Gap. You will grasp that concern when you choose to walk into his presence and rest. You will know that he cares deeply about your Half Family.

We need to know that despite the reality of our external world, he loves us and is right beside us. He will lead us over, around, and through the Cold Hard Facts and across the Income Gap Chasm. Even though we may not feel his presence, Jesus is always there for us.

One of the most difficult spiritual lessons I had to learn on my own personal journey is that faith has little to do with "feeling" Jesus and everything to do with "knowing" Jesus. Learning that lesson is crucial at this point in our journey. It is difficult to look at a bleak financial picture for as far as your eye can see and believe that Jesus cares. You may not feel like he loves you and your children. If he really loved us, why are we on this brutal journey? We don't feel his presence.

And we get it wrong. Faith is not about feeling his presence. Faith is about knowing his presence. And the only way to grow in faith and know the loving presence of Jesus is to spent time with him. The reality is that if you ever needed to know Jesus, that time is now. It is impossible to successfully travel through the Cold Hard Facts and across the Income Gap Chasm without knowing the love of Jesus. You need to know that no matter how bleak your financial picture, Jesus knows your situation and he deeply cares for your Half Family.

I want you to do something different with your self-care instructions for the Spiritual Margin of Faith. I want you to stretch your faith muscles by practicing "resting in Jesus." It takes practice to learn to rest.

Choose to take the step of knowing Jesus by walking into his presence and resting. Right now, Jesus has prepared a rest area on the side of the road for you. So I want you to take off your CEO hat and go to a solitary place. Take your income statement, the physical piece of paper, and prayerfully give it to Jesus. Don't ask for answers. Just give your income statement to Jesus. Then rest and find some Bible verses to comfort you. Sit with Jesus and read scripture to him. It does not matter where you start in the Bible. Our Lord loves to hear us read his Word back to him. If you choose, you can begin with this verse.

> Come to me, all you who are weary and burdened, and I will give you rest. Take my yoke upon you and learn from me, for I am gentle and humble in heart, and you will find rest for your souls. For my yoke is easy and my burden is light. (Matthew 11:28)

CHEAT SHEET

Facing the Cold Hard Facts

The Truth

1.   The Cold Hard Facts are not personal, but the journey is personal.

2.   Face the Income Gap.

The Hope

1.   We are the CEO of Half Family, Inc.

2.   We can find hope in the income statement for the Cold Hard Facts.

The Love

1.   Walk into Jesus' presence.

2.   Give him the income statement and then rest.

12

Discovering the Facts that Surround the Cold Hard Facts

You are to be congratulated. It took a lot of courage to face the whole financial picture of minimum income and maximum expenses, to understand and accept that these Cold Hard Facts are not personal, and to face the Income Gap and accept your vulnerability of sliding into this Chasm. Your courage will be rewarded because you are one step closer to managing the Cold Hard Facts and crossing the Income Gap.

That first step on this external road has taken us a long way. Before you took that step and faced the Cold Hard Facts and Income Gap, you saw only that boulder in front of you. You reacted to it and the next one in the cold hard rain. Often due to your narrow vision, you did not see the slippery slopes of the Chasm until it was too late. Now you have chosen to expand your vision. You now see the whole road. You have faced the Cold Hard Facts and the Income Gap. You have the whole financial picture.

Now I want you to take another look at that Cold Hard Fact in front of you. Look closely, there is something surrounding that boulder in front of you. What is clinging to it? There are "Facts" surrounding that Cold Hard Fact, that boulder. Do you see them? No? Well, don't worry; shortly these facts will be clear to you. You just need some time to focus your vision. You see, these clinging facts are never truly visible until we face all the Cold Hard Facts and Income Gap. As strange as it sounds, until you choose to see the whole financial picture, the whole road, you will not see the detail on the road. Only when you choose to expand your vision will you see the "Facts" that surround the Cold Hard Facts.

Now I am certain that you have probably had your fill of "facts" about your external world. But these new "facts" are different from the Cold Hard Facts. These facts are warm and will give you the much-needed hope for your harsh external journey through minimum income and maximum expenses. They will provide you with valuable information that is required to create your management plan for the Cold Hard Facts. And I am quite certain that no one ever explained these facts to you. Certainly, no one ever explained them to me.

The Truth

As I so often have done on my own Half Family journey, I stumbled across the truth about the facts that surround the Cold Hard Facts. At first, I simply missed the truth about these facts. Then I caught a glimpse of the truth but I chose to ignore it. Every time I encountered a Cold Hard Fact; I encountered these other facts too. Finally, I could no longer dismiss the truth. And as I studied the truth, I was enlightened. How could I have been so blind? It became clear that if I wanted to manage the Cold Hard Facts and cross the Income Gap, I must move from enlightenment to acceptance of the truth about these new "facts." That acceptance has been a journey for me as it will be for you too.

The Soft Facts

The truth is we have Soft Facts that surround the Cold Hard Facts. These facts are right in front of us but are quite easily missed on the road. Always, when we react to the Cold Hard Facts, we completely ignore the Soft Facts. Or quite frankly we often glance at them and simply dismiss them as optional information. We incorrectly determine that the Soft Facts are of little importance on this journey. The truth of "real" boulders and cold rain is more critical, and we are wrong. The Soft Facts are also important. In fact, if we choose to stop reacting to the boulders in the road and choose instead to prepare a management plan for the Cold Hard Facts, we cannot miss, ignore, or dismiss the Soft Facts. We cannot learn to manage the Cold Hard Facts without the Soft Facts—because these facts cannot be separated.

The "enlightened" truth I discovered is you will never encounter a Cold Hard Fact without Soft Facts. These Soft Facts surround and cling to the Cold Hard Facts like soft green moss. The hard boulders and cold rain on our road is the perfect climate for this soft green moss to grow and thrive. Moss covers all the boulders on our road. We were so occupied with maneuvering that boulder in front of us that we missed the moss. We need to stop reacting and focus our vision.

Here is what I want you to see. We know that our income statements reflect the Cold Hard Facts. This picture of minimum income and maximum expenses reflects the financial condition of our external world in black and white numbers on a page. Certainly those numbers show all the boulders, the Cold Hard Facts in our way, but this picture is not complete. All we see are the numbers that represent minimum income and maximum expenses. If our external world were only numbers on a page, our management of the Cold Hard Facts would be reduced to a simple "five-step" formula. There would be no difference between the way each of us manages these Cold Hard Facts. But the truth is our external world is not just numbers. And there is no one-size-fits-all formula for maneuvering this difficult road. There are no black and white answers because our external world also includes personal choices.

And those personal choices are driven by the Soft Facts. What are the Soft Facts?

The Soft Facts are who we are as women and mothers in the Half Family. They are the soft green moss that surrounds the Cold Hard Facts, the boulders. Who we *are* creates green growth in our external world. Who we are as women and mothers creates warmth in a far too cold external world. The warm, soft green moss of Soft Facts surround the Cold Hard Facts and makes this Half Family journey personal.

Yes, the Cold Hard Facts may not be personal, but the Soft Facts are. These Soft Facts drive the personal choices that we make on this external journey. For example, many of us may work to generate income. That income is a Cold Hard Fact, but our occupation is a Soft Fact. The actual income number on our income statement is not personal. It is a Cold Hard Fact, but it does not represent who we are. Who we are is reflected in our occupations, and our choice of occupation is personal. Some of us are teachers, teacher's aids, nurses, receptionists, sales people, waitresses, clerks, managers, scientists, software programmers, etc. Those choices reflect who we are as women and mothers in the Half Family, the Soft Facts.

Are you beginning to see the Soft Facts right in front of you? It is so obvious, isn't it? Yes, but many of us neglect or sacrifice "who we are" in order to make money. We ignore the Soft Facts or we dismiss them as of little importance as compared to the need to pay our overwhelming expenses. The truth is we react to the Cold Hard Facts and the Income Gap and sacrifice who we are as women and mothers, on the altar of "money." I worked in sales for years and I truly do not have a salesman's personality. I ignored who I was. I dismissed and sacrificed myself as a woman and mother to make money, and I was absolutely miserable most of the time.

Certainly, we need to work to earn money and support our families. Certainly, we need to pay our expenses. Here is the harsh truth; any attempt to manage the Cold Hard Facts without accepting the Soft Facts is simply reaction. We manage nothing. Ignoring or dismissing the Soft Facts will not make them disappear. The moss is still on the boulder, so the journey will still be personal, but the road will be brutal and barren and full of cold hard rain. We will simply continue to react to the boulders on the road and wonder why we feel so hopeless.

Our external world is not just the Cold Hard Facts; it is infused with who we are as women and mothers in the Half Family. We will never be able to create an effective management plan for the Cold Hard Facts without embracing the truth about the Soft Facts. More importantly, we will never be able to manage the Cold Hard Facts without embracing who we are.

Now I could write pages about the Soft Facts and their importance, but I think you need to write your own story. You need to see it on paper. You need to see who you are as a woman and mother in the Half Family. And you need to get these facts deep in your gut before you can move forward on this external journey. You need to open your eyes, focus your vision, and see the warm, soft green moss that surrounds the boulders on this road. You need to begin this journey into the acceptance of the Soft Facts.

The Hope

This acceptance will be a journey into the hope of the Soft Facts. We need to discover the hope that grows in the Soft Facts of who we are as women and mothers in the Half Family. Actually, we will not have to look too far. We have an income statement that represents the Cold Hard Facts of minimum income and maximum expenses. Therefore, it is logical that we will begin to see who we are as women and mothers in the Half Family as we examine each of the Cold Hard Facts in our income statement. Specifically, we are going to discover the Soft Facts that surround each income and expense item on that statement. This process is probably going to stretch you and take some time because it is not about making a Soft Fact list.

I don't know what it is in this country, but we like to reduce everything to lists and formulas. For me, lists and formulas as related to who I am as a woman and mother have never been beneficial on my own Half Family journey. Discovering the Soft Facts of who you are is not about creating a neat straightforward list or taking some personality test. Who we are as women and mothers in the Half Family does not fit into some tidy little box with a green ribbon. Does moss look the same on every boulder? Is it the same shade of green? Is it the same thickness and texture? Does it grow in the same area on every boulder? The answer is no. The same is true for us. Who we are is just as unique and different as soft green moss. Lists do not work.

This process is going to stretch you for another reason. In fact, we all have this reason in common. If you have missed, ignored, and dismissed the Soft Facts on your journey, you have programmed your brain to resist discovering who you are. You may have been blinded to the Soft Facts and missed them. Now your eyes are beginning to see something and your brain is censoring that vision. Even now, you may be thinking about ignoring this whole step as silly or a waste of time. Even when you decide to trust your new vision, you will struggle with a desire to dismiss yourself. You may begin to think who you are in relation to the Cold Hard Facts is simply unimportant.

When this temptation emerges in your brain, you will need to use some positive input from your mental margin to reprogram your thoughts. Remind yourself that you are the most important asset in the Half Family. Think about it this way, we all acknowledge that having enough income to pay our expenses is necessary to maintain our Half Family. Money is only a tool to manage the Cold Hard Facts. We are the manager. Which is more important the tool or the manager?

If you have never looked at who you are as a woman and mother in the Half Family, it will take time for this person to become clear to you. Just take it one step at a time. It is simple. Just as you faced each Cold Hard Fact, each boulder on the road, you need to discover the Soft Facts, the unique formations of soft, green, warm moss, on each Cold Hard Fact, boulder. To assist you in this discovery process, I will point you in the right direction and provide you with "sample" information for Soft Facts that surround the Cold Hard Facts. From the income statement, we will look at Soft Facts for jobs (income) and Soft Facts for housing (expense). Please, please remember, this information is a "sample." We are all unique. Therefore, there is no right or wrong Soft Fact. There is only who you are. And remember, this is only a "fact-finding" mission; do not edit your facts.

Soft Facts for the Job. Chances are the main source of income for many of us is our job. We are all unique in our work schedules and occupations. Some women have well-established professional careers, some have never worked, and some are struggling to get by working in a retail environment. But we probably have these two things in common; we are trying to squeeze every penny of income out of our jobs, and with money as a priority, we don't think about ourselves.

When your relationship died, who you were as a mother changed. Your wound and/or healing changed who you are as a woman. Those changes impact your job. For example, the need for income drives us each to different reactions. We think about going from part-time to full-time work or working overtime, or working two jobs. And we make income decisions based solely on the need for more money, ignoring who we are as women and mothers. Ladies that is a wrong turn on this road. Before you make any decisions about jobs, you should carefully consider the Soft Facts. Only when you have all the "facts" can you make the best decision for your family and you. To help you determine your Soft Facts for the job, here are some questions for you to answer

Who are you emotionally right now? Be brutally honest with yourself. If you are newly separated from your partner, are you an emotional mess? You may look great on the outside, but the inside is not so great. I am an educated woman and have had a professional career. However, when I left my husband, I struggled to answer a telephone without emotionally falling apart. I struggled daily and some-times hourly to control the emotional turmoil inside of me. I would cry easily. Get angry easily. Get my feelings hurt easily. Who are you emotionally right now? And it is not only the newly separated woman who should ask this ques-tion. We are on a brutal journey that can rip us apart emotionally. Emotional tur-moil and the wrong job is a recipe for disaster. If you are considering working ten, twenty, or thirty hours of overtime a week or working two jobs? Can you do this? Even if you have more money, will you be so emotionally drained that you make mistakes managing the Cold Hard Facts?

Understand how you respond emotionally as a woman. When I reflect on my son, I so clearly see who I am as a woman. I used to say if emotions were an orange, you would see the difference in emotional responses between my son and I. I would peel the orange, squeeze it dry, and sleep with the rinds. My son would examine it and then play basketball with it. I feel deeply, completely, and pas-sionately, and you see it all over me. I am transparent. My son also feels deeply, completely, and passionately, but a casual observer cannot see his emotions. Nei-ther response is right or wrong. It is simply who we are. The point is to under-stand who you are emotionally. What makes you laugh? What makes you cry? What makes you angry? Who we are as women and mothers in the Half Family can often emotionally drain us and we need to carefully consider this Soft Fact in any job choice. If you choose to work in a confrontational work environment and are overly sensitive and cry easily, you might want to reconsider that choice. If you choose to work in an environment that requires a caring, sensitive touch and you have compassion but struggle to communicate that compassion, you might want to reconsider that choice.

Who are you physically? Are you energetic or lethargic? Are you overweight? Are you too thin? Do you exercise? Do you tire easily? Are you healthy? Do you have a disability? What is your physical condition? Where you are physically will have a huge impact on the type of work that best suits you as a woman and a mother. If you have five small children, you are probably physically exhausted most of the time. You might want to think twice about taking a position as a construction worker no matter how high the pay rate. If you are overweight, you might find it difficult to be on your feet all day in a retail environment.

Where are you mentally? I am absolutely convinced that it takes more mental energy to raise children than emotional or physical energy. Those little minds are always ready for mental gymnastics with mom and the games can change from day to day. So be honest with yourself. Where are you mentally? If you have small children or teenagers, you are undoubtedly mentally exhausted. What can you mentally handle in a work environment? If you are absolutely, mentally drained from your work schedule, what other areas of your life will suffer?

When we make decisions about work; we can choose to ignore who we are emotionally, physically, and mentally, and our ignorance will have consequences. We will eventually burn out the most important asset on the journey.

Who are you as a mother? Who do you need to be as a mother to your child or children? What do your children need from you? For example, if you have three small children, what do you need from a job (not money) in order to be a mother? Do you need to be home for breakfast or bedtime? Do you need Saturday morning to play with your children? If you have older children, do you need to be there to help them with their homework? Do you need to be available for your children's activities or sports events? Think about each child in your family and the family as a whole. Who are you as the mother?

What are your dreams? Too often we do not allow ourselves to dream or we let others rob us of our dreams. We all need the hope that lives in our dreams. In the business world, we say, "We need to think out of the box." I like to say "Don't be trapped by what you know; be open to the possibilities." Dare to dream. I know it is hard but forget about money for a moment. What do you want to do? When you were a little girl, what did you dream about doing as an adult? What gets you excited? What are you just naturally good at doing? Write down a description of your dream job—not an occupation. Just let the words come out. For example, I might write that I love to be creative. I get excited when I can tell a story that inspires people. I love to search my brain to create word pictures. I enjoy sitting for hours all by myself, and writing about things that I think are important. Writing energizes me.

Forget about money and let your thoughts flow onto the paper. Since this type of dreaming tends to be difficult for us, we will work on this "dream job" some more at our next step, creating a management plan for the Cold Hard Facts.

Really spend some time on your Soft Facts for your income. Repeat this exercise for income from government assistance as well as child support. Ask yourself questions to discover who you are. Do you need to leverage your government assistance to relieve some stress? What is the cost to you emotionally, physically, and mentally to chase more child support?

Income is a Cold Hard Fact, but how we earn it is personal. I know the temptation is to ignore the Soft Facts when you face overwhelming bills. Actually, I am facing that situation as I write this book. I have made a choice to follow this personal dream that Jesus put in my heart. And I am struggling to balance that personal choice to write this book with the cold reality of my need to work for income. It has not been easy to do both. I have made mistakes, but I know that I cannot surrender who I am as a woman and a mother in my own Half Family. So if you are reading this book, you know I made it to end of this journey. And you can too. Don't surrender who you are.

Soft Facts for Housing. I am going to assume that housing is near the top of the list of glaring expenses that drain your income. We may attack this expense by determining that we need to live in "cheap" housing. That may be a true statement, but it is not the only factor in making a housing decision. Where we live is not determined by cost alone; we have Soft Facts that need to be considered.

Who are you as a woman? I am guilty of ignoring this Soft Fact as related to housing for too many years. It has only been in the last few years that I have truly come to understand the importance of who I am as a woman as related to my choice of housing. It has taken so long because, like you, I absolutely sacrificed who I was for the cost of housing. This expense, this Cold Hard Fact, completely drove my decisions. You may have experienced that same situation. I did not think I had another choice.

I have watched two-parent families in awe for many years. They have a variety of housing options due to their income: the more income the more options. Even two-parent families with minimal income had more options than I did. The result was they could easily make housing choices based on who they were as a family.

I did not have a variety of housing options. That does not mean I should have to completely sacrifice who I am as a woman. For example, I do not like living in a big city with the noise, the large population, and the concrete. I am a solitary person. I need green trees and flowers around me. I need quiet space.

It is extremely important that you allow yourself to explore who you are as woman as related to your housing needs. What type of environment is most comfortable for you? What type of environment will allow you to rest emotionally, physically, and mentally? What type of environment represents a "safe" haven for you? Forget about the housing expense. Avoid inputting any negative thoughts like I will never be able to afford this type of house. Remember positive input only. More importantly, don't think of the physical structure of a house; think in terms of a living environment. It is not the four walls that matter; it is the environment that reflects who you are as a woman.

Who are you as a mother? These Soft Facts are critical for us to be able to raise our children. For example, school districts are important. Who are you as a mother in relation to your child or children's educational needs? As mothers, we are sensitive about our children's education: schools and school districts. Again, this Soft Fact is not about money. Does your child need to be in a gifted program? Is your child in need of special attention physically, emotionally, or mentally? Does your child need small classes? Or is your child like mine? My son is extremely social, and he loved large schools and large classes. No matter the age, write down your child's educational needs. Those needs may have an impact on where you live. Those needs reflect who you are as a mother.

Also, think about your needs. Do you need to live close to your child or children's school? If you live close to your child's school, you can save some precious travel time. Wouldn't you like to capture more time? If you work, you will have a short trip in the morning to school. If you are not working, you will have a short trip to those parent-teacher conferences, a sick child, or a misbehaving child.

What are the physical requirements for your housing? What do you need as a woman and a mother in the Half Family? Now this question may appear to reflect a Cold Hard Fact. What does space have to with Soft Facts? Well, it may be cheap for your five children and you to live in two rooms, but what will the impact be on all of you emotionally, physically, and mentally. In other words, do not jump to the "financial" conclusion immediately that your five children and you will only be able to afford a one-bedroom apartment. Who are you as a family? Think through your specific needs not wants. Now you do need to censor your brain a little on this Soft Fact. Do you *need* three bedrooms and two baths? Do you *want* a house in Malibu on the beach? There is a difference between need and want. And only you can determine the difference because housing needs will be different for all of us. My son is grown. I do not need a lot of space. Our housing needs as related to physical space are personal. So spend some time thinking about your children and yourself. What are the physical requirements for your housing?

You need a safe neighborhood. I want you to write down this Soft Fact. There are millions of mothers of Half Families living in unsafe neighborhoods. Unfortunately during my son's youth, I lived in neighborhoods that were not as safe as I would have liked. I do not have the answer to this tragic trend in our country. No matter your situation, put safety down as a Soft Fact for housing.

Do you need a place of your own? Again who are you as a family? Over the years, I have had many well-intentioned married couples with children give me advice on housing. Their advice was to find a roommate or take my son and move into a room in someone's house. Like some of you, I have had to do both of those things. This advice was based solely on money, the Cold Hard Fact of housing expenses. Taking this advice should truly be a last resort. First and foremost, you need to develop a family unit and that is going to take all your energy. If you move in with someone, even a loving family member, you will have to divert energy away from your Half Family to deal with the other relationships in the house. You will be faced with other outside people giving you advice on raising your children or even correcting your children. They may be correct, but that kind of interference can be confusing for both your child and you. It is imperative that you really think through the Soft Facts around living alone as a Half Family. What does your family need?

Is it starting to make sense that Soft Facts are important? Obviously, these Soft Facts are only samples. I just wanted to get you started on the thought process. Look at every item on your income statement and write down for each item your "personal" Soft Facts, who you are as a woman and mother of a Half Family. Think about each item. Trust me, I know from experience the cold, barren journey of reacting to the Cold Hard Facts because I chose to ignore the Soft Facts.

It will be a journey. It will take time to retrain your brain to accept who you are as a woman and a mother in the Half Family. If you have never put down on paper who you are, I encourage you to write down everything that comes to your mind. Do not worry about the format or the words and do not eliminate anything. Write whatever initially comes to your brain. When you have the first "draft" of Soft Facts, you can move on to the love.

The Love

Quite often, we simply do not see ourselves as Jesus sees us. We think who we are as women and mothers is somehow insignificant as compared to the brutal external road that we travel each day. In many cases, we have been stripped of basic necessities like homes, food, and clothing. Minimum income and maximum expenses have stretched us to the limit emotionally, physically, and mentally. In that condition, we think that money is more important than who we are. We need more money. That is true, but it does not mean we need to sacrifice who we are. We do have a choice. No one or nothing can take who we are as women and mothers unless we allow it.

When we ignore or dismiss who we are on the altar of money, we grieve Jesus. That is what we do every time we ignore the Soft Facts that surround the Cold Hard Facts. We grieve him because we make the wrong choice. Jesus does not see us as insignificant women who should be sacrificed for money. He loves us. Sadly, there have been many, many times on my own Half Family journey, that I did not trust this "love."

If Jesus loves me, why am I hungry? If Jesus loves me, why can't I pay my bills? How can I even think about myself in this situation? I was so blind to the truth. I did not see his love because I had a heart condition. I had a heart condition that did not allow me to see who I was through his eyes.

You may have the same heart condition as I. Maybe you need to be enlightened to the truth and see who you are through Jesus' eyes. I warn you, if you think that the discovery process for the Soft Facts in our hope part of the journey stretched you, you haven't seen anything yet. This little walk through Jesus' love is not only going to stretch you but will flat out challenge you to think quite differently about your heart. If you accept the challenge, you will begin to see who you are through Jesus' eyes. From Jesus' own lips, he turns our thinking right side up and shows us our hearts. So take a little "Bible" walk with me.

> Do not store up for yourselves treasures on earth, where moth and rust destroy, and where thieves break in and steal. But store up for yourselves trea-

sures in heaven, where moth and rust do not destroy, and where thieves do not break in and steal. For where your treasure is there your heart will be also. The eye is the lamp of the body. If your eyes are good, your whole body will be full of light. But if you eyes are bad, your whole body will be full of darkness. If then the light within you is darkness, how great is that darkness.

No one can serve two masters. Either he will hate the one and love the other, or he will be devoted to the one and despise the other. You cannot serve both God and money. (Matthew 6:19–24)

What has this got to do with who we are as women and mothers in the Half Family? Actually, it has everything to do with who we are. The source of who we are is found in who we are spiritually. All the Soft Facts flow from that source. And who you are spiritually is reflected in your heart condition.

The first step toward seeing ourselves as Jesus sees us is to examine our hearts. Does Jesus live there or money? For you see treasure, or money, lives in our hearts. Money is nothing more than paper. It is a lifeless object. Money becomes a treasure as we move it into our hearts. We give it value there. And if we pursue storing it up, it will consume our hearts. It will consume us and blind us to who we are.

This truth applies to the materially rich and materially poor. Yes, even a poor person can be consumed with accumulating money. As related to the mother in the Half Family, it is impossible to discover the Soft Facts of who you are if you are consumed with the need for money. If you pursue money and sacrifice yourself, you have put yourself in the position to love the money and hate God. So Jesus confronts us with a choice. With our hearts, we either pursue God or money. We either store up God or money in our heart. You cannot do both. If you try to serve both masters, that pursuit will result in a love/hate relationship. And yes, pursuing money from your heart makes money your master. So we have a choice: either our heart is set on treasures in heaven and we choose to love God, or we don't.

You will never know who you truly are until you see yourself through Jesus eyes. And you will never see his vision until you make a choice about the condition of your heart. Who do you serve, money or God?

Faced with minimum income and maximum expenses, the choice between God and money seems impossible. You need the money. And that is the key mistake that we make. The choice is not about having money to pay your bills. The choice is about trust. Do you trust money or do you trust Jesus to meet your needs?

Therefore, I tell you, do not worry about your life, what you will eat or drink or about your body, what you will wear. Is not life more important than food, and the body more important than clothes? Look at the birds of the air; they do not sow or reap or store away in barns, and yet your heavenly Father feeds them. Are you not much more valuable than they? Who of you by worrying can add a single hour to his life?

And why do you worry about clothes? See how the lilies of the field grow. They do not labor or spin. Yet I tell you that not even Solomon in all his splendor was dressed like one of these. If that is how God clothes the grass of the field, which is here today and tomorrow is thrown into the fire, will he not much more clothe you, O you of little faith?" (Matthew 6:25–30)

Jesus is challenging us to examine our heart condition. He is challenging us look up from our boulder-filled, rain-soaked road and look at the owner of that road. Jesus owns this world. He created and meets the needs of every creature and every plant. How can we possibly think that we are not important? We are much more valuable than anything else in creation. Jesus wants us to know the depth of that statement. He wants to know who we are in him: who we are as women and mothers in the Half Family. If we trust his love, he will move the boulders in our road and help us cross the Chasm. This is his promise to us.

So do not worry, saying, 'What shall we eat? or What shall we drink? or What shall we wear?' For the pagans run after all these things, and your heavenly Father knows that you need them. But seek first his kingdom and his righteousness and all these things will be given to you as well. Therefore, do not worry about tomorrow, for tomorrow will worry about itself. Each day has enough trouble of its own. (Matthew 6:31–34)

Do you see the blessing in these verses? I know you may not be feeling blessed right now but you are. Here is how I know you are blessed. When you read that scripture, does it capture you? Does it make you cry? Does it grab your heart and give you a sense of hope? Does it feel like Jesus is speaking to you personally? Yes? Do you know why? Because we are never closer to Jesus than when we are at our greatest need. When we have exhausted every external source for monetary answers and we are at the end of ourselves, Jesus meets us there. When we choose Jesus, that place is a blessing. That place of almost feeling his physical presence is the greatest blessing we can receive as a human being. You have been honored by his presence and you will now know the secret about blessings. *Blessings have absolutely, positively nothing to do with money.* That lie is spread by a world in love with money. Blessings are those moments that Jesus' love envelopes our hearts and we see who we are through his eyes. We become enlightened and know his love.

Seek and pursue Jesus and he will meet your needs. Seek and pursue Jesus, if you want to truly know who you are as woman and mother in the Half Family. If you want to see yourself through Jesus' eyes, you need to choose to let go of the need for money and choose to embrace Jesus who meets our needs. He loves us. He is grieved every time that we ignore or dismiss who we are because we are then ignoring and dismissing Jesus in our lives.

There is so much to learn from these words of Jesus. In fact, this scripture will become an important cornerstone for managing the Cold Hard Facts. So when we reach that part of our external journey, we will take another walk through these verses in Matthew.

For right now, just take one small step of faith. Release your heart grip on money and make a choice to embrace Jesus to meet your needs. Begin to see yourself through his eyes.

Seeing yourself through Jesus' eyes is a totally personal experience. Therefore, I can go no further with you. It is time for you to pick up your Soft Facts and take a walk with Jesus by yourself through the Bible. Read his Word and discover how he views women, the poor and oppressed and the single mother. Discover the miracles in the Bible. Sit with him and be enlightened by his personal revelations of who you are as a woman and mother in the Half Family. You may discover new depth in your Soft Facts. Let his Word refresh your weary heart.

CHEAT SHEET

Discovering the Facts that Surround the Cold Hard Facts

The Truth

1.   The Soft Facts surround the Cold Hard Facts.

2.   The Soft Facts are who we are as women and mothers in the Half Family.

The Hope

1.   The self-care instructions for positive input for positive thoughts

2.   The Soft Facts for our job, income

3.   The Soft Facts for our housing, expense

The Love

1.   We will not surrender who we are as women and mothers in the Half Family.

2.   We will see ourselves through Jesus' eyes.

13

Creating a Plan for Managing the Cold Hard Facts and Crossing the Income Gap

Proactive not reactive. I want you to memorize these words. Because these words truly define our steps on this external journey. We took proactive steps at our last two stops. When we faced the Cold Hard Facts, we took a proactive step. We chose to stop reactively climbing over boulders in the rain and sliding into the Chasm. We chose instead to take a step back and look beyond that boulder in front of us to view the whole road. We chose to look beyond that expense staring us in the face and view our whole financial situation. Once we saw the whole financial picture, we took another proactive step to discover the "Facts" that surround the Cold Hard Facts. We chose to stop missing, ignoring, and dismissing the soft green moss that surrounds those boulders in front of us. We chose instead to focus our vision and be enlightened to the Soft Facts that surround the Cold Hard Facts. All of those choices represent proactive steps.

Now that we have all the facts, it is time to take another proactive step. We have an income statement, which reflects all the Cold Hard Facts, and we have the Soft Facts, which reflect who we are as women and mothers in the Half Family. We are now ready to create a management plan for our journey through minimum income and maximum expenses. This plan will provide us with the information needed to make intelligent, methodical, logical decisions about difficult financial situations that we will encounter as we manage the Cold Hard Facts and cross the Income Gap.

We need to take a proactive step and develop a plan. But similar to the Soft Facts, I think that we dismiss the concept of planning. Our assumption is we do not have time to create a management plan. Let's face it. We are in the middle of a muddy road surrounded by boulders, and it is starting to rain again. Besides, we have all the facts now. Certainly, we can manage our financial road. We need to take action. Yes, but any action without a plan is nothing more than reaction. We may have all the facts, but how can we hit the road running before we have a plan of attack for the boulders and are fitted with the appropriate rain gear? Do we think brute force will move the Cold Hard Facts? Do we really think we are that strong? No, we are not that strong, and assuming that brute force will move anything is simply an emotional reaction. Having all the facts is not enough; we need to proactively use those facts to create a management plan.

That proactive approach makes sense to us. The problem is that the temptation to react to minimum income and maximum expenses is still with us. And unfortunately, we are going to continue to feel that temptation as we travel down this road. We will feel it because the Real Fear from minimum income and maximum expenses is ever present. We can feel the Real Fear, but we need to learn how not to react to that fear. *Proactive not reactive.*

You probably can see the value in being proactive rather than reactive and intellectually it makes sense. But moving that knowledge from your head to your feet will take time. It will take time to move from reactive behavior and develop proactive behavior. And here in lies the truth that we need to see at this stop on our external road.

The Truth

The Bad Habit

We need to examine the truth about each behavior: reactive and proactive.

In order to grasp the importance of moving to proactive behavior, I want to share some truth that we need to understand and accept about our reactive behavior.

We know that daily we may face a crisis like an unexpected car repair or a doctor's bill for a sick child. It is a crisis because the last thing we need is an unexpected expense that we cannot pay. Or we pay it and sacrifice a basic necessity like food or electricity. We are in crisis and are forced into Crisis Management.

Now remember our definition of Crisis Management? Crisis Management is a method for handling an unexpected critical situation or problem that requires immediate attention and a solution. And effectively managing a crisis requires gathering all the facts, clearly identifying the problem or crisis, carefully looking at the options to resolve the crisis, determining a logical recommendation, and making a "clear headed" decision on the proper course of action.

Crisis Management takes a tremendous amount of energy. No one can maintain the stamina needed to effectively manage a crisis day in and day out. Unfortunately for mothers in the Half Family, Crisis Management seems like a normal lifestyle, but this lifestyle cannot be maintained. At some point, we will break down. We will end up reacting to the crisis rather than managing the situation. This crisis lifestyle will result in daily visits to the edge of the Chasm. This lifestyle will eventually mean a slide into the Income Gap or worse—an escape jump off the edge.

We have traveled far enough on this Half Family journey that I am sure you see yourself in this picture. At some point on this harsh external road, we have all been worn down by daily Crisis Management and ended up in reactive behavior mode. That is the truth.

But at this point on the road, we need to move this truth from our head to our gut. Daily Crisis Management means we have accepted crisis as a normal lifestyle. We may not verbalize this but our reactive behavior shows the truth. The logical consequence of accepting crisis as a normal lifestyle is a reactive behavior lifestyle.

That's right, we have created a pattern of reactive behavior. We have programmed our brains to react to our external world. We see the Real Fear of the Cold Hard Facts in the road and we allow our emotions to drive us to react. We reactively try to move or climb over the slippery boulders in the rain, then slide to the edge of the Chasm and see no option but escape. We react to the Cold Hard Facts. Oh our fear of the Cold Hard Facts is real, we should be afraid of minimum income and maximum expenses, but we need to stop reacting to that fear. We need to stop this reactive behavior, which will take time. Why will it take time? Our reactive behavior is now a habit.

The human brain is amazing. It does what we tell it to do. If we consistently have reactively climbed over boulders in the rain, our brain has been programmed to tell us to behave this way. We have created a self-destructive habit. If you do not think that you own this habit, I want you to think back to the last financial crisis in your life. How did you handle that situation? Did you react to the Real Fear by running away? Did you get drunk or did you escape into the Chasm of "shop till you drop"? Did you take it out on your children with anger? If you are not proactively managing financial crisis, you are reacting. Reaction has become a habit. If we choose to create a plan for managing the Cold Hard Facts, we need to be proactive rather than reactive. If we choose to manage the Cold Hard Facts and cross the Income Gap, we need to be proactive rather than reactive.

You are probably preparing a mud pie for me because the last thing you want to hear right now is that you have a bad habit. Great, your mud-throwing reaction means that the truth has made it to your gut. You feel this truth. I simply put words to your feelings.

Now comes the challenge, you need to take another step and move this truth from your gut to your feet. Unfortunately, we cannot simply resolve not to react anymore to the Real Fear of the Cold Hard Facts. We cannot just tell our brain that reactive behavior is not acceptable. We need to create a new habit. We need to replace that reactive behavior with proactive behavior.

If you have ever tried to change a bad habit, you know that this change process can suck. Your brain is programmed to go down the bad habit road and you want it to go down the new habit road. It may be slow to move from reactive to proactive. It will take time and be challenging. Therefore, to make this change process a little more appealing, I have some wonderful truth about developing proactive behavior as a new habit. Choosing to put "feet" to the truth and develop proactive behavior on this external road puts you in *control*.

Think about your reactive behavior. When you react to the Real Fear of the Cold Hard Facts in your road, what are you feeling at that moment? Don't you feel like you have no control over the situation? Do you feel like this fear and the road are in control? Of course, you do. Our reactive behavior is a desperate, futile attempt to gain control over the Cold Hard Facts. You will never gain control by reacting to minimum income and maximum expenses.

So how do you gain control? You gain control by being proactive. The truth is you have proactively faced and uncovered the facts for the whole financial road. Whether you realized it or not, you have already begun to change that "reactive" habit. You have already gained control over a part of the road that used to control you. Therefore, if you take those new facts and figure out how to proactively manage minimum income and maximum expenses, who is in control: the road or you? If you face Real Fear on the road but have a plan to manage that fearful situation, who is in control: the fear or you? Your proactive actions to the Cold Hard Facts will give you control.

Now I am not saying you will never encounter a crisis and Crisis Management. I am saying that a crisis will become the exception, not the rule. You will not live in daily Crisis Management. So when that crisis does come, you will be better prepared to manage it rather than react to it. More importantly, if you are not accepting crisis as a normal lifestyle, you will break that bad reactive habit. You will have created a new proactive habit in your brain. You will have a new lifestyle and control.

But our forward movement will be challenging because our reactive lifestyle has become a comfortable tool to attack boulders and dodge rain. In a twisted way, we even think we have a functioning management tool. In fact, reactive behavior is not a management tool and it needs to be replaced. Even though it will be challenging to embrace a new habit, we need to learn to walk in proactive behavior in order to manage the Cold Hard Facts and cross the Income Gap. We must be proactive rather than reactive.

The Hope

There is much hope in the little phrase proactive rather than reactive. *It means you can be in control rather than out of control on the road*, you can be prepared rather than surprised by the road. You will have choices rather than no options on this road. This hope means you can create a management plan to maneuver the boulders and rain and cross the Chasm. I am certain it will come as no surprise to you that we need to roll up our sleeves and go to work again. Trust me, this work will be worth it.

With a management plan we have the hope that we can turn minimum income and maximum expenses into maximum income and minimum expenses. Wouldn't you like to be able to pay your bills and have money left over? Of course you would. We all want that kind of freedom, but it requires some work.

We are going to develop a plan for managing the Cold Hard Facts and crossing the Income Gap. That plan will consist of three strategies designed to give us a proactive approach to management of our external road.

As with our last two stops, you need to go into this process with a positive attitude. In fact, we will need all our margins to keep us on the development path. In other words, if you are emotionally and physically drained, do not attempt to prepare this management plan now. This strategy development is going to take your mental, emotional, and physical energy. This energy is needed because this proactive approach to the Cold Hard Facts is the absolute opposite of our reactive behavior. Therefore, your brain may resist, your emotions may react to the Real Fear, and your muscles may tense up as you begin this strategy development. Remember, we are not only creating a plan we are taking steps into a new habit. Therefore, make sure you, the most important asset, are as prepared as possible for this development process.

Also creating a plan for managing the Cold Hard Facts and crossing the Income Gap cannot be accomplished in one development session. In the business world, I have never been able to write a business case or marketing plan in one sitting. It takes time to write, edit, and finalize any management plan. And those "business" tasks are not as difficult as this personal strategy development. Again, this plan will take some work, but the resulting hope from this process far outweighs the effort.

So if you are ready, I am going to show you how to develop the Short-Term and Long-Term strategies for your new management plan. To begin, I want you to put your CEO hat back on and pick up your income statement.

Short-Term Strategy

Our management plan begins where we are right now: in the middle of the boulders and cold hard rain of minimum income and maximum expenses. Our goal in the short term is to minimize some of the boulders and reduce the rain. So our Short-Term strategy can be summed up in two words: *cost containment.*

You may not agree with this proactive approach. Our normal first "reaction" may be to try to increase our revenue to cover expenses. Seems like a logical first step, but is it? As the CEO of Half Family, Inc., we know this approach is only a reaction. Think about it, if we do not contain our operating expenses, how will we know how much revenue to generate? If we do not control expenses, those expenses will continue to eat up more and more revenue. We will end up reactively throwing money at the Income Gap. Increasing revenue by working more hours or taking a second job is a short-term solution to a long-term problem. Therefore, we need to focus first on cost containment.

We are going to develop a Short-Term strategy for containing our operating expenses. This strategy may look like a budget, but I do not want you to think about it that way. For too many years, we have viewed a budget as the answer to the Cold Hard Facts. We need to change our thought process about a budget. It is not the answer. It is a tool. I want us to start thinking about a budget as a Short-Term strategy for cost containment.

Strategy Development. Our income statements are the starting point in this strategy development. However, this process will not be as straight forward as facing the Cold Hard Facts and creating an income statement. In order to develop a workable strategy, we will need to surround those Cold Hard Facts with the Soft Facts. You will get dirty and muddy on this part of the road. It is muddy because each woman's Short-Term strategy is different. There is no one-size-fits-all answer to this strategy development. Only you, as the mother in your Half Family, can make the personal choices in the short-term that are best for your family. I will give you direction, but you must develop the appropriate strategy.

So take out another sheet of paper and create this form.

Monthly Expenses	Current	Containment
Housing		
Food		
Transportation		
Health Care		
Child Care		
Credit Cards		
Other Expenses		
Monthly Income		
Contained Expenses		
Monthly Net Income		
Long-Term strategy cost		
New Total (Net Income)		

Divide all the operating expense items on your income statement by twelve and write down the monthly number for each line item on this form under Current. In other words, if your annual expense for housing is $7,200, write down $600 on the form next to Housing under the word Current. Also put down any other expenses that were not covered in our income statement. These expenses are any costs that are recurring on a monthly basis throughout the year such as an installment loan, school fees, attorney fees, etc.

Once you have the numbers down on paper, we need to look for the "short-term" hits item by item that can reduce our expenses.

Housing

As CEO of Half Family, Inc., we would think long and hard about moving the business from one facility to another in order to save money. We should give the same consideration to our housing decisions. Do not immediately assume this expense can be contained by moving. When you look at the Soft Facts for your housing expense, what do you see? Doesn't your physical environment look like a long-term commitment? Yes, which means that moving is *not* a Short-Term strategy. You may have to make that choice down the road, but it is a last resort in the short-term. There are other aspects of your housing expense that can be contained.

Remember, we added electricity, gas, water, sewer, and phone expenses to our overall housing costs. We need to find ways to contain these costs. For example, does your gas or electric company have a "budget" plan that you can use to keep your costs from fluctuating during the winter and summer months? Check to see if there is some financial assistance that is available to reduce your gas or electric expense. Take a long hard look at your phone expense. The telecommunications industry is very competitive right now. Shop around. You may be able to get a better rate at another company. Also consider just using a wireless phone with voicemail and long distance charges included in a flat rate. Before you make any decisions, make sure you are not ignoring the Soft Facts as related to these expenses. For example, if you, as a mother, know your children look forward to that weekly long distance phone call to their father, you do not want to cut that expense. You want to get the best rate, but do not sacrifice your children to save money. Make an educated, realistic decision on how much cost can be reduced from your housing expense. Now write down the new expense number for Housing under Containment.

Food

Be realistic. If your food budget is $700 a month, you are not going to save $400. If you have decided to change your eating habits i.e., eliminating fast food or pre-pared foods, you will discover this change is not an event written on a piece of paper. Who we are as women and mothers in the Half Family needs to be considered as related to the food expense. In other words, it takes time to change a habit. Therefore, accept the fact you will not eliminate fast food and prepared foods from your food expense. Rather, focus on containing this expense. If you tend to use fast food on those days you work late or your children have activities around dinnertime, you can give yourself permission to use fast food. Try to contain this expense to those specific times. Do the same exercise with your purchases at the grocery store. Be realistic. Move towards healthy eating and cost containment. It is a journey. Determine the amount you can save and write down the new number for Food under Containment.

Transportation

This expense is necessary to keep our business operating on a day-to-day basis. Therefore, we may only have minimal impact on this cost. Find those expenses that can be contained. I would recommend you locate the cheapest gas station and a reliable, fair mechanic. In fact, if you have an older automobile that breaks down all the time, try to work out a payment plan with your mechanic. Shop around for the best automobile insurance. Do not attempt to contain expenses by eliminating those nights out you as a woman and mother need to go to classes, or Bible study, or the movies. You need these "margins" away from the external road. Now write down the new number for Transportation under Containment.

If you use public transportation, you will probably only be able to contain your costs by eliminating any unnecessary trips. Be careful; don't eliminate those trips that are related to play or an MHD. Now write down the new number for Transportation under Containment.

Healthcare

I have a slight twist for cost containment on this operating expense. As CEO of Half Family, Inc., what if we decided to contain costs by eliminating some benefits for healthcare? What if we decided to only provide major medical insurance for our employees (no co-pay on doctor's visits or medicine) and we eliminated any sick days from our benefits package? What do you think would happen? Besides having a lot of unhappy employees, this situation would cost us more money. Some employees would quit. Other employees would come to work sick. Chances are good that many of those sick employees would get sicker or make other employees sick. In that situation, it would cost us money to replace employees that quit, and it would cost us money for lost productivity from sick employees. Now I know that this situation makes no sense. What employer would be so short sighted? Yet we, as mothers, do the same thing.

Here is what I mean. Often we wait until the last minute to go to the doctor with a sick child. We go to work sick. We do these things to save money. In reality, it is costing us money. A sick child may require tests or medicine that could have been eliminated by an earlier visit. The one sick day from work that we could have taken may turn into a week and lost wages because we did not stay home from work that one day.

Here is my point on cost containment for healthcare. We need to take care of our children and ourselves as soon as we get sick. We need to move toward preventative care i.e., regular physicals, dental visits, etc.

After you think about this operating expense, you may not have any "number" changes for your Short-Term strategy, but you may have a mind-set change.

Childcare

Be careful with this operating expense. Who we are as mothers in the Half Family is more important than money. Our children's well-being and safety are in the hands of other people; therefore, do not sacrifice your children to save a few dollars. With that thought in mind, cautiously determine any costs that can be eliminated or contained from your childcare expense. Can you find a child-care facility closer to your work? You might be able to save some money on gas. Do you qualify for subsidized childcare through a government program? Is there a trusted single mom who does not work or works different hours than you who will watch your child or children? Also, be careful not to eliminate that babysitter expense unrelated to work hours. In other words, as the most important asset on this Half Family journey, you need an occasional night out to get somewhat refreshed and relaxed. So contain this expense, but do not eliminate it. Write down the new number for Child Care under Containment.

Credit Cards

Credit cards are not "free" money. Yet many of us view a credit card that way. We may not verbalize it, but our actions demonstrate the truth of that statement. A credit card is not free money. I am not saying you should not use a credit card in an emergency. I have used my credit card to keep the gas or electricity on in my home. But I realized paying that expense created another expense: a credit card bill and interest. I had no other alternative. It was winter and I needed heat. I made the best decision I could under the circumstances. Here is my point. You may be faced with using a credit card to pay a bill. Just understand you are paying an expense with an expense. Guess what? You are not alone. Struggling companies use their credit the same way.

But there is an expense associated with credit cards that we need to contain; it is *escape* shopping. Look at your income statement, how much credit card expense is associated with escape shopping. Take a long hard look and make a choice to contain your impulse to jump off the edge into the Chasm of a credit card escape. In looking at the Soft Facts, I stated it would be beneficial to know where are you emotionally right now. Escape shopping is an impulse jump based on where we are emotionally. If you understand and accept this Soft Fact, you will know when an escape jump is near and you will be prepared to control that "impulse." But elimination of escapes will be a journey.

If you are using the illusion of "free" money to escape the Cold Hard Facts, you have created a wrong path, a bad habit. You need to change that habit and create a different path. Each time that you get pushed to edge of this Chasm by the Cold Hard Facts, you will need to make a choice. Do I want the "familiar" feeling of escape shopping or do I choose to hold onto Jesus and walk across this Chasm? Escape is never a solution. Just keep choosing Jesus in these difficult moments, and over time you will stop choosing escape. You are still going to get pushed to the edge of Chasm, but you will learn how to avoid escape jumps.

Determine how much money you can contain from escape shopping with credit cards. Set a realistic goal for yourself concerning escape shopping. Write down that new goal, new number for Credit Cards under Containment.

Other Expenses

As I have mentioned before, we may have expenses in common, but we are still all unique. Therefore, some additional operating expenses may need to be examined. What other monthly costs can be contained in the short-term? Write down those new numbers for Other Expenses under Containment.

Once you have the cost-containment numbers for your Short-Term strategy, divide your annual income by twelve and write down that number next to Monthly Income. Now add up your contained expenses, write that number down next to Contained Expenses, and subtract those expenses from your monthly income. Write down that number next to Monthly Net Income. You now have a Short-Term strategy for cost containment. Unfortunately, I imagine the majority of us still need to increase our income to cover even the contained expenses. We will address this need for income a little later on. The good news is we now have a realistic view of how much income we need to cross the Chasm. We have our Short-Term strategy for cost containment. It is now time to create our Long-Term strategy.

Long-Term Strategy

Any CEO will tell you that doing the same thing over and over again will not produce different results. If a struggling business has contained operating expenses and is still struggling to survive financially, it needs more revenue. However, if the revenue stream is drying up even though the sales force keeps working harder and harder, a change needs to occur. The company needs to find a new revenue stream, a new direction, but this will take planning and will require a Long-Term strategy.

For the mother in the Half Family, we face the same situation. Whether you are separated, divorced, or unwed, you lost a revenue stream when your partner left. You need to replace that lost income. Therefore, our Long-Term strategy can be summed up in three words: *new revenue stream.*

However, we are not going to look at money as the starting point for developing this Long-Term strategy. The Cold Hard Facts surrounded by the Soft Facts drove the development of the Short-Term strategy for cost containment, but our Long-Term strategy for a new revenue stream will be driven by the Soft Facts of who we are.

I learned this approach from my own failure. For years, I followed the money rather than who I was. I pursued any long-term strategy that would bring in more income. It was a wrong path that left me cold and miserable. In fact, following the money only made money more illusive. As I mentioned earlier, I chose to work in sales for the potential of a larger income. However, I am not a sales person. It is not who I am. The harder I tried to make myself a sales person, the more miserable I became and the less productive. And I did not make that larger income.

I know it is hard not to focus on income, but it is crucial you first know who you are in relation to your Long-Term strategy. Only then can we examine potential future income. So we are going to forget about money for the moment. Instead, we are going to develop a Long-Term strategy for a new revenue stream based on who we are as women and mothers in the Half Family, the Soft Facts.

The reality is that most of us are going to need to work to generate this new source of income. We are either going to be self-employed or we are going to work for someone. Therefore, we need to look at who we are in relation to a job.

Right now, I want you to give yourself permission to dream. That's right, you are going to reach down inside of you and uncover your dream job. We all have certain passions, talents, and desires about what we want to do. Forget about that paycheck. What are your dreams? I know it may be hard. Many of us have buried our dreams so deep, we are not certain we can dig them out. So I want to point you in the right direction and walk you through a thought process for uncovering your dreams.

Strategy Development. In discovering our Soft Facts, we began to explore our dreams as related to income. I want you to look at that Soft Fact, and let's uncover your dreams, your talents, and your desires. Begin by asking yourself some basic questions. What do you like to do? Do you like to be outside or inside? Do you enjoy doing physical work? Do you enjoy working at your computer? Do you enjoy reading? Do you enjoy being surrounded by and interacting with people? Do you desire to paint, write poetry, or play the piano? Does solving mathematical problems or investigating some new scientific discovery energize you? Do you enjoy following or leading others? Do you want to work alone or with other people? What do have a passion to do?

Ask yourself questions to dig out your dreams. Now take all those answers and write down a description of a dream job. Do not write down an occupation, but do write down a detailed description of your dream job and do not censor your mind. For example, maybe you dream of working with a group of women to create, develop, and patent new products. Or do you dream about teaching under-privileged children about art, poetry, and music to capture their imagination and show them their own dreams. Write down a description and put it aside.

On another sheet of paper, I want you to write down an occupation. Do you want to be a construction worker? Do you want to be a lawyer or a doctor? Do you want to be an advertising executive or a computer programmer? Do you want to be a teacher or a teacher's aid? Do you want to be a writer or a sales person? Again, do not censor yourself. Be as specific as possible. Write down what comes to your mind.

Here is the acid test. I want you to match up that occupation with the dream job description. Does it match? It should. If the description and occupation do not match there is a problem. If you want to work at something creative and you wrote down an analytical occupation, like an accountant, I don't think we have a match. If you don't like confrontation, then you should not have written down trial lawyer. The point is if your dream job description and occupation do not match, we have a problem. The most common reason for this mismatch is that the dream job may reflect who you are, but the occupation reflects money. Don't get discouraged. It is hard to ignore our need for income. Our gut tells us we need to make money in order to support our families. That is the very reason why this third step is so crucial. I have seen many women get sucked into multi-level marketing schemes and work at home scams because of "big" money. If it looks too good to be true, it is. This step can really help you determine if your desired occupation is driven by who you are as a woman and mother in the Half Family or by money. The dream job description and occupation should match. If possible, I want you to look at your dream job description and come up with two occupational choices that match who you are.

Now we can talk about income. We cannot ignore the need for money, but we can only look at income after we determine our dream job and put an "occupation" name to it. So I want you to get a general idea of salaries for your one to two "matched" choices. This process will take a little bit of work. If you have access to the Internet, you can find some good web sites that provide average yearly salaries for positions. The local library can also provide this information. At this point in our Long-Term strategy development, we are looking for an educated estimate. This income number will be refined the closer you travel towards your dream.

Choose a dream. Now I want you to make an educated decision at this point. You have some good information that will lead you towards a good decision. Even if you have never expressed your dreams, those dreams were inside you. Hopefully, you were able to come up with two dream job options. Ask yourself "what do I really want to do?' Choose a dream but keep the other option.

Now you need to determine what it will cost to make your Long-Term strategy a reality. That's right, there is always an expense associated with a new stream of revenue. You may need to get further education and training to move into a new occupation. Make an educated guess of the cost on a monthly basis. If you do not know the exact number right now, it does not matter. We just need the awareness that the cost for our Long-Term strategy will impact the cost-containment for our Short-Term strategy. So go back to the form for your Short-Term strategy and write down the estimated monthly cost for your new job next to Long-Term strategy cost. Subtract it from the Monthly New Income and write down the new figure next to New Total (Net Income).

Now let me explain reality here. We have just gone through a "beginning" exercise for your Long-Term strategy. You have an awareness of your dreams, what you want to do, and what it will cost to get there. This strategy only becomes real as you begin to take steps toward your dreams. As you walk, this Long-Term strategy will become clearer, more complex, and more expansive. You will need to make adjustments and changes to this strategy as you move forward. That is normal. If you do not need to make course corrections, it will mean you are not moving and your dreams are just words on a piece of paper. Changes to your Long-Term strategy are a good thing.

Now that we have the Short-Term and Long-Term strategy, we need to step back and look at the plan so far. First, do you clearly see how we thought our way through this process? We took a proactive approach to this strategy development. By using positive input for positive thoughts, we surrounded the Cold Hard Facts with Soft Facts to create a Short-Term strategy. We found the short term "hits" that would drive cost containment without sacrificing who we are as women and mothers in the Half Family. Then we determined a Long-Term strategy for a new revenue stream based on the dreams of who we are as women and mothers. Also, did you notice that when you have all the facts, putting a plan of attack together is relatively simple? It is always easier in the long run to be pro-active rather than reactive.

We have developed two of our strategies for our plan, Short-Term and Long-Term. We have the hope that we can contain costs in the Short-Term and we have the hope that the dream job of who we are in our Long-Term strategy will lead us to maximum income and minimum expenses. Unfortunately, we may still have an Income Gap between these two strategies. In other words, after you sub-tract all your contained expenses and the cost of your new revenue stream (new occupation) from your current income, you may be facing an Income Gap. In fact, it may be worse than before you contained some expenses.

There is a Chasm separating where you are right now from where you want to be. Right about now, you may be thinking what kind of a management plan is this? It has created or widened the Income Gap. Believe it or not, we do have solid strategies and we do have a good plan so far. It was built on the rock-solid truth of the Cold Hard Facts of minimum income and maximum expenses and the Soft Facts of who we are as women and mothers in the Half Family. It is a good plan because we took the truth and proactively developed a plan that gives us hope to manage the Cold Hard Facts on this external road. It is a good plan because it focuses on the parts of the road that we can control.

That's right, this plan gives you a measure of control. I want you to reflect back on our travels thus far in our external world. We have slowly and methodi-cally been identifying what we have control over on this road. We now have con-trol over facing the Cold Hard Facts. We now have control over discovering the Soft Facts that surround the Cold Hard Facts. We now have control over a Short-Term and Long-Term strategy in our management plan. We have logically thought through everything that is in our control on this road and we own that part of the plan.

But there is one part of the road that we do not own. We do not have control over one part of the journey, the Chasm. The strategy for crossing the Income Gap, that part of the management plan, belongs to someone else. Someone else has control over Income Gap.

The Love

Jesus has control over the Income Gap and he owns the third strategy of our management plan. Now given the *very real danger* of the Income Gap Chasm, you are probably not very enthusiastic about this approach. In fact, you probably have a strong desire to retain some control over this strategy. Let go of that desire because Jesus owns this strategy.

Actually, the foundation of this strategy for crossing the Income Gap Chasm is not new to us on our Half Family journey. From the beginning, we have been learning about Jesus' strategy. When we are standing on the edge of a Chasm with no visible means to cross this gapping hole in the road, we have learned to take a step of faith onto the invisible bridge. In our internal journey, by faith we learned how to walk across the Chasm of unforgiveness. By faith, we learned how to walk across the Chasm of difficult relationships, but learning to take steps of faith across the Income Gap will be a different challenge.

Faith walking on this invisible bridge will be challenging because we face Real Fear and a visible Chasm, the Income Gap. Our temptation to revert to our reactive behavior will challenge our faith. We will be challenged to release our desire to control this part of the journey and trust our invisible confidante, Jesus, with our visible external world.

If you are like me, your first reaction to this Income Gap strategy is that it does not make "human" sense that we should give up control of the visible Income Gap to an invisible God and an invisible bridge. Even if we try to contemplate stepping out in faith to cross this Chasm, our emotions start to boil as we react to the Real Fear of the Income Gap. I mean the reality is we are facing Real Fear and need Cold Hard cash to get across the Income Gap. What is Jesus going to use to get us across this Chasm, invisible cash? That was my reaction to this ridiculous concept. I was focused on the solution rather than the strategy. I wanted control because I truly did not understand the Income Gap strategy. I did not understand because I did not ask Jesus. In his love, Jesus has provided a very clear explanation of this strategy and the necessary strategy development process for crossing this Chasm. We simply need to take a proactive step in his direction and ask for his explanation and directions.

Income Gap Strategy

This Income Gap strategy can be summed up in four words: *Who do you trust?* Having crossed a lot of "financial" Chasms in my lifetime, I know I have taken steps of faith. But what motivated me to take those steps onto the invisible bridge? Again and again, in my mind, I have traveled back to those moments as I stood on the edge of the Income Gap Chasm. Why did I take a step forward? What was I thinking? I now realize my mind was struggling with the answer to the question: Who do I trust? The Income Gap strategy requires me to trust Jesus and believe there is a bridge across this Chasm. No matter how impossible the financial situation in human terms, nothing is impossible in spiritual terms. When we come to the end of ourselves, who do we trust?

To know the truth of this explanation, I simply need to look at one of the most worn pages in my Bible and a passage that has been highlighted and tear stained: Matthew 6:24, "No one can serve two masters. Either he will hate the one and love the other, or he will be devoted to the one and despise the other. You cannot serve both God and money."

Who do we trust: God or money? When we are standing on the edge of the Income Gap Chasm, we all struggle with this question. Don't think so? Well, let me give you a glimpse into my own experience and see if you can relate. Facing the Real Fear standing on the edge of the Income Gap Chasm, I have experienced terror. When I have faced the very real, visible possibility of no food, my utilities being shut off, or my car being repossessed, my fearful reaction was to search for Cold Hard cash. Surely that is the way to cross this Chasm. So I would pray for Jesus to drop money on me. In other words, I had the solution and I wanted Jesus to fill up this Chasm with money. If I only had enough money, I would be okay. The problem is the more I focused on the Income Gap; the more the Real Fear terrorized me. The more I focused on filling up the Chasm with money, the more I tried to control this fearful situation. I was reactively hanging onto the money, and I would not surrender control to Jesus. In fact, I could not even see Jesus. He was right in front of me, but I was staring at the Income Gap. I had the answer. Why was Jesus not answering my prayer? There was no prayer. There was only my answer to Income Gap: money.

It has taken me many years to understand that the Income Gap strategy has nothing to do with money and everything to do with trust. Do we trust money or God? And I know the agonizing struggle in that choice. It does not make human sense to trust the invisible Jesus with our visible money problems. When you have done everything you can that is within your control and you are standing on the edge of the Income Gap, the only other choice is to trust Jesus with your external world.

Now you may not like this Income Gap strategy. In fact, if you are honest, robbing a bank sounds less risky than trusting Jesus. If that thought has crossed your mind, then I know you understand the choice. Jesus is asking us to ignore everything that our human eyes see and trust him. And you are blessed to be in this position. What? Blessed, how is this choice a blessing? It is because you are in the special position to truly know your faith. Very few Christians in this country have had the rare privilege to test their faith this way—to choose between money and God. In fact, when I was well fed with a home and a steady paycheck, I would profess my faith in Jesus. But that faith was only a word until I stood on the edge of my own Income Gap Chasm, and I had to ask myself, do I really believe Matthew 6 when Jesus states that he loves us and desires to meet my needs? If I believe that Jesus cannot lie, the logical decision is to choose to trust Jesus.

The Income Gap strategy means the solutions to crossing this Chasm belong to Jesus. And I will twist your brain even more; Cold Hard cash is not always the solution to the Income Gap. What do you think is a better strategy for crossing this Chasm, stepping onto an existing bridge or attempting to fill up this massive hole with money?

I know that this strategy seems impossible, but nothing is impossible with Jesus. He truly knows the struggle. And in his love, Jesus asks for only small choices, small proactive steps. In our internal world, we only need to make one small choice to trust Jesus, and we manifest that choice by taking one small step of faith in our external world. And those small choices give us access to the expanse of this amazing strategy for crossing the Income Gap Chasm.

Strategy Development. Jesus has already developed an Income Gap strategy for each of us. We simply need to ask Jesus to teach us. He does not ask us to choose to trust him and then leave us to our own human knowledge to cross the Chasm. No, if we only ask, he will guide us in the strategy development process for faith walking across the Income Gap. That development process requires us to create an ongoing dialogue with Jesus to learn three key principles of faith: it's intelligent, logical, and orderly.

My understanding of the Income Gap strategy was turned upside down through my own dialoguing with Jesus. My most profound learning was the realization that faith was intelligent, logical, and orderly. We exercise our faith by using our God-given intelligence as we step onto the invisible bridge. Those steps will be driven by Jesus' biblical, logical instructions as he directs us through prayer across the Chasm in an orderly manner one step at a time. This learning took my understanding of faith from the invisible to the visible. And this learning process begins before we are standing on the edge of the Chasm.

If this strategic faith development for crossing the Income Gap requires intelligent, logical, and orderly decision making, the edge of the Chasm may not be a good learning environment. Think about it. If I begin a dialogue with Jesus at this point, where do you think my vision is focused? I will stare down into the Chasm and focus on the money I need. In that reactive condition, do you think that this beginning dialogue will be productive or result in any proactive steps of faith? Probably not.

So it makes sense that we need to learn about this strategy away from the edge of the Chasm. So where do we begin? We begin this dialogue with Jesus about intelligent, logical, orderly faith walking by discussing the other side of the Chasm.

Here is what I mean. Why are we crossing the Income Gap? Yes, we have an unpaid expense and no income, but ultimately, why are we crossing the Income Gap? Are we not crossing it to get to our Long-Term strategy, our dream job? Yes, our hope is that our dream job will provide us with a new revenue stream so we can stay on the other side of Income Gap Chasm. From this present point on the road, it is only a hope. How clearly do you see the other side and that dream job? Is it a little fuzzy? Is it but a shadowy vision? Of course it is. In fact, if you have never allowed yourself to dream or imagined that your dream job could be a reality, you may even doubt your limited vision. What if you are wrong about this dream job? What if you made a mistake? How do you know that you are really headed in the right direction? Maybe it would be a good idea to spend some time with the one who built the invisible bridge and clearly sees the reality of your dreams.

Jesus owns the bridge across the Income Gap Chasm. He clearly sees the right direction. Since Jesus built the bridge, he knows our destination. Jesus not only knows our destination, but he intimately knows who we are as women and mothers in the Half Family. He knew your dream job before you did. Therefore, it is logical that we begin our ongoing dialogue with Jesus about the Income Gap strategy by taking a step of faith and trusting him with our dream job. In other words, if we cannot clearly see the other side of the Chasm, we should talk to one who does see it.

I know that this approach may have twisted your brain. How is this going to help you cross the Income Gap? It will because it is *proactive rather than reactive.* Our reactive behavior tells us we learn about faith walking on the invisible bridge at the edge of the Chasm. Proactive behavior means that we have learned the Income Gap strategy before we face the Real Fear of the Chasm. So let's move away from the edge of the Chasm and get a clearer vision of the other side and our dream job.

Our Dream Job

If you choose to dialogue with Jesus, he will lead you through a process of intelligent, logical and orderly steps to embrace your dream job and see the other side of the Chasm. Here are some discussion points to begin the dialogue with Jesus.

First, Jesus will never guide us to a dream job, an occupation that violates his truth and his love. Obviously, an occupation that causes you to lie, cheat, or steal is not a good choice. An occupation that drives people to greed and lust is not a good choice. But there are more subtle violations that we need to uncover in a dialogue with Jesus. For example, an occupation that requires long workweeks or extensive travel will hinder your ability to be emotionally, physically, mentally and spiritually available for your family. An occupation that violates the truth of who you are as a woman is not a good choice. Spend time with Jesus reflecting on who you are as a woman and mother in the Half Family. Trust me, if you faithfully ask Jesus to reveal who you are in relation to your dream job, he will reveal the truth. So test your choice against the Bible. Literally, look up passages on truth and love. How does your dream job measure up to his Word?

Second, Jesus will always lead us to a dream job, an occupation that honors him. Here is what I have discovered in my ongoing dialogue with Jesus. I have found out who I am through Jesus' eyes. In my still moments in his presence, I discovered myself. And it was in those still moments I realized how important the Soft Facts are to each of us. Who we are is a gift from Jesus. *Who we are as women and mothers can make a difference in this world and bring honor to Jesus.* If we know who we are in Jesus, we will honor him in what we do. If you know you are a teacher and you follow that Long-Term strategy, you will honor Jesus by making a positive difference in young lives. If you know you are a construction worker, you will honor Jesus by providing homes for people. Honoring Jesus in our work has absolutely nothing to do with a "Christian" occupation; it has everything to do with seeing who we are in Jesus' eyes and reflecting that vision in our daily lives. Every occupation should be a Christian occupation.

Third, trust Jesus with your dream job. You need the support, guidance, and encouragement of your most trusted confidante who will gently hold your dreams. You need Jesus' counsel especially at the birth of a dream. Dreams are fragile at birth. You do not yet clearly see this dream. It is not a reality. In the beginning, the safest place for your dreams is in Jesus' arms. Protect your dream and be smart about who you tell. In other words, if our dreams are still fragile, we should not put them in the hands of people who will break them. Even now, I am almost finished with this book but few people know I am writing it. This process is physically, mentally, emotionally, and spiritually exhausting. I do not need to risk sharing my dream with anyone who will drain more energy from me.

Fourth, make a "heart" commitment to spend time with Jesus, the Bible, and prayer concerning your Long-Term strategy. This commitment is the most important aspect of the Income Gap Strategy. This time will build a trust relationship and you will begin to clearly see your dreams. Your Long-Term strategy will become real internally before it is a visible reality. In those moments when you are facing the Income Gap Chasm and the Real Fear, you can look up and see the other side of the Chasm. You see it because daily Jesus has been revealing it to you. Daily you have been walking towards that dream. On the edge of the Chasm, you will see Jesus' outstretched hand waiting to embrace you as you step forward in faith. You will have built a communication bridge. As you walk in faith, you will begin to trust what your eyes do not see. So even when you are standing in the middle of invisible bridge and you begin to doubt, you will only have to look behind and see the bridge that faith is building.

When you are standing on the edge of the Chasm, you can make choices that reflect your trust in Jesus. In that precarious position, an escape jump may look like your only option. You can ask yourself, "Is this choice in line with the truth and love of Jesus"? "Will this honor Jesus?" "Am I trusting him?" and "Am I surrendering to his presence?" You will ask these questions because you have created a proactive dialogue with Jesus. It is a dialogue that began before you reached the edge of the Chasm. I tell you from personal experience, Jesus' Income Gap strategy has never failed me. I may have failed to trust, but Jesus never failed me. Even times that looked like failure were really my greatest successes.

CHEAT SHEET

Creating a Plan for Managing the Cold Hard Facts and Crossing the Income Gap

The Truth

1. The Crisis Management lifestyle has created a bad habit—reactive behavior.

2. New proactive behavior gives you control.

The Hope

1. The management plan for maximum income and minimum expenses

2. The Short-Term strategy for cost containment

3. The Long-Term strategy for a new revenue stream

The Love

1. The strategy for crossing the Income Gap Chasm: who do you trust?

2. The strategy development: dialogue with Jesus to learn intelligent, logical, and orderly steps of faith.

3. Begin the dialogue with your dream job.

14

Managing the Cold Hard Facts across the Income Gap

Even as I wake I am weary. Another tough day lies in front of me. As I glance out the window, I do not see the beauty of the morning sun streaming through the leaves on the trees nor do I feel the warmth of its light. All I see is a long ominous rocky road filled with treacherous mud pits. I do not see the sun. I see only the dark clouds filled with cold rain. And the memory of damp air rushes over my aching body. It starts to drizzle on this road as I reach for my Bible. As I open this well-worn book, I cry out to Jesus, "I can't do this anymore. I am too tired. It is too hard. I can't think anymore. Please just make it be over." I search through the pages for comfort, strength, courage—answers. Yes, answers. I don't want comfort or strength or courage anymore. I want to be off this road. "And need I remind you, Jesus, I am not the only one on this road. What about my son, Lord?" My thoughts drift to my sweet little boy and I cry. It is not fair that he must suffer too. Those thoughts of my son jolt me back to the reality that I have to keep moving for him. Even if I think that I can't do this anymore, I must do it for him. "So yes, Lord, I do need your comfort, strength and courage. I can't do this but I must believe that you can." I struggle to focus and absorb his Word. Slowly, the words invade my heart, fill my soul and I begin to feel some peace settle my spirit. It is warmth from the cold reality of my external world. I have entered Jesus' presence and I want to stay curled up all day in this cocoon.

But I must face the day, so I get to the truth of my external world. "What do I do, Lord? Do I pay the electric bill or the gas bill? We need the lights but we need heat too. I have squeezed every penny out of this month's income. And I am thirty days behind on these bills." The Real Fear of being without electricity or gas is terrifying because I have lived without lights and heat. And I do not want to go through it again. I am so tired of facing this lack of income, this Chasm. The truth is I have done everything I can do. "There is nothing else for me to do but

199

trust you, Jesus. So the real question is what will you do, Lord? Despite my fatigue and fear, I know you will take care of my son and me. So I will do the only thing that I can do. I will trust there is an invisible bridge across this Chasm. I am weary of walking through this Real Fear. But I won't run away. Oh Lord, you have rescued me before from the Chasm. Please do it again. I am frightened for my family—help me. You are my only hope."

That is the reality of the managing the Cold Hard Facts across the Income Gap. It is gut wrenchingly personal. It is deeply and profoundly personal. And anyone who tells you differently is either lying to you or has never traveled this road. It is the darkest, most treacherous part of the Half Family journey because it is so daily. The Cold Hard Facts will wear you down into the mud, and you will face the reality of the Income Gap many times. But when you face the mud pits, boulders, and Chasms on this road, you will also have the rare privilege to experience the deep personal touches of grace and mercy and know a peace beyond your brutal reality that can only come from Jesus' presence. When the brutality of the road has beaten you down into the mud, you will not be defeated because Jesus will lift you up.

For no matter how devastating our circumstances, we can never travel beyond the love of Jesus. I want you to hold on to that fact even if you do not believe it right now. Hold on to this love as we begin this part of the journey by walking through some painful truth.

It is painful truth. But it is truth that is familiar to you because you live with it daily. If you are like me, you may have tried to ignore it, but you keep stepping in it on the road. Given this painful familiarity, you will probably not have a problem understanding the truth. It is the acceptance of it that will be difficult. Yes, the truth about this personal journey of managing the Cold Hard Facts across the Income Gap will be difficult to accept. In fact, you may feel that accepting the truth has left you neck-deep in the mud in the middle of the road. But actually in our acceptance, the love of Jesus will lift us out of the mud with a precious blessing for our personal journey. It is a blessing that can only be received after acceptance of the truth and will transform our journey. There are two truths that we need to understand and accept about managing the Cold Hard Facts across the Income Gap.

The Truth

There Is No Answer to Why

I have struggled for months with putting this first truth down on paper. It has been frustrating because quite frankly, I did not know how to put the truth into words. I understand my struggle and frustration now because no one ever verbalized this truth to me. I came to understand and accept it in the depths of my soul as I cried out to Jesus. I never verbalized it to anyone else, but I could see other mothers on the same journey as I. They too were silently struggling with the truth: an unspoken truth. It is a question that demands an answer; but it is a question that we will never be able to answer. Why?

When we begin to manage the Cold Hard Facts across the Income Gap, we cannot avoid the question: Why? Why should we be faced with choosing between food and electricity or between putting gasoline in our car or paying the rent or mortgage? Why should our children be hungry? Why should we, who live in the richest country in the world, be prevented from seeing a doctor because we have no medical insurance? Why should our society classify our children as broken? Why? Why? I don't know. Oh I could answer the *why* question many different ways. In fact, our society as a whole may answer these questions in simplistic terms. In my unguarded moments, I would ask someone, "Why"? Please tell me why?" Unfortunately, some of the common answers only pushed me deeper into the mud. We have all heard the answers like: we, as divorced or unwed mothers, are living with the consequences of our actions or we face minimum income and maximum expenses because we simply do not work hard enough. These answers and others are simplistic and flawed.

But even flawed answers are better than no answer. For without an answer to the question of why, this part of the journey just seems unfair, which makes us angry. It is not fair that millions of Half Families in this country live in horrific environments without food, water, electricity, or gas. It is appalling and it should make you angry. The bottom line is that it is not fair. No one should have to live in poverty without basic necessities. Anyone would be angry in this situation.

That is the truth. You understand it. You have felt it in your gut for a long time. I just put in black and white. You have searched for an answer to *why*. But there is no answer to why we are faced with this journey. It is unfair and we are left with our anger. And…what do we do with this truth? We have been on this journey long enough to know that once we understand a truth, we need to accept it. Yes, we accept it. Let that sink in for a moment.

For me, I could not accept this truth. I could understand it, but I simply could not and would not accept it. So there I was neck deep in the mud of this unanswerable question.

Therefore, my progress was very slow. When I did somehow get out of the mud, I stumbled, fell, and got injured as I struggled to manage the Cold Hard Facts across the Income Gap. Angry about the unfair nature of my journey, I spilled that anger on everyone and everything. I managed nothing and reacted to everything most of the time.

It is true. If we cannot accept that there is no answer to why and we allow this unfairness and anger to simmer inside of us, it will boil over into reaction against the Cold Hard Facts and result in "Chasm" jumps into the Income Gap. And we will pass that anger onto our children. Clearly, we have come too far on this journey to turn back to our old ways. Therefore, rather than react to this truth, we need to accept the truth.

That's right, just like every other truth on this journey; we need to accept this truth about managing the Cold Hard Facts across the Income Gap. This acceptance is not easy. For me, it took a lot of prayer and Bible study to accept the truth. The Bible is full of stories of men and women who walked difficult, unfair roads and never knew why. They accepted the truth. We need to accept the truth that we will never fully understand why we have had to travel down this difficult road with the Cold Hard Facts across the Income Gap. We need to accept that it is not fair and it makes us angry. Those feelings are valid and real. That statement does not diminish our need to accept the truth: there is no answer to why.

Here is why that acceptance is so difficult. You need to accept that there is no answer to why which means you will also accept that it is not fair and it will make you angry. Are you neck deep in the mud yet? If you are honest with yourself, you will think that accepting the full depth of this truth is impossible.

When I faced this truth, I thought that it was impossible. How could I accept the unfairness? How could I accept I was angry about this situation but not react? How could anyone accept the oppression and injustice of the situation? The fact of the matter is that in and of myself I absolutely could not accomplish that acceptance. I needed Jesus and his courage. When I accessed his courage, I became aware that holding on to the unfairness of my situation and my anger paralyzed me in the mud on the road. And if I wanted to get out of this mud, I had to accept that there was no answer to "why me" and "why us." Basically, I needed to surrender my need to know why and stop demanding an answer from Jesus. I had to accept I did not know why but Jesus had the answer. And he may choose to never tell me the answer as long I walked on this earth. I had to surrender the unanswered question of why and the unfair journey and my anger to Jesus and trust him.

But that acceptance was a journey because I had to face the truth every day. Every day I could see that managing the Cold Hard Facts was not fair and some days I could feel the boiling emotion of anger. Each time these feelings emerged and I began to question why, I cried out to Jesus to calm my emotions. I kept moving forward. When I finally walked into acceptance, he gave me an amazing blessing, which is available to every mother in the Half Family. But before we can receive this blessing, we need to face one more truth.

The Long Journey

As if the truth about "why" was not enough, I have struggled for months with the truth about the journey. How do I share this truth with you? I have written and rewritten this explanation. It has been an agonizing experience. I am a veteran at managing the Cold Hard Facts across the Income Gap. But how do I put the truth down on paper?

I think that this continuing struggle came from my desire to take away your pain. I mean I lived this part of the journey. Certainly, I did some things right, and hopefully, I learned from my mistakes. Therefore, I should be able to show you the way to avoid the boulders, the mud, the rain…the Chasm. Surely, I can show you the way so you do not have to suffer or endure any pain. Now I realize the greatest gift I can give you is the truth about the journey. Only when you understand and accept this last truth will you have access to the blessing.

Just like our first truth, I lived with this second truth about managing the Cold Hard Facts, but I could not accept it. I could not accept that I was on a long journey. I not only tried to ignore it, but I actually tried to change the truth. I tried to change it to something I could accept. See if you relate to my experience.

As I began to manage the Cold Hard Facts across the Income Gap, I was absolutely terrified. Therefore, I would share my Real Fear and the reality of my harsh external world with people. The majority of people would say to me, "You're just going through a rough time, it will get better." In other words, you are divorced. It will just take you time to adjust to this new lifestyle. It is just a rough time, right now. I liked that answer. To me, a rough time meant that this situation would pass. This rough time was just a bump in the road and it, my external world, would get better. So I accepted this version of the truth that was spoon fed to me. Unfortunately, the rough time did not get better. In fact, at times, the "rough time" got worse. One month went by, then six months, and then a year. No matter what I did, it did not get better. I would read self-help books and seek financial counsel and use "gimmicks" to get through the rough time. I would get around one Cold Hard fact only to face another and another. If I was just going through a rough time, why was I still struggling with my financial road? What was I doing wrong?

My firm belief in the "rough time" theory convinced me I was doing something wrong. If I was doing the right things, surely my financial situation should be getting better. I was following financial advice. I was working hard. I was not spending money on anything other than necessities. Yet, I was still staring at minimum income and maximum expenses. The Real Fear of my situation began to overwhelm me and I became convinced that the Cold Hard Facts were my fault.

I began to focus so much on that Cold Hard Fact, that boulder in front of me, that I lost sight of the road. I reacted to the Real Fear and determined that only brute force could move these boulders. I needed more income. That was the answer. I was in this situation because I was just not working hard enough. I just needed to work more to get more income.

If I worked more hours or two jobs during this "rough time," I would be able to pay my bills. I could fix this situation, the lack of income, by working more hours. That approach worked for a time. But since I viewed my situation as a rough time, I believed I would be able to go back to a normal workweek at some point. Unfortunately, that was not reality. I was not dealing with some bump in the road: an unexpected medical bill, house repairs, etc. I was facing overwhelming everyday expenses, like housing, childcare, food that could not be "fixed" with a short-term extra job. Therefore, I began to get tired emotionally, physically, and mentally from long workweeks. I was drained internally, my external world was not safe, and the Cold Hard Facts were very personal. In that condition, standing on the edge of the Chasm, you don't think that escape looked like a viable option. Of course, it did. My life became a downward spiral into the Income Gap Chasm.

Deep down I knew the truth. I just could not accept it. Facing a long journey with the Real Fear of the Cold Hard Facts was too much for me. I wanted to believe it was a rough time. I wanted to believe that people and those self-help books were right. It was just a rough time. Unfortunately, a rough time is an unexpected expense or a temporary lack of money that will pass in a few weeks or a few months. A rough time is a bump in the road. The Cold Hard Facts are minimal income and maximum expenses. Look at your income statement. Does that look like a rough time that will pass? No, it is a harsh road strewn with boulders and pounding rain, not a bump in the road. I was not going through a rough time; I was on a long journey with the Cold Hard Facts.

Can you relate? Oh, you may have never used the words "rough time" to describe the journey, but what do your actions say? Have you really accepted the truth that you are on a long journey managing the Cold Hard Facts? Deep down you know this truth because you live it every day. Is accepting this truth almost impossible for you? It was for me. I knew the truth. It was with me every moment of every day. And the more I fought it, the more I lied to myself, the more difficult the road became for me. The rocks grew sharper, the mud deeper, and the rain colder. Do you know that feeling? The truth is that managing the Cold Hard Facts across the Income Gap is a long, personal journey. You cannot side step this truth or try to minimize the impact. It is a long journey.

For me, I don't think that I accepted the truth so much as I finally surrendered to it. I was just plain tired of fighting against it. And in that surrender, I found an incredible blessing.

The Blessing of Acceptance

Yes, from the pain of accepting the truth is a blessing to help us manage the Cold Hard Facts across the Income Gap. It is a painful process of accepting that there is no answer to why and that the journey is long. In fact, in my experience, facing these two truths was like ripping all hope from my being. If there is no answer to why, then life is just unfair and that makes me angry. If this rough road is not a rough time, I am facing a long journey with the Cold Hard Facts. To me, this acceptance was loss—loss of hope. From our human perspective, it is loss. But from God's perspective, when you have nothing else to loose, that is the moment you have everything to gain.

And it is at that crushing human moment that Jesus always gives his greatest blessings. Since I was not expecting to find anything remotely positive in surrendering to the truth, it took me awhile to even see the blessing and accept this wonderful gift.

Are you ready? The blessing from Jesus is simple and available to all of us: "The truth shall set you free." Not what you were expecting? I know that it sounds strange but if you accept the truth, you will find freedom. Trust me; freedom is the perfect blessing for the unfair, long, personal journey with Cold Hard Facts across the Income Gap. If you choose to accept this blessing, it will transform your journey.

If you accept that there is no answer to why, you will be freed from continually demanding an answer. If you accept that life is unfair and choose not to react in anger, you will be freed from the paralyzing mud. Even though the journey is unfair and it makes you angry at times, you will have access to the freedom to walk around the mud. Your freedom gives you the option to manage the Cold Hard Facts, not react to them.

If you accept the long journey and stop lying to yourself, you will have the freedom to see beyond that boulder in front of you. This freedom will mean the journey through the boulders and the cold rain will not surprise you. In other words, you will not enjoy facing the boulders of the Cold Hard Facts, but you will know that it is part of the long journey. You will know that if there is one boulder in front of you, chances are good that another boulder will be right behind it. You will know that this journey is not a bump in the road. In fact, a bump in the road would be a welcome encounter. You will also not enjoy the cold rain of daily financial crisis, but it won't be unexpected.

Freedom does not mean that you will not face Real Fear on this road. Do not be deceived, the road of managing the Cold Hard Facts across the Income Gap requires us to face Real Fear quite frequently. But freedom does mean you will have the choice to walk forward and not be trapped by the Real Fear.

The freedom that is found in accepting the truth is a blessing that is too often dismissed. If we are honest; in relation to the journey through minimum income and maximum expenses, we would consider money a far better blessing. However, you will discover that the blessing of freedom is worth more than any amount of money. Money can disappear in an instant, but freedom only grows. The more you access this blessing and walk in freedom, the more it expands. It empowers you on this unfair, long personal journey. It is this freedom that we will carry with us into the hope for this journey.

The Hope

I want you to hold onto your newly found freedom and say out loud, "I can do this." I truly believe that the most courageous path you can choose as a mother in the Half Family is the choice to manage the Cold Hard Facts across the Income Gap. It is a dangerous road but not impossible. I made it and so can you. I am telling you this right now because we are getting ready to take our first steps in managing minimum income and maximum expenses. There is no doubt that our journey will be extremely difficult and our forward movement will be slow and painful at times. Despite the difficulty, we will move forward because we will have the hope found in a new thought process: wisdom.

The Hope of Wisdom

Managing the Cold Hard Facts across the Income Gap will be a new thought process for most of us. In our past reactive states, we may have let the Nightmare Fear from our internal world drive our financial decisions based on our emotional turmoil. Or we may have reacted to the Real Fear of our external world, which resulted in decisions based solely on the Cold Hard Facts. Our forward movement was either a reaction to internal pressure or external pressure.

Managing the Cold Hard Facts requires us to balance our internal and external worlds. We have learned from our last three stops that managing the Cold Hard Facts is more than trudging through the daily financial mud. Our lives are not black and white numbers but rather reflect the color of who we are as women and mothers in the Half Family. From this understanding, we developed a management plan. It is a plan that balances our internal world, the Soft Facts, and our external world, the Cold Hard Facts. It is a good plan, but it will take wisdom to implement it. It is this hope of wisdom that will transform us from reactors into managers of the Cold Hard Facts.

How do you begin this transformation from reactor to manager? First, wise decisions are made logically, methodically, and orderly. Whether you realize it or not, we have been following a logical, methodical, and orderly process as we walked through our external world. We faced the Cold Hard Facts, then the Soft Facts, and then balanced these external/internal facts to develop a management plan. We have made some wise decisions. So we have already begun the transformation. To complete the transformation from reactors to managers, we need to use the hope of wisdom to make the tough, personal decisions to manage the Cold Hard Facts across the Income Gap. Before I give you some practical information to point you in the direction of wise decisions about where to step on the road, I want to share some thoughts about wisdom.

Most important, neither I nor anyone else can give you this hope. Wisdom is a hope that is learned. Only you can gain wisdom. Each time you choose to make a tough personal decision and take a step on this difficult road, you will gain wisdom. With each step in managing the Cold Hard Facts, no matter how painful or difficult, you become wiser. Even in your missteps, you will grow in wisdom. Actually, my most profound learning about wisdom has come from my biggest missteps on the road like my Chasm jumps. If you choose to learn from every step forward, your wisdom will grow.

So let's hit the road. I want to assist you in learning to make wise decisions about managing the Cold Hard Facts. Given the harshness of our road, we are going to break down our decision making into two different processes. We will make tough, personal decisions about 1.) leveling the road and 2.) managing daily.

Leveling the Road. It is true; we have actually acquired the ability to level the road. We have accumulated a lot of knowledge about our financial road. That knowledge has given us the foundation to make wise decisions that can move some boulders out of our way. We can't eliminate all the Cold Hard Facts from our path, but we can move some facts out of our way. However, we need to make a wise choice about where we spend our energy. In other words, we need to move those boulders that will have the biggest impact in leveling the road in front of us.

To accomplish this task, we will need our Short-Term and Long-Term strategies from our management plan. We will use these strategies to help us reduce our maximum expenses and increase our minimum income. I will guide you in a logical, methodical, and orderly process to use the knowledge from your management plan and help you make some wise personal decisions. We will begin with reducing maximum expenses.

Reducing Maximum Expenses—Housing

As you view your financial situation, you may see that your Short-Term cost-containment strategy has reduced some expenses, but you may still have a visible Income Gap. In fact, that gap may have widened due to the expenses associated with your Long-Term strategy. You may have additional training or education costs on a monthly basis. Therefore, you will need to wisely make some tough decisions to minimize expenses and narrow the Income Gap.

In my experience, there is one expense that is proportionately larger than other expenses and tends to absorb income on a monthly basis. It is our housing expense. Therefore, we are going to methodically walk through a process that will challenge you to balance who you are as a woman and mother in the Half Family with reducing your housing costs. In this process, you will be challenged to make the wisest housing decision for your family that balances your internal and external worlds.

1. We need to look at our internal world first, our Soft Facts for housing. You discovered these facts two stops back. These facts, not housing expenses, must be our starting point. We are going to prioritize the Soft Facts for housing. So pick them up and number each one in order of importance.

For example, Safety #1, School District #2, Size of Housing #3, etc. Take the time to do this exercise. If you need to go back to our stop with the Soft Facts, do it now. Reread the section on Soft Facts for housing, and write down your facts in the order of importance to you. It is critical that you know what is important to your family and you as related to housing. You may be faced with making a tough, personal decision related to this expense. In order to reduce housing costs, you may need to sacrifice some of your Soft Facts. This type of sacrifice is going to be difficult. If you have wisely prioritized your housing Soft Facts, you will be able to make a wise choice about what you are willing to sacrifice. If you do not have the facts in order of importance to you, you risk making a reactive decision based on Real Fear and may sacrifice your family on the altar of money. A decision based on money will ultimately hurt, not help your children or you.

Once you have determined your housing priorities, I want you to sit down with Jesus and discuss it. Ask yourself, am I letting money drive my priorities? I cannot emphasize enough the need to sit with Jesus and ask this question. The reality is that we daily live with financial stress. Whether you realize it or not, that stress takes an emotional, physical, mental, and spiritual toll on you. We all need Jesus to calm our world-weary spirits and give us counsel. Jesus will never ask us to sacrifice our children for the sake of money. And money has nothing to do with this first step. Your priorities for the Soft Facts should be driven by who you are as a woman and mother in the Half Family. Trust me, if you spend time with Jesus and have faith that he will lead you, you will know what is important for your children and you. And never forget that Jesus is the source of all wisdom. Only after you finish this first step, can you look at the cost of housing.

2. Now we can look at our external world—the cold, hard economics of housing. The bottom-line question is: can you save money by moving into cheaper housing? This step will take some research. If you own your home, do you need to sell your house and move into a smaller one? Are there less expensive homes for sale in your area? Will you need to move to another town? In order to answer these questions, I would recommend seeking the counsel of a trusted realtor. This means someone who can give you good advice, not someone who is just interested selling you a house to get a commission. Do your research and determine your options for less expensive housing.

If you live in rental property, do you need to move from one rental property to another? If you are locked into a lease, is there a cheaper apartment in the same complex? Are there homes for rent that are a less expensive solution than an apartment? Apartments will normally cost more per square foot than rental property from a private owner. Remember, you are gathering all the facts and looking for options to reduce your rent.

There are other housing options. Can you save money by having a roommate? Can you save money by moving in with friends or family? How much will you save on a monthly basis?

Find all the housing options that will save you money. Then on a sheet of paper prioritize the list from the greatest cost savings to the least. Now sit down with Jesus and discuss it. He is very concerned about our financial situation. In fact, some of my most creative solutions have come from my discussions with Jesus. You may discover some options that you missed. So do not dismiss this prayer time from this process.

3. Now you are ready to balance your internal world with your external world. We will walk through balancing your prioritized Soft Facts against your housing options to make a wise tough decision that could move a financial boulder from your daily path.

On a sheet of paper, write down the cost savings at the top, such as $500, and under that write down a brief description of the property. Underneath this description draw a line down the center and write Pro on one side and Con on the other side. Create as many sheets as you have housing options. Begin with the housing option that has the greatest cost savings. Each sheet for housing options should look something like this:

Cost Savings	$
Description of Property	
PRO	**CON**

Now take your prioritized Soft Facts for housing. Based on the description of the property, put each fact and its corresponding number in either the pro or con column for the housing option. If safety is a priority 1, put "safety #1" in either the Pro or Con column. At this point, the process will get muddy because only you can determine "pro" or "con." But be honest, a bullet-ridden, rat-invested apartment is not safe. Therefore, "safety" should be in the Con column. Place all your prioritize Soft Facts in either the Pro or Con column.

Whether you own or rent property, you will need to complete a Pro/Con sheet for every housing option. This process is time consuming and tedious. Your time will be well spent. For only when you follow a logical, methodical, orderly process are you able to wisely make the tough, personal decisions that balance your internal and external worlds.

Housing Options (Example)

Cost Savings	$200
Description of Property	2 Bedroom/ 2 Bath
PRO	**CON**
Close to school (#2) Enough room (#3)	Safety——not safe (#1)

4. Making this housing decision is truly the muddiest portion of this process. You will need to balance your internal (Soft Facts) with your external (Cold Hard Facts). And this balancing act will be very personal and difficult. If you are fortunate, one of your housing options will be a clear winner. It is more likely that you will need to make a tough personal decision. Chances are you are faced with sacrificing some of who you are as a woman and a mother. In other words, balancing of our two worlds is rarely even. Only you can do the balancing that results in the wisest decision for your family.

The key to determining what you are willing to sacrifice is found in your priorities. For example, let's assume that you can save $200 per month by moving into a smaller apartment. However, all but 2 of your Soft Facts for housing are listed in the Con column. You are probably sacrificing too much of who you are as a woman and mother to save $200 monthly. Another example, maybe you can save $600–700 a month by moving in with your family. You may decide that you can sacrifice some of who you are as a woman and mother because you can then finish training (Soft Fact–Long-Term strategy) in six months rather than one year. And you are willing to make this sacrifice in the short term. Or, maybe after reviewing all your housing options, you decide not to move. You determine you would have to sacrifice too much as a woman and mother for a few dollars in savings.

Again, this process may be time consuming and tedious, but it works. When you take time to prioritize your Soft Facts for housing and research all the cost savings for housing options, it is in the light of day. There is nothing hidden anymore. You have logically, methodically, and orderly balanced your internal and external world. You are in control now and can make a wise, tough personal decision. If you sacrifice some of who you are as a woman or mother, it is a proactive choice. You understand what you are giving up and for how long. You will make a wise decision based on all your knowledge.

5. Before you act on your decision, visit with Jesus again. We have a logical and intelligent confidante in Jesus. You can trust his counsel. I found that it helped me to literally talk through my decision. In fact, you may need to visit with Jesus several times. Choosing a housing option under difficult financial circumstances and making the wisest decision for your family can be soul-wrenching. I know. Before you make that decision, let Jesus' wisdom invade your soul. He will guide you to the wisest decision for your Half Family.

We went through a process for leveling the road by reducing our housing expense. I recommend you use a similar process for other expenses such as transportation. Balance your internal world, the Soft Facts and your external world, the Cold Hard Facts. With Jesus' guidance, make a wise decision on reducing your expenses.

Increasing Minimum Income—Job

Another way to level the road is to increase your income. When you have done everything that you can to contain costs, you may have no other choice than to increase your income. Did you get that? You can only look at this option after you have attempted to decrease maximum expenses. Increasing your income is a last resort.

The truth is that if a higher paying job was available, you would not be thinking about increasing your income through other means. The majority of mothers in Half Families have limited options for additional income and the most common option is to work more hours. If we are not careful with this option, working more hours can be trap, not a solution.

Here is what I mean. We have done our homework and have a Long-Term strategy to move us from minimum income to maximum income. But in order to reach our goal, we need time. We may need hours each week to train or study to reach our goal, our dream job. But if we use all our precious time to work additional hours, what happens to our Long-Term strategy? In my opinion, the only thing that we have less of than money is time. We must not forget what we have learned. Working more hours is a short-term fix for a long-term problem.

How do we maximize our income in the short-term? We know all too well the trap of focusing on the job and money first without considering who we are as women and mothers in the Half Family. We surrender our internal world for the sake of our external world. Therefore, we need to begin this process not with the job or the money but rather our time. We need to understand how much extra time we really have to work more hours. So instead of sacrificing yourself for money, try walking through the following steps to make a wise decision.

1. Finding extra time is more than determining a "number." We need to understand the impact extra time has on us as women and mothers. So ignore your need for income at this point. Instead, ask yourself some questions about the most important asset. What can you handle emotionally, physically, and mentally from additional work hours? If you already work forty hours a week, how many more hours can you work? What will the impact be on you? Can you handle it emotionally, physically, and mentally? If you take more hours out of your week, will you surrender some of those margins? Will you have time to play or exercise? Understand, if you work more hours, you will need all your margins.

    Then ask yourself: what will the impact be on my family? Who will watch my children? Will you miss breakfast, lunch, or dinner? Who will help your children with their homework? How much am I willing to sacrifice? This first step is about awareness. No one else but you is going to work additional hours to bring in more income. Take the time to become aware of the impact that time or lack of time has on who you are as a woman and a mother in the Half Family.

2. How much time do you need for your Long-Term strategy? That's right, your new occupation will not just happen. It will take time. Will it take time each day, each week, each month? Do you need training or schooling? How much time do you need each day, each week, each month to reach your long-term goal? *Do not sacrifice the long-term for the short-term.* No matter how tempting; no matter how many people tell you to work two jobs, the time you need for your Long-Term strategy is more important than any short-term fix.

3. After you have completed steps 1 and 2, you need to make a rough esti-mate of the extra time you have each week for extra work. This process will again be muddy because right about now you may be wondering how to stretch nothing into something. You are looking for time where no time exists. You may feel like you will need to sacrifice all of who you are to increase your income. Do you know why that feeling is surfacing? You have already jumped to the solution and that part-time job at the local shopping mall. You are looking for time in the wrong place. Forget about that job. Did I even mention job? No, I stated that you needed to determine how much extra time you have each week. Therefore, based on who you are as a woman and mother emotionally, physically, and mentally, how much extra time do you have each week? Based on your Long-Term strategy, do you have any extra time? Ask yourself these questions. Do you have a couple of extra hours in the morning or do you have extra time at night once the children are asleep? Do you have extra time while your children are in school or playing or at basketball practice or at ballet lessons? How much extra time do you have? Write down a number for the extra time each week on a piece of paper.

4. Now I want you to think "out of the box" and be creative. Remove "job" from your brain and replace it with "work." For example, is there work that you can do from home on your own schedule? Can you stuff envelopes for businesses at night? Can you do computer work or cus-tomer service work for a large company from home? Can you read books on to tape for the blind in your spare time (I have done this)? Can you clean houses or offices at times that fit your schedule (I have done this)? Can you deliver newspapers in the morning or evening? Can you

do wedding rehearsals at the local church (I have done this)? Remember, *don't be trapped by what you know; be open to the possibilities.*

Don't be a slave to a part-time job or work longer hours and sacrifice yourself and your family for the job. Those sacrifices normally cost more than you earn in terms of baby sitters, and travel. Discover your extra time and creatively make the job work for you. In fact, some of these jobs don't require a babysitter or travel and your children can help. We live in a technology driven world. Make this new world work for you. Spend the time to research the possibilities.

One word of warning. Stay away from "opportunities" that require you to invest money to make money. These opportunities are not a wise choice for you at this time. If it looks too good to be true, beware. Look for new ways to earn more income without sacrificing yourself or your money.

5.   Guess what? You know where I got my own creative ways to earn more money? I spent quiet time with Jesus. He knows our talents, abilities, and experience. He will guide you to creative ways to earn money that complements who you are as a woman and a mother. In his presence, you can learn to balance your need for income and your external world with the beauty of who you are and learn to make the wisest decision for your family.

Leveling the road will stretch your wisdom muscles. It will drain you emotionally, physically, and mentally. But you and only you can wisely make tough, personal decisions that result in leveling your path. The road will not be totally clear of the Cold Hard Facts or the Income Gap, but it will be easier to maneuver. Trust me, there is great freedom in choosing to make wise decisions and taking the steps that grow your wisdom. And nowhere will you see that growth of wisdom more than in daily managing the Cold Hard Facts.

Managing Daily. I began this chapter with a personal memory; a memory which is reality for many mothers in the Half Family every day. The daily struggle with minimum income and maximum expenses can take a toll on any woman emotionally, physically, and mentally. It takes a tremendous amount of energy and courage to wisely manage the Cold Hard Facts across the Income Gap. But we have prepared ourselves for this part of the journey with hope. We have the Hope Roadmap and the hope of the management plan. We now have our new freedom and the hope found in wisdom. How do we appropriately use all this hope to make wise decisions on a daily basis? The best way to answer that question is to take a walk through a hypothetical day.

A Day in the Life of Managing the Cold Hard Facts across the Income Gap

The Cold Hard Facts are in our face from the moment we wake in the morning to the moment we go to sleep at night. But there is something else that will be in our face quite often on a daily basis. It is something that can only be experienced as we walk this road with the Cold Hard Facts. It is the Real Fear. In our preparation time for this journey, I briefly mentioned the Real Fear. We could not explore the depths of this fear any sooner than right now because it only exists on the personal journey. It only lives on the road with the Cold Hard Facts. The Real Fear is an internal warning signal that there is danger on the road. If we are not careful to heed this warning, Real Fear can drain us emotionally, physically, and mentally. It is always lurking around some boulder waiting for us. It can paralyze us in the mud. Therefore, as we learn to manage the Cold Hard Facts on this personal journey, we also must learn to manage the Real Fear. We must learn to use this warning signal to move us forward rather than to paralyze us. Large doses of hope will always empower us to walk through the Real Fear. So let's take some proactive steps to walk through a day of managing the Cold Hard Facts across the Income Gap by wisely using the appropriate doses of hope.

Waking Up

Even when you do not feel like it, start your day in prayer (*Spiritual Margin of Faith—spiritual exercise—Hope Roadmap*). There were plenty of mornings I did not want to spend time with Jesus. Sometimes I was mad at him, or I was too tired, or I overslept. Sometimes I had wrestled with Real Fear all night in dreams, or rather nightmares. No matter what, it is absolutely imperative you spend time with Jesus.

Let me give a little insight into my prayer times. Quite frankly, I didn't spend time with Jesus to be more spiritual; I needed his help often to just get out of bed in the morning. After a tough night wrestling with Real Fear, I wanted to pull the covers over my head and escape. So those prayer times normally started with a lot of crying or complaining or fearful words. And that was good. Yes, who better to spill all that emotion onto than Jesus? And the emotion will come out. So would you rather spill it on your children first thing in the morning? Or do you want to spill on your boss or co-workers? However, you do need to give yourself a time limit for this raw spewing with Jesus. So I recommend you allow the emotion to flow to Jesus for no more than ten minutes. Then get down to business with him and I do mean business.

I recommend you talk with Jesus about any issues with your job, bills that are due, missing income, homework for school *(Management plan—Short-Term and Long-Term strategies)*. Then based on this conversation, write down actions for the day: the things you can control. You should list the toughest, most fearful actions first, like a late electric bill. Then you can add items such as a new cost containment idea or test related to your dream job. And make the list manageable. I would recommend no more than one to four daily items for managing the Cold Hard Facts across the Income Gap. Also, I would not recommend that normal bill payments be included in your daily list. If at all possible save this weekly or monthly activity for your days off.

After you complete your list with Jesus, pray for your children *(Spiritual Margin of Faith—Love—Hope Roadmap)*. Jesus knows your children's needs and your heart. So share your heart with him. Pray for your little family. Cover your day in scripture. My favorite scripture verses for protection are Ephesians 6:10–18. With some discipline, you can accomplish this waking process in thirty-forty minutes.

Waking Your Children

In my past reactive state, I would struggle to get up on time and rarely spent any prayer time with Jesus. Therefore, I was normally late getting my son up and would constantly verbally jab him to keep moving. We would eat breakfast in the car. In other words, I spilled minimum income and maximum expenses on him. That is exactly what I did. I had not spent time with Jesus, so all my thoughts and any Real Fear came down on my son.

Take wise control of your time. If you know that it takes your child or children forty-five minutes to get up and get ready in the morning, do not cut that time to fifteen minutes and wonder why a child is not moving fast enough.

Breakfast Time

It is important to eat breakfast with your family *(Physical margin—you are what you eat–Hope Roadmap)*. I know it takes time to schedule breakfast, but we all do too much eating on the run. We intuitively know eating a good breakfast can get our children off to a good start in the morning. In fact, something else besides good nutrition happens during a mealtime, we talk to our children. We can encourage them for their day *(equipping them with Love)*. We can pray with them *(Spiritual Margin of Faith—spiritual exercise—Hope Roadmap)*. This time can also provide positive communication with your family away from any Real Fear *(Mental margin—positive input for positive thoughts—Hope Roadmap)*. Breakfast does not need to take a lot of time. It is the small doses of hope that make a difference to our children. Whether you realize it or not, children feel the effects of managing the Cold Hard Facts across the Income Gap. They may not verbalize it, but they feel it. Small doses of hope can reassure them and calm their spirits.

Also, if you make a sack lunch for your children, make one for yourself. It will only take a few extra minutes and can save you money *(Short-Term strategy—cost containment—Management plan)*.

The Daily Hit List for Managing the Cold Hard Facts

After your children have gone to school and before you go to work, do your first difficult action item from your list like that late payment to a creditor. The reality is there is never going to be a good time to deal with the tough, personal decisions related to managing the Cold Hard Facts. I used to procrastinate in calling creditors. I would wait until 5:00 p.m. and then call. By then, I had been dealing with the Real Fear all day. I was worn down and tired.

We need to wisely choose a time to deal with this action list. From my experience in the morning before work is a wise choice. We have privacy for difficult creditor conversations. Based on those conversations, we have the rest of the day to work on solutions. We are emotionally, physically, and mentally at our best in the morning and not worn down by ignoring the danger signal–Real Fear *(Emotional, physical and mental margins—the Hope Roadmap)*.

Clearly, you need to set aside time for these conversations and I know it is not easy. So let me give you guidance. If you work in retail, you probably do not need to be at work before 9:00 or 9:30. So you may have an hour or so after you drop off your child or children at day care or school. If you work in an office environment, you may not have that much flexibility. If you get an hour for lunch, try to negotiate a half-hour lunch in order to come in a half hour later in the morning. Maybe you can drop off your child or children at daycare or school a half hour earlier. No matter your situation, try to capture at least a half hour in the morning to address the toughest item on your action list.

Here is a sample action list from the prayer time with Jesus:

a.   The electric bill is due and you do not have the money.

   b.   Registration and payment for classes needs to be done.

   c.   Adjustments need to be made to utility payment plans.

Obviously, the first item is the toughest—Real Fear. The electric bill is due and you do not have the money and you need to call the electric company *(Income Gap strategy—Management plan)*. This type of action item was probably the most difficult call that I had to make to a creditor. Clearly, you need to call the electric company for a very important reason. This action item represents the Real Fear of living without electricity. If you choose to call the electric company in the morning, you will be acknowledging the danger signal by taking some action. If you procrastinate, the Real Fear will drain you emotionally, physically, and mentally during the day.

Now this bill is a Cold Hard Fact. So the conversation with the electric company should be non-personal. For example, "My electric bill is due today and I do not have the money. Can I get an extension? What are my options?" Do not assume you know the options. Once when I knew that I would never get another extension on my electric bill, I still asked for the options. The customer service rep told me about a non-profit organization that paid utility bills for people in need. (I am certain that Jesus was whispering in her ear) I had no idea that such an organization existed in my area. No matter the outcome of the conversation, chances are good that you will get at least twenty-four hours to pay the bill.

This conversation applies to all creditors. If your rent or mortgage payment is going to be late, call your landlord or lender. If your car payment is late, call the bank. Quite frankly, I would limit these conversations to no more than one per day. A bad interaction with a creditor may leave you extremely upset and crying. If it does, call your confidante before you go to work *(Emotional margin—Find a confidante—Hope Roadmap)*. If possible, let her know in advance about your situation. Have her pray for you and let her know you may call her after the conversation. Actually, a loving confidante will insist on a call.

At Work

If you have done the tough task on your action list and done everything in your control, focus on your job. When you are at work, make sure your mind and emotions have followed your body to work. In other words, when you are at work, be at work. No matter how minimum the income, it is income. So do not jeopardize your job. I have had way too many days of just being a warm body at work. Be productive for your employer. Now you may never have thought about being productive as a mental margin, but it is *(Mental margin—positive input for positive thoughts—Hope Roadmap)*. Think about it, don't you feel better mentally after having a good day at work? Just doing your job to the best of your ability is a mental margin. If you are focused on being productive at work, you will not be focused on the Real Fear.

Lunch Time

Make sure you take a lunch break. Now I know that many of us tend to use our lunch breaks for running errands. It is understandable, but try to run those errands on your days off. You need to capture your lunchtime for other important items. You can use this time to work on your daily action list.

The remaining items on the sample action list:

1. Registration and payment for classes needs to be done *(Long-Term strategy—new revenue stream—management plan)*. Remember, we discussed that there may be a cost associated with our Long-Term strategy. If you need to deal with any of these costs, put them on your daily action list. These conversations can include getting information on grants for training, payment of tuition through your employer, school loans, etc. Obviously, these conversations can be more encouraging and pleasant than creditor conversations. So try to balance your action list with priorities that don't always make you face the Real Fear.

2. Adjustments need to be made to utility payment plans *(Short-Term strategy—cost containment—management plan)*. Our Short-Term strategy can fluctuate. As you grow in wisdom, you may discern new and creative ways to deal with cost-containment. Maybe you went on a payment plan for your gas bill a year ago. That plan was based on your projected consumption and maybe you used less gas than projected. Therefore, you need to call the gas company and get a reduction in your monthly plan. Don't forget to revisit the Short-Term strategy periodically and determine if there is further cost containment.

Again, these two action items do not generate any Real Fear. The last thing that you need in the middle of the day is more Real Fear. After you have done these two tasks, eat lunch and no desk-top dining (eating lunch at your desk as you work). I was notorious for doing this. Get up from your desk, eat lunch, and take a short walk *(Physical Margin—exercise is not a dirty word—Hope Roadmap)*. Eat lunch and do homework *(Mental Margin—positive input for positive thoughts—Hope Roadmap).* Eat lunch and listen to music *(Emotional mar-gin—learn to play—Hope Roadmap).* We need to apply doses of hope whenever we have the opportunity. These doses in the middle of the day can empower you to get through the rest of the day and not be so tired at night.

Lunchtime is about capturing your time. If you have an hour for lunch, you can easily accomplish the example above. If you have a half hour, do one action item and eat lunch. I would discourage you from going out to lunch. This use of your lunchtime should be the exception not the rule. Think about it, going out to lunch will take your time, money, and maybe some hope. That's right; I have gone to lunch with co-workers only to experience a "complain about work" session. You truly do not need this negative input.

Leaving Work

Be disciplined about leaving work at a normal time each day. Some of us (like me) use work as an escape. Normally, I could easily leave my office at 4:30, but I would stay until 5:15 and then speed to pick up my son. Be more disciplined than me, if you are scheduled to work eight hours, then give your employer a solid eight hours of work and go home.

Dinner

Try to plan dinners in advance on the weekend. I know it takes time and work, but it will make life easier during the week. You will eat healthier and maintain the cost containment on your food budget *(Short-Term strategy—management plan).* Make every effort to sit down as a family for dinner. You will need this time to relax briefly before you continue with your day.

The Rest of the Day

Yes, as mothers in Half Families, our days do not end after dinner. We may still have four to five hours left. And I think nighttime is the most stressful time for us. We may be exhausted from our long day of dealing with creditors, our bosses, and now our children. Yet, our day is not done. We may have to work for an additional source of income. We may have classes to attend for our dream job. We may need to take our children to basketball or ballet. We may need to spend time with a child who is struggling with homework. Nighttime can be a real bal-ancing act.

If you need to go to class and your child needs help with their homework, what do you do? Can you miss a class? Can you get up early in the morning and help your child with their homework? Our children need to be a priority above managing the Cold Hard Facts across the Income Gap, which is easier said than done. Only you can determine when you cross the priority line. If you have a class one night a week, you have certainly not crossed the line. If you are out of the house every night during the week, you may want to rethink your priorities.

We need to make the wise, tough, personal decisions that balance our families' needs and the needs of our external world. Do not try to do everything because you will end up accomplishing nothing.

As we put our children to bed, we should not forget to pray with them and for them *(Spiritual Margin of Faith—Hope Roadmap)*.

After Your Children Go to Bed

If you have any work associated with extra income or homework for your dream job *(Short-Term and Long-Term strategy—management plan)*, I recommend you do it after your children are in bed. If your child or children are young, then bedtime is probably 8:00 or 8:30, which gives you a few hours for you. If your children are older, then establish a reasonable hour that marks the beginning of your private time. This time can be used for any doses of hope. You can do some work for extra income. You can work on your dream job. You can take care of the most important asset in the Half Family by reading a good book, exercising, or talking to your confidante *(The management plan or the Hope Roadmap)*.

To Bed

I have not forgotten about that unpaid electric bill. You may have done everything in your control to find a solution–the money. The reality is you may head to bed with this Real Fear still in your face. I know our human desire is to continue to cry out to Jesus about the unpaid electric bill. He really did hear you the first time earlier in the day. Often I knew Jesus had heard my cry for help, but I felt like I should remind him that we only had a few hours left before the electricity would be off. Clearly, it is not a good idea for me to fall asleep in an anxious state because chances were good I would be wrestling with Real Fear all night. However, continuing to plead with Jesus to meet my need did not relieve the anxiety.

It took me awhile to realize that in order to find the peace to go to sleep, I needed to use my bedtime to grow in my intimate knowledge of God. *(Spiritual Margin of Faith—know God—Hope Roadmap)* When I chose to take my narrow focus off my need and focus on knowing God, I began to see the expanse of his grace, mercy, and love. As I stretched my spiritual muscles, God's peace would flow through me. Choosing to *know God* has filled me with peace that far surpassed my prayers based on *meet my need*. He will do the same for you.

Choosing to know God is a personal journey, and you do not need to be a scholar to know God. Start in Genesis…"In the beginning". God will reveal himself to you based on where you are. He will honor your steps to know him with an ever-expanding vision of who he is.

There is absolutely nothing easy about managing the Cold Hard Facts across the Income Gap. It requires us to carve out time to pray. It requires us to make logical, methodical, and orderly decisions about which facts to manage daily. It requires us to use the appropriate doses of hope to manage the Real Fear. It requires time and discipline. We need to use hope to just keep moving through each day. It is not easy. And the only way to manage the Cold Hard Facts across the Income Gap is to access our freedom, cling to Jesus' love and apply the knowledge from the Hope Roadmap and our management plan to make wise, tough, personal decisions about where to step.

The day that I described above is pretty typical for most mothers in the Half Family. And the majority of the day, we had control to make wise decisions that resulted in a step forward with the Cold Hard Facts. But there was one aspect of the day that we did not have control over: that electric bill. We may have gone to bed with no solution and the Real Fear of living with no electricity waiting for us the next morning. We spent time to know God and gained some peace to sleep. But an Income Gap has opened up in front of us, and we will be standing on the edge of that Chasm in the morning. We are going to need Jesus to make it across this Chasm *(the Income Gap strategy—management plan).*

The Love

When I stood on the edge of the Income Gap, I could not ignore the Real Fear. The Real Fear loomed in front of me as it emerged from the Chasm of no income. Unlike the Chasms in our internal world, this one is visible. We have no income and have no more options other than to believe that there is an invisible bridge across this visible Chasm. We are faced with the Real Fear of no electricity or no car or no home.

Our only hope is the Income Gap strategy, which means we need to answer the question, who do we trust, God or money? The tough personal decision about where we step next is determined by the answer to that question.

Unfortunately, I have chosen money in the past. The truth is I need $150 to pay the electric bill. When I have chosen money, I have taken some wrong steps that were actually Chasm jumps. I have overdrafted my checking account. I have borrowed money from ungodly men. I have accepted gifts that were really loans in disguise. Painfully, I have learned I cannot beat off Real Fear with money; this approach only feeds my fear. You will discover, as I did, that if you try to beat off the fear, the next time that you face the Income Gap, the Real Fear is even more menacing because we have determined that money is the only answer to the Income Gap. In essence, we have tried to take control of the invisible bridge, and we have shut out Jesus.

We need to choose God—Jesus. When we choose Jesus, he will teach us how to walk through the Real Fear onto the invisible bridge across the Income Gap. We need to use wisdom, self-control, and perseverance.

Wisdom

We need to believe and not doubt that a faith bridge extends across our Income Gap and we need to use wisdom to know where to step. But not our definition of wisdom, we need Jesus' definition. "But the wisdom that comes from heaven is first of all pure; then peace-loving, considerate, submissive, full of mercy and good fruit, impartial and sincere. Peacemakers who sow in peace raise a harvest of righteousness" (James 3:17–18). This definition should guide our actions as we face the Income Gap. I will give you an example. If we need $150 to pay that electric bill, we should not just write a check and play hopscotch with our checking account. In other words, we pray that the check will not clear before we get our paycheck in the account. And we can deceive ourselves that we are exercising faith. Is that approach wise? Is it a wise step based on God's definition of wisdom? No. Don't try to twist scripture to match an unwise step. I have tried that approach as well as the hopscotch maneuver and it does not work.

Therefore, before we take any steps forward, we need to determine if our steps are wise. We need to search the Bible and ask Jesus in prayer to reveal wisdom to us. If you read the Bible for wisdom, request wisdom from Jesus, and do not doubt, you will know where to step. If you come out of this time with Jesus and doubt that a certain step forward is wise, do not take a step. I doubted that hopscotch with my checking account was a wise step, but I took it anyway. The painful good news is I gained wisdom to clearly know it was an unwise step.

Self-control

Once you have guidance from Jesus on a wise step, you will need to exercise self-control. Self-control is all about keeping our eyes on Jesus. "Therefore, prepare your minds for action; be self-controlled; set your hope fully on the grace to be given you when Jesus Christ is revealed. As obedient children, do not conform to the evil desires you had when you lived in ignorance" (1Peter 1:13–14). If you have not guessed by now, I have ruined your desire for escape jumps. As you have traveled down this road as a Half Family, you have discovered the invisible bridge of Faith and you are no longer ignorant. Therefore, when we take wise steps onto the invisible bridge across the Income Gap, we cannot revert to our old ways.

We need self-control to keep our eyes on Jesus and not look into the Real Fear of the Income Gap Chasm. It is not easy. In fact, it is impossible without Jesus. Therefore, it will take all your self-care instructions from the Spiritual Margin of Faith to exercise self-control. I am much more self-controlled today than I was twenty years ago. However, I still have to practice self-control every time I cross the Chasm because I cannot cross the invisible bridge without it.

Look back at the day in the life of minimum income and maximum expense. In my own reality of a late electric bill, I knew the wise step forward was to call the electric company. I had no idea about the outcome of that conversation, but it was the first step on the invisible bridge across my Income Gap. My electricity was due to be shut off that day at 1:00 p.m. and I could not see any options. Jesus knew the option. I had to use self-control to keep my eyes on him and trust his love. Despite the temptation to beat off the Real Fear, I needed to take another step in self-control.

Perseverance

Once we take a wise step in self-control onto the invisible bridge across the Income Gap, we need to persevere. Perseverance means we keep moving on the invisible bridge of Faith. "Blessed is the man who perseveres under trial, because when he has stood the test, he will receive the crown of life that God has promised to those who love him" (James 1:12). No matter how wide the Income Gap, we must persevere. And perseverance is not about never wavering on the invisible bridge. It is not about always standing firm and walking tall. It is movement forward in any form. We may stumble, fall, or crawl at times. That is true perseverance. It is forward movement in spite of the Real Fear. Perseverance is moving towards the love of Jesus.

I mentioned that in my own phone conversation with the electric company, the customer service rep directed me to a charitable organization that would pay my bill. I did not know that when I took steps onto the invisible bridge. It took enormous perseverance to ask for options. At that point, I was right in the middle of the bridge. I could not go back, and I was starting to glance down into the

Chasm of Real Fear. But Jesus knew that someone I did not know would pay my electric bill.

Accessing the Income Gap strategy to cross the Chasm requires us to use wisdom, self-control, and perseverance. By using this strategy, I can see many parts of the invisible bridge. Yes, Jesus has given me spiritual vision to see the invisible. In other words, each time I have traveled the invisible bridge with Jesus, I have grown in wisdom, self-control, and perseverance. I have learned a great deal about the right and wrong way to walk across the Income Gap. Certainly, you will need to learn from your own personal journey. But there are some key learnings I would like to share with you.

Meeting Our Needs

Having walked the invisible bridge across many Income Gaps, I now see a clear pattern in how my needs were met by Jesus. My needs were met either by people motivated by the love of Jesus, or by waiting on Jesus.

People Motivated by the Love of Jesus. If you are like me, another person actually giving me money to cross the Income Gap sounds like a preferable way to cross the invisible bridge across this Chasm. And it is Jesus' choice as well. He knows our material needs, our need for income. He knows we will need an electric bill paid, the mortgage or rent paid, or money to go to the grocery store or put gas in the car. Therefore, when we are on the invisible bridge crossing the Income Gap, Jesus wants to work through his followers to meet our needs. Jesus will use other people to extend his love to us. Great news!

Yes, unfortunately, not everyone will be open to demonstrating the love of Jesus. The quickest way to find out who knows and who does not know the love of Jesus is to ask for money. You are going to encounter many people who will not help you, and you need to pray for them. We do not need to judge them; we need to pray for them. Because their inability to demonstrate the love of Jesus to meet your need; hurts them far more than it will ever hurt you. For when Jesus returns, he will judge everyone not on the basis of their words but their actions. In particular, we will be judged based on our willingness to help the needy and oppressed. Read Matthew 25:31–46. And remember, we should reflect Jesus' love to others in need because we will also be judged by this passage. Jesus' love should flow through us to others.

So it is Jesus' responsibility to judge everyone, but it is our responsibility to discern the love of Jesus. As you will find people that will not help you, you will find people who will offer money to you. Just because someone offers you money, it does not mean that this offer was motivated by the love of Jesus. It does not mean that all offers of money will "meet your need." Knowing what I know now, I would rather have someone refuse to help me than to deceive me. For an offer not motivated by Jesus' love is deception. Therefore, we must wisely discern who is motivated by Jesus' love and who is not. And it is imperative we learn this discernment because discerning a person's motivation is the difference between crossing to the Income Gap and falling into the Chasm. Learning this discernment has been a long and painful process for me. I have accepted money, which not only did not meet my needs but actually made the Income Gap wider. As I have grown in wisdom, self-control, and perseverance, Jesus has educated me to discern which people are his followers in love.

Therefore, if you are getting ready to accept money for another person, let me give you guidance. It begins with our definition of Jesus' love. Love is deliberate, selfless, and sacrificial acts to meet the needs of others. So before you accept a monetary gift to meet your Income Gap need, ask yourself these questions:

1.   *Is it deliberate?* If you look in the dictionary, you will find definitions of the word deliberate: "Said or done intentionally, voluntary, and purposefully." Someone who is compelled by Jesus' love to meet another person's needs chooses to walk onto the invisible bridge with them. This person truly understands the consequences and chooses to step out in love. This person takes their own deliberate step of faith to reach out to a needy person. I want you to think back to the story of the Samaritan woman and Jesus. We encountered this wonderful story at the forgiveness stop on our journey to wholeness. "Now he had to go through Samaria" (John 4:4). Jesus did not have to go through Samaria to get to Galilee because it was the only route. No, he had made an intentional, voluntary, and purposeful decision to meet the needs of a Samaritan woman. It was a deliberate act to walk onto her invisible bridge across her Chasm.

A clear indication of a deliberate act of love is that it is void of judgment. When Jesus chose to extend his love to meet needs, he did not judge the needy person. He saw a need and took a deliberate step to meet it. So be careful to avoid people who see you drowning and want to teach you to swim instead of throw you a life preserver. In other words, a person who requires an interrogation of your financial situation to determine if you deserve to have your need met is not taking a deliberate step of love to meet your need. Judgmental offers of help will only fuel your Real Fear of your external world, stir guilt in your internal world, and can push you into the Chasm. Certainly, our own ignorance or mistakes may have contributed to the Income Gap. But using this information to avoid helping a person pay an electric bill is a judgmental act void of Jesus' love. A deliberate act of love seeks to meet a need, not judge a person.

2. *Is it selfless?* Is the offer of money motivated by love to meet your need, or is this person motivated to meet their need? Are they using your situation to get something for themselves? Jesus is very clear about giving to the needy. Matthew 6:2–4 "So when you give to the needy, do not announce it with trumpets, as the hypocrites do in the synagogues and on the streets, to be honored by men. I tell you the truth, they have received their reward in full. But when you give to the needy do not let your left hand know what your right hand is doing, so that your giving may be in secret. Then your Father, who sees what is done in secret, will reward you." A person who offers money with a selfish motivation will never be able to do it in secret.

If you are still not sure if an offer of money is a selfless act motivated by the love of Jesus to meet your need, ask yourself these questions. Is this person offering money based on *what you really need* or *what they want to give*? Are there conditions on the offer? In other words, if you do something for this person, they will give you money to meet your need. I tend to visualize a selfish act as a person who is standing on the edge of the Chasm and sees you on the invisible bridge. This person wants to help you in order to have "good feeling" or to "look good" to others, but only if they do not have to step onto the bridge with you.

For example, watch out for men who want to give money to you in exchange for sexual favors. I think this situation is one of the most common escapes for us. If we are facing the Income Gap Chasm with a painful wound from our partner, a man with money certainly looks like a "gift from God." Even if we are healed internally, this same man can be a temptation. Now not all men will take advantage of your situation. But you need to be able to discern. So if you are unsure of a man's motives, do not take the money. If you have trouble seeing this trap, do not accept money from any man.

3.   *Is it sacrificial?* Jesus has called people to give to those in need. Read the Bible. Over and over Jesus calls those people with material possessions to share with those people in need. In his giving, Jesus always erred on the side of love. The ultimate act of sacrificial love to meet another person's need is demonstrated by Jesus' cruel death, knowing full well that the majority of people would never accept the gift of salvation. A sacrificial act of love to meet another person's need is always an unconditional gift.

If a person professes to be helping you in the love of Jesus but lends you money, it is not from Jesus. This sounds harsh, but it is the truth. An act of love requires sacrifice. Lending money to a desperately needy person is not a sacrificial act. The lender expects to get the money back. The love of Jesus does not motivate this person; money motivates them. When Jesus talks about meeting the material needs of another person, he never uses the word lend. He always says give. Unfortunately, there are many religious organizations in this country that will require you to justify your need and then require you to pay back the money. Do not accept this money. No matter the justification for this loan, it is not motivated by the love of Jesus. When Jesus walked on this earth, he never lent to the needy. His purpose was to ease people's burdens not add another burden. A needy person does not need an additional burden, another debt.

In general, do not borrow money. When we are desperate for money, we may be tempted to borrow money from institutions or people. When I was in great need, I borrowed money to meet my expenses. However, I really did not get more income. I just got another expense, the borrowed money. And I was not going to be able to pay it back for a long time. If I was in a position that I needed to borrow money just to meet my monthly expenses, I was not in a position to pay that money back any time soon. That borrowed money became another boulder in my path that I had to try to maneuver.

Also watch out for individuals who want to give you money with other conditions. A monetary gift with conditions is not a gift. It is a loan disguised as a gift. If you do something for this person, he or she will give you some money. For example, if you change your job or housing based on this person's personal judgment, he or she will give you money. If you attend this person's church, he or she will give you some money.

Now if you want to accept the conditions for the money, go ahead and take it. Just see it for what it is. It is not a sacrificial act of love to meet your need.

Waiting on Jesus. There will be times when no one steps forward in Jesus' love to help you financially. In those moments, all we can do is wait on Jesus. I know that those times will really test your faith. If it is 12:55 and your electricity is due to be shut off at 1:00 p.m., it is hard to believe that Jesus will meet your need. If your car is going to be repossessed today and you do not have the back payments, it is hard to believe that Jesus will meet your need. I have been in all those situations. And I have been told by people that we have a "last" minute God, which means at the last minute Jesus will shower us with money. However, when we view God in this way, we miss what it means to wait on Jesus. Waiting on Jesus has nothing to do with meeting our need for money but rather meeting our need for trust.

Remember, the Income Gap strategy is all about who do you trust: God or money? And when we choose God, then waiting on Jesus is all about walking the talk. Our actions will reveal the decision in our heart to either trust Jesus or trust money.

Now when I first came face to face with waiting on Jesus, I was standing in the middle of the invisible bridge. When my material world around me was collapsing and nothing was in my control, I looked around me for some money. There was none. Alone on the invisible bridge convinced I was going to fall into the Income Gap Chasm, I struggled to cling to my faith in the love of Jesus. Think about that situation for a moment.

For me, it was a relatively easy step of faith to give my son to Jesus, or give Jesus the outcome of getting a job. But to take a step of faith and release control of my very visible basic needs in my material world to an invisible Jesus and an invisible bridge was absolutely terrifying. Only women who have faced this situation know the absolute terror that grips you at that moment. It is a difficult, solitary choice to wait on Jesus.

Once you make that choice, you will begin a spiritual transformation. What I know now is that money was not the only need I had as I faced the Income Gap. Certainly, Jesus knows our need for money; but he also knows our unrequested need. We need to have our faith transformed into trust. It is only trust in the love of Jesus that empowers us to walk the invisible bridge across the Income Gap. How do we transform ourselves from faith walkers into trust walkers? We practice waiting on Jesus.

Waiting on Jesus will be a struggle at first. Frankly, in the silence of waiting on Jesus, I used to see it as a punishment. I would replay in my mind any missteps that had gotten me to this dangerous place. It was not punishment; it was an opportunity to take a faith step. It was a privilege to be transformed from a faith walker into a trust walker. It was a privilege that is very visible to me now. Do you think that I could write this book if I had not walked this path?

Waiting on Jesus by trusting in his love can get us across any Income Gap. When you trust in his love, you open heavenly solutions. I have seen Jesus get me across many Income Gaps without money. I have seen him work through complete strangers to forgive debt, extend payment dates, accept partial payments for bills, open their homes to me, and give me groceries. Never underestimate the power of the love of Jesus. It is always, always with us.

Therefore, when you are faced with Income Gap and have done everything in your control, you need to wait on Jesus. It is a silent, solitary place that will stretch your faith muscles. It is a spiritual transformation into trust in the love of Jesus. In the silence of waiting on Jesus, you may begin to question his love for you. So hold fast to the Holy Bible. Trust the truth of Scripture; read it, absorb it, and memorize it. Can anyone or anything separate us from the power of the love of Jesus?

> "No, in all these things we are more than conquerors through him who loved us. For I am convinced that neither death nor life, neither angels no demons, neither the present nor the future, nor any powers, neither height nor depth, nor anything else in all creation will be able to separate us from the love of God that is in Christ Jesus our Lord" (Romans 8:38–39).

CHEAT SHEET

Managing the Cold Hard Facts across the Income Gap

The Truth

1. There is no answer to why.

2. The long journey is not a bump in the road.

3. The blessing of acceptance is freedom.

The Hope

1. The hope of wisdom to make the tough, personal decisions about managing the Cold Hard Facts across the Income Gap

2. Leveling the road (Short-Term and Long-Term strategies from the management plan)

3. Managing daily with doses of hope (The management plan and the Hope Roadmap)

The Love

1. Use wisdom, self-control, and perseverance to cross the Income Gap (the Income Gap strategy: who do you trust?).

2. Meet your need through people motivated by the love of Jesus.

3. Meet your need by waiting on Jesus.

15

Facing and Conquering Trials

"What I feared has come upon me; what I dreaded has happened to me. I have no peace, no quietness, I have no rest, but only turmoil." (Job 3:25–26)

Trials…will happen to us. It is inevitable. In the Bible, the story of Job describes how he lost everything: his children, his business, his wealth, his health. He was thrust into a dark valley of emotional, physical, and mental pain. And even spiritual pain. Yes, as he faced this trial, he seemed to be alone and abandoned by God. Job struggled to survive amidst horrendous circumstances. In the end, he conquered the trial.

We will all face trials of one kind or another; hopefully not as devastating as Job's. We all can be thrust into a period of turmoil—a trial. It is part of the human journey through life. As much as we would like to sidestep trials, we will experience a period of turmoil.

Trials can come in many different forms: the loss of a loved one, disease or illness, or a natural disaster. There is a particular trial that we have in common. In fact, it is all too familiar to the mother in the Half Family. It is a financial trial. And it is this type of trial that we need to learn to face and conquer at this stop on our Half Family journey.

Now you may think that managing the Cold Hard Facts across the Income Gap is a trial: a trial by fire. Amen to that statement. Unfortunately, a financial trial is much worse.

Here is what I mean by that statement. When we faced the Cold Hard Facts, those financial boulders were visible and scattered on the road in front of us. We could see minimum income and maximum expenses, and the Income Gap loomed in front of us. It was predictable. Even that unpaid electric bill from our last stop of managing these Cold Hard Facts was visible.

A financial trial is unpredictable. We often do not see it until it is in our face. It is invisible until we are suddenly and sometimes violently thrust into the turmoil. It is unpredictable. It is invisible. It is extremely dangerous. A financial trial is unlike anything we faced on our Half Family journey thus far and preparing for this type of turmoil is easier said than done. Certainly, we can prepare ourselves with the truth about a financial trial, the hope to face it, and the love to conquer it. This preparation will guide us through the trial. But how do we prepare ourselves for the unpredictable, invisible, and sudden appearance of danger on our path? At other stops on our journey, we could clearly see the danger in the road. Therefore, the truth, hope, and love prepared us well for each step. Unfortunately, we can't see a trial. Is it possible to see the danger before it is upon us?

Actually, it is. We are going to take a slightly different approach at this stop. Before we examine the truth about a financial trial, we need to learn about the dangerous path that leads us into this type of trial. I learned just how critical this information is from my own experience. In the middle of my own turmoil, I found myself asking these questions: "How did I get here?" or "How did this happen to me?" Unfortunately, those answers would not have helped me. I was already in the dark valley of a painful financial trial. Clearly, that information would have been helpful before I was thrust into financial turmoil. How did I get there? How did I end up in a financial trial?

I wanted to know the answer to those questions. So when I conquered my own trial, I retraced my steps to find the path that leads to a financial trial. And I uncovered that path. It is a path, which we have in common. The messy details of a financial trial will vary from mother to mother in the Half Family, but the unpredictable, invisible path that leads us into this dark turmoil is common to us all. Therefore, before we examine the truth about a financial trial, let's shed some light on this dangerous path. It will reveal that we are thrust out onto this path the minute we step on the first landmine. Yes, the path that leads to a financial trial begins by stepping on a landmine.

Stepping on Landmines

The road of Cold Hard Facts is a volatile place. It is full of boulders, which we have learned to maneuver. We have learned to make tough, personal decisions about managing minimum income and maximum expenses. We have made choices about where to step on our rocky road. We have learned to use the Income Gap strategy to get across this Chasm. But what do we do about the unpredictable, unforeseen expense or loss of income? What happens if we step on this invisible, dangerous spot? What if we step on a financial landmine?

A financial landmine is different from the boulders of the Cold Hard Facts. We have spent many stops looking at minimum income and maximum expenses.

We can clearly see these boulders now, but a landmine is buried in the ground out of our sight and sensitive to any movement. We don't know that it is there in front of us. It is unexpected-unpredictable. A financial landmine can be unemployment, an unexpected medical bill due to sickness or injury, an automobile accident, or a major home repair due to a natural disaster. Anyone can step on this type of landmine, not just the mother in the Half Family.

Certainly, stepping on one landmine can create a financial crisis that needs to be managed. For example, both a mother in a two-parent family and a mother in a Half Family can step on the landmine of unemployment. For a two-parent family, this situation can create a crisis that needs to be managed, but it is not necessarily a trial. There is still a spouse who can earn an income. There is still an extra margin. The mother in the Half Family does not have that margin. We are the only source of income. There is no spouse margin.

We have little or no margin for error as we manage the Cold Hard Facts. We have nothing extra. Therefore, when we step on the landmine of unemployment, we have stepped on the path that leads to a financial trial. The path of landmines is very dangerous.

For us, stepping on the landmine of unemployment can quickly escalate from a crisis to a trial. We are on a path where one landmine can set off a chain reaction of exploding landmines. Unemployment (boom) can trigger no more income (boom), which triggers past due bills (boom), which can trigger shut off utilities (boom), or car repossession (boom), or no food (boom), or eviction/foreclosure (boom). There are bombs going off everywhere in our external world which can also trigger landmine explosions in our internal world.

For example, you may be newly separated from your partner and have a throbbing, open wound. You are feeling vulnerable and are prone to Nightmare Fears. In that condition, when you step on the unemployment landmine, you step on an emotional landmine of fear and vulnerability (boom). You have the Real Fear situation with all the Nightmare Fear swirling around inside of you. You could easily find this situation unmanageable. The Real Fear from your external world can collide with the Nightmare Fear from your internal world (boom).

Even veterans of the Half Family journey are vulnerable to this type of collision. There is no doubt that traveling with the Cold Hard Facts can wear us down emotionally, physically, and mentally. In that condition, when you step on one or more "unexpected" landmines, you may begin to take them personally. You begin to imagine the worst and see the situation as your fault or just see the situation as impossible. You too can step on the landmine of Nightmare Fear in your internal world (boom). You too can find that the situation is unmanageable.

The Real Fear from your external world can collide and explode with the Nightmare Fear from your internal world.

It is the collision of our external and internal worlds that results in a massive explosion that blows you into a financial trial (BOOM). In this situation, your physical, emotional, and mental margins will quickly disappear. The impact of stepping on landmines and the resulting explosions will leave you in a desperate survival mode. You are not standing on the edge of the Chasm; you have been blown over the edge. On your descent into this abyss, you reach out for the edge and cling to it by your fingernails. You are in grave financial turmoil. As you look down, you see only the blackness of a trial. And as you look up, there does not seem to be anyone around to help you up to safe ground. You loose your grip and fall into a financial trial.

How did you get there? You stepped on a financial landmine that set off a chain reaction of landmine bombs in your external and internal worlds that resulted in a massive explosion that blew you over the edge of the Chasm and into a trial. So how do you get out?

The Truth

The massive explosion that has blown you over the edge of the Chasm is just the start of a trial. The very nature of a trial means you will not be able to cling to the edge. You will fall into the darkness. And in the darkness, you will find the truth of a financial trial. It is a hard truth that I painfully learned in my own darkness. I can shed light on this truth, but it won't be real to you yet. For the reality is you will not fully understand and accept the truth until you are in your own time of trial. It is then that this hard truth will become real.

Testing your Faith

A trial is all about testing your faith. And testing your faith has nothing to do with getting to the end of a trial but has everything to do with your journey through it. In other words, do you trust God no matter what you loose, how you feel, what you experience, or what you think that you know about God? In a financial trial, you will not be able to escape the question: do you trust God?

Even if you do not have a relationship with Jesus, you will face this question in the depths of your soul. Just read any story about a personal trial or watch personal tragedies play out on the national news, you will hear the questions from desperate people. "Where is God?" "God help us?" When human beings are faced with a trial, they ask spiritual questions from the depths of their souls.

When our emotional, physical, and mental margins are gone, we will face the same question. Do we trust God? A trial is always about testing our faith. Still need convincing?

At the beginning of the book of Job, we can find this truth revealed in a conversation between Satan and God. It is a rare conversation that I have been unable to find anywhere else in the Bible. Therefore, these passages are often overlooked as literary prose or something mystical. I believe that these passages are a real conversation and an amazing gift from God: a rare insight into the truth that a trial is about testing our faith.

> Satan came into God's presence. God asked Satan, "Have you considered my servant Job? There is no one on earth like him; he is blameless and upright, a man who fears God and shuns evil".
> "Does Job fear God for nothing?" Satan replied, "Have you not put a hedge around him and his household and everything he has? You have blessed the work of his hands, so that his flocks and herds are spread throughout the land. But stretch out your hand and strike everything he has, and he will surely curse you to your face."
> The Lord said to Satan, "Very well, then, everything he has is in your hands, but on the man himself do not lay a finger." (Job 1:8–12)

So Satan goes out and destroys Job's business and kills his servants and children. Job gets the devastating news and his reply is, "The Lord gave and the Lord has taken away; may the name of the Lord be praised" (Job 1:20). Now here is an important point. We have the advantage, the gift, of knowing the conversation between Satan and God. Job had no idea. He does not know that this devastation is at the hands of Satan. He thinks that God has done it, and he makes the choice to trust God despite what he sees and Satan fails.

> Satan returns to God and God says, "Have you considered my servant Job? There is no one on earth like him; he is blameless and upright, a man who fears God and shuns evil. And he still maintains his integrity, though you incited me against him to ruin him without any reason." (Job 2:3)
> But Satan has an answer. "Skin for skin!" Satan replied. "A man will give all he has for his own life. But stretch out your hand and strike his flesh and bones, and he will surely curse you to your face." The Lord said to Satan, "Very well, then, he is in your hands; but you must spare his life." (Job 2:4–6) So Satan goes out and inflicts Job "with painful sores from the soles of his feet to the top of his head. (Job 2:7)

This last attack by Satan thrusts Job into a trial. He becomes the innocent victim of landmine explosions that devastate his external and internal worlds. He does not know that God allowed this turmoil to test his faith. And he begins the struggle to face and conquer his trial.

As humans we belong to a material world. Whether we realize it or not, we rely on that material world to provide us with food, clothing, and housing. Satan knows this reality. That is why he basically said to God, if you want to know where Job's loyalty really lies, take his material world away. It is the ultimate test of faith to have our material world ripped from us. Will we curse God or trust him?

For the mother in the Half Family, a financial trial will rip our material world from our grasp. We will face a graduate level test of our faith. Do we trust God? It is either a yes or no answer. When I was faced with this choice, I was devastated. My human existence had been destroyed by an unpredictable and invisible set of circumstances. I stepped on landmines that resulted in a massive explosion. I lost my grip and was falling into the abyss of darkness…and God allowed this to happen. How could I trust a God who allowed this trial? But the real question should have been how could I not trust God?

Look back again at the conversation between Satan and God. God says, "Very well, then, he is in your hands; but you must spare his life." God allowed Satan to take everything from Job but his life.

For me, in the middle of my own trial, the destruction of my physical world lay in piles of shrapnel at my feet. Not unlike Job, the only thing standing, barely, was me. And that is the point; Job's trial was about testing his faith. My financial trial was about me, not my physical world. It was about my faith. The only way to truly answer the question do I trust God or not is to remove anything that stands between God and I. For me, this hard truth was difficult to accept as I stood in the wreckage of a financial trial. Sporadically, I was only able to cling to my faith through the words of the Bible. And my favorite passage became:

> Consider it pure joy, my brothers whenever you face trials of many kinds, because you know that the testing of your faith develops perseverance. Perseverance must finish its work so that you may be mature and complete and not lacking anything." (James 1:2–4)

I not only held tight to the verses in James, I memorized the entire book of James. It was the only way for me to hold onto my faith in Jesus. Holding onto

Jesus was extremely difficult during the faith test of my financial trial, but it was almost impossible as I faced the next truth.

The Silence of God

Persevering through the testing of your faith is difficult. In the middle of a trial with the shrapnel of your world scattered around you, you need to hear a word of encouragement from God. You need to hear that you will survive. You will want some tangible sign that there is a financial rescue. All you may hear is the silence of God. In fact, I think the most painful suffering in a trial is the spiritual journey through the silence of God. In the silence, you will feel abandoned. The pain of this silence will rip through to the core of your soul.

That pain can be felt in the words of Job. After seven days of suffering and feeling the impact of his loss, "Job opened his mouth and cursed the day of his birth." (Job 3:1). Job did not just want to die. He wished that he had never been born. He was feeling not only the trial but the silence of God. Job sat for seven days with no communication from God. That silence must have been devastating for Job, who had an intimate relationship with God. Job could handle the loss of everything, but the loss of God's voice was too much.

Even Jesus knew the pain of the silence of God during his crucifixion, his trial. "From the sixth hour until the ninth hour of darkness came over the land. About the ninth hour, Jesus cried out in a loud voice, "Eloi, Eloi, lama sabach-thani?—which means my God, my God, why have you forsaken me." (Matthew 27:45–46)

God will be silent in a trial. Anyone who has been through a trial will experience this silence. It may be a day or a week or months or years, but God will be silent. That does not mean God has abandoned us. God is always there. Jesus will never leave us. He will hear our prayers, our cries for help. Except there will be silence.

In reality, I am convinced that the most difficult test of our faith is the silence of God. We must persevere through the silence and believe the promise in the Bible that he will never leave us. We must know that nothing can take our faith in God. Not even the silence of God can take our faith. His silence does not mean that he has abandoned us. He is always present. Given the hard truth about the testing of your faith and the silence of God, the final truth about a trial should come as no surprise.

The Solitary Struggle of a Trial

You will struggle during a financial trial: that is the absolute truth. Do not be deceived by people who tell you differently. Anyone who dismisses your struggle in a trial is dismissing the truth. You will struggle during a financial trial. And it will be a solitary struggle. So do not be surprised by the range of emotions and even your actions during it. Your emotions can range from sadness to hysterical crying and from anger to rage. You may scream and rant and rave at creditors, friends, and even Jesus. You may throw things and hit walls. There is nothing pretty about the journey through a trial. It will be a struggle emotionally, physically, and mentally, but the human struggle is merely a symptom. For in reality this is a spiritual struggle.

It is the spiritual nature of the struggle that makes it so solitary. It occurs deep in our souls. It is a struggle that comes from the truth about the testing of our faith and the silence of God. These two truths will cause you to struggle spiritually.

You may begin to see the trial as a punishment. If only you had handled those landmine explosions differently, maybe you would not be here. If only you had not let fear get the best of you and tried to escape, maybe you would have avoided this. You become convinced that your mistakes, your sins have caused this trial. So you ask for forgiveness. Surely Jesus will forgive you and show you the error of your ways, and you will be released from this dark valley. There is only silence. So you begin to bargain with Jesus. If he will release you from this trial, you will never do it again: whatever the sin was that resulted in a trial. There is only silence.

Or maybe you begin to realize that this financial trial was not the result of your actions. Certainly, you made some mistakes, but the truth is you stepped on landmines. How could you have foreseen unemployment or illness? So why are you being punished? You know people who have cheated or lied financially and they do not experience financial turmoil. They have sinned but have not been punished. So why are you? You become angry with God. You are a follower of Jesus; why are you in the middle of a trial?

> Though I cry, 'I've been wronged! I get no response; though I call for help, there is no justice. He (God) has blocked my way so I cannot pass; he has shrouded my paths in darkness. He has stripped me of my honor and removed the crown from my head. He tears me down on every side till I am gone; he uproots my hope like a tree. (Job 19:7–10)

We will struggle in a trial because we equate the testing of our faith as something we don't deserve, we want to find the way out of the pain, and we feel trapped or abandoned by God.

A trial is a solitary spiritual journey. Others can be affected by it. Your children in particular will feel the effects. However, you and you alone experience the weight of it. Walking through a trial seemingly alone is a gut-wrenching journey. The depth of this hard truth will be difficult to accept. If God is silent, you will long for comfort and companionship of your friends at least. Sadly, even friends will fail you. Friendship during a trial requires long-suffering support, and unfortunately some friends, for whatever reason, will desert you emotionally and/or physically during a trial.

"Now you too have proved to be of no help; you see something dreadful and are afraid (Job 6:21)." Even Job's friends deserted him. Oh they were present, but their support did not help. Their words only rubbed salt in Job's wounds.

The truth is that if you, who are going through the trial, are struggling to deal with the situation, how can you expect an outsider, no matter how close that friend, to deal with it? In the midst of a trial, you will need to accept you are on a solitary, spiritual journey. You will be needy. As much as you will want friendship in the painful turmoil, you will not have the energy to work at a relationship. You will not have the strength to listen to people who only rub salt in your wounds with judgmental words or actions. Therefore, you will need to let go of friends who cannot be long-suffering with you. The solitary nature of a trial is a hard truth to accept, but it is a fact. It is a truth that you can know now and that you will only accept in the middle of a financial trial.

The hard truths about a trial are: testing of your faith, the silence of God and the solitary struggle of a trial. The journey through a trial is a messy, painful experience that cannot be avoided. A trial is part of the human journey. But there is hope to face a financial trial.

The Hope

Unlike Job, we know something that he only hoped in his trial. He hoped that God did not abandon him. We only need to look again at the beginning of the story of Job to know that hope.

God Is in Control

We have the hope that God is in control. The most formidable, powerful evil in this world is Satan. You can't see him, but his fingerprint is seen in everyday life:

in poverty, oppression, injustice, and murder. Through his devastation, it may appear he is in control. But look closely at the story of Job. Satan could only inflict a trial on Job because God allowed it. In essence, Satan had to ask permission. God allowed him to take everything but Job's life. Satan was not allowed to kill Job. Oh, Satan could terrorize Job and try to push him to take his own life. Ultimately, Job belonged to God and Satan could not have him.

For a moment, forget about the fact that God allowed this trial and focus on the fact God is in control. When you are in the middle of a trial with everything around you being blown up, you will need to hold on to the hope found in the knowledge that God is in control. God may be testing your faith, but he is in control. He wants to test our faith not destroy our spirits. He knows our limits. God may be silent, but he is in control. He knew about the landmine and allowed you to step on it. He knows about the explosions that have blown you over the Chasm, but if you are a child of God, he is in control of your life. Actually, even if you are not a child of God, he is still in control. And if we have the hope that God is in control, we also have the hope that we are not alone.

You Are Not Alone

As Job struggled through his turmoil emotionally, physically, and mentally, God was there. We know that because God finally broke his silence and spoke to Job. The very nature of a trial and the silence of God will make us feel like we are alone, but God will never leave us. Look again at the beginning of the story of Job. When Satan returned to God's presence, did God have to ask what Satan had done to Job? No, he knew the facts. When God told Satan he could not take Job's life, was Satan able to kill Job? No, God's protection was on Job and he never left him. God's silence does not mean that he has abandoned us. No, we have the hope that we are never alone.

In fact, I want to share the fullness of this hope with you. It is a fullness that you will not experience until you walk through a trial. It is a hope that will fill you with a peace that transcends any human experience. Not only are we never alone during a trial, we are never closer to Jesus than when we are in one. For you see, Jesus walks among Christians daily, but Jesus lives with the oppressed, broken, wounded, and rejected in this world. Jesus was born on the bottom of society in a feeding trough for animals located in a cold cave. He spent his ministry walking among the bottom of society and died between two thieves. When he was resurrected, he appeared and proclaimed that good news to those same people. Jesus lives on the bottom of societies. When we have been blown over the edge, Jesus is there waiting to embrace us. We may fall into the darkness, but

Jesus is waiting at the bottom to catch us. No one knows the pain of trial better than Jesus. He may be silent but he is there with us. He is our hope.

Hold onto the hope that God is in control and you are not alone. You will need this hope to face a financial trial but only love will conquer a trial. At no other point on this Half Family journey is it more important to prepare ourselves with love.

The Love

Love will conquer every trial. To understand that statement, we need to clearly see what does not constitute conquering a trial. Conquering a financial trial has nothing to do with money—the end of a trial. So if you were waiting for some financial answers, I do not have them. Conquering a financial trial has everything to do with walking through the trial by choosing love and choosing not to escape. You see I think you can get around financial trials by escaping. We can choose to basically sell our souls for money by borrowing it, marrying a man with it, or stealing it. We could emerge from this trial, but you can never conquer a trial in this way: by escape. A trial is not about financial solutions, it is about testing our faith. If facing a trial is about the hope found in trusting Jesus, then conquering a trial is about the embrace of Jesus' love to conquer a trial.

Job's faith was certainly tested in his trial. And though he struggled, he did not choose escape. He kept coming back to God. Though he did not know it, he was never out of the embrace of God's love. In the end, he conquered his trial. The story of Job is the story of anyone who has been through a trial. And just like Job, in the middle of the turmoil, it is difficult to know the embrace of Jesus' love will conquer any trial.

In order to see the love that conquers trials, I think that we need to bring the experience of a financial trial a little closer to home. So I want to share my own financial trial.

It was a journey through turmoil that is forever edged in my heart, mind, and soul. It was a time of devastation and blackness and a journey of excruciating pain that led me to the brink of an unthinkable Chasm jump. More importantly, it was a journey into the depths of love that ultimately led me to conquer the trial.

And it all began when I stepped on an unexpected medical problem with my son. At first, this landmine seemed relatively harmless and manageable. Unfortunately, this one landmine started a chain reaction of landmine explosions in my external world i.e. medical bills, low cash for other bills, and missed work. As the medical problem continued, I started to get worn down emotionally, physically, and mentally, and I experienced internal landmine explosions. Emerging from the smoke of each external explosion was a Nightmare Fear that we were not going to survive this situation. This fear grew as I continued to step on landmines in my external world. Finally, my external and internal worlds collided and created a massive explosion.

I had reached a point of complete helplessness clinging to the edge of the Chasm. Then the worst thing that I could have imagined happened. Unable to manage anything with a clear head, I lost my grip on the basic needs for my external world. I lost my car; then I lost my home and I had no job. As I clung to the edge of a dark Chasm, I managed to find a family who was gracious enough to allow my son to live with them. I managed to get our few possessions into a storage unit but was unsure how I would pay the monthly fee. And I fell into the darkness of the financial trial.

Homeless, I went weeks, spending one night in a friend's house and another night at someone else's house. Sometimes, I would get a gift of $30 to stay in a hotel for a night. With only sporadic transportation, I walked everywhere. Once a week, I would get access to a phone to call my son. I didn't eat everyday.

Finally, I found some temporary shelter in a small, run-down efficiency in the back of someone's garage about thirty miles from my son. I had no job, no money, no food, and no transportation. I wanted to die. There was no reason to go on living.

Committing suicide became part of my daily thought pattern. Each day, I took a walk to try to think and find a solution to my situation. I would pray and cry out to Jesus for an answer but the only answer was silence. I would contemplate suicide, but thoughts of my son would jolt me back from the edge of this Chasm. I loved him. How could I hurt him even more? How could I leave him? His life so far had been hard and my suicide would devastate him. So I would return to my temporary living space in as much pain as I was before I went for the walk.

When I could no longer bear the material struggle, I would sit alone in the dark and cry out to Jesus for help. I would struggle for hours spiritually only to hear silence! I concluded that the silence meant that this situation was my fault. I was getting what I deserved. So I cried for forgiveness and tried to "pull myself up by the bootstraps" and get out of the trial. Nothing worked. Again, I would cry to Jesus for help. Silence! Where are you Jesus? Why have you abandoned me? I am a child of God. As days turned into weeks, I felt helpless, guilty, trapped, and hopeless. I really did want to kill myself. I thought that everyone would be better off. I was positive this situation was my fault. I didn't deserve to live.

One day, I felt dangerously close to acting on this suicide thought. So I dragged myself out of bed and took a walk. I had not eaten in a day; I had no money, no phone to call my son, no transportation, and no job. As I looked around me, I thought how different our society looked from my devastated vantage point. As I looked up from the bottom of our affluent society, I was amazed how much people took for granted. There were grocery stores on every corner, but I was hungry. There were vacant apartments everywhere, but I was homeless. There were cars on every street, but I had to walk. I was also amazed how oblivious people are to the needy right in front of them. There is great poverty in this country, and yet, the hungry and homeless are almost invisible, or at best, stereotyped. I was certainly invisible. After months of this financial trial, I knew I had been locked out of this affluent society. I was on the bottom and invisible. Unfortunately, those thoughts only fueled the hopelessness of my situation with feelings of being isolated, forgotten, and judged.

As those thoughts invaded my mind, I again judged myself. I thought how could I, an educated woman, be in this situation? How could I have been so stupid and careless to allow this situation to happen to me? Therefore, it was my responsibility to find a solution to my financial turmoil. So I will try one final time. I began the material struggle again. But what do I attack first? I need a job. But I have no transportation, no phone, and I don't even have an address. How do I get work? Well, if I had a car or access to public transportation, I could work. But I can't get a car without an income and I need money for a bus or taxi. Well, if nothing else, I need food. But I have no money. When I ask for food, individuals make me feel like a beggar, and food pantries either ask why I keep coming back or restrict my access. I was even denied food stamps because I did not have an address. People know my situation. Why don't they just bring me some food? I do not have the energy to ask anymore. The more I searched for a solution, the more frustrated I became. And as I had so many times before, I began to cry out, "Jesus, if you will just help me, I will not make any more mistakes. I will do whatever you want." Silence!

My friends say I am strong and a survivor, but at that moment, I had truly come to the end of my external and internal worlds. There was no struggle left in me. I had nothing to hang on to externally. Everything was gone. I was empty internally. I felt dead emotionally. I was physically barely moving and my brain was useless. I had finally come to understand I could never take my life. It belonged to Jesus. I was completely helpless. So I just gave up. I don't remember my exact audible words at that point, but I do remember the state of my spirit. I felt helpless, guilty, trapped, hopeless, isolated, forgotten, and judged. Basically, I told Jesus please either let me die or save from this trial and I do not care which one. I could no longer handle the emotional, physical, mental, and spiritual pain. No matter what he did or did not do to me, no matter whether he saved me from this turmoil or not, whether I lived or died, I was in his hands. Where else could I go than to him? I completely surrendered myself to Jesus. I had come to the end of myself.

At that moment, I came face to face with Jesus; there was nothing or no one between us. Suddenly, I became aware of his presence. It was overwhelming. I stopped, frozen in the middle of the sidewalk. Tears began to fill my eyes. I could not see him but I *knew* he was there. I could not speak but there was a spiritual conversation going on deep in my soul. And it was not about money. It was about Jesus and his love. I *knew* that I had never been out of the embrace of Jesus' love. More importantly, nothing else mattered to me than his love.

If you are fortunate enough to experience the moment of nothing between Jesus and you, your relationship with him will be changed forever. For me, it was a profoundly personal moment that put me on the path of love that leads out of a trial.

Conquering a trial has everything to do with embracing the love of Jesus. Conquering a trial is about purification of our faith in the fire of adversity and coming out the other side in a deeper love relationship with Jesus. It is the only way to conquer a trial. Jesus love led me out of my trial. And you will begin to know this love the minute you stop the struggle to get out of your trial and surrender to the embrace of Jesus' love.

The Miracle of Love

Jesus quite literally lifted me out of the darkness of the Chasm. The moment I came to the end of myself, Jesus moved in amazing ways in my life. He gave guidance and courage to walk through my trial. He opened doors for food, a job, a car, and housing. I experienced profoundly personal changes in my financial situation that were absolutely the result of the touch of Jesus. Prior to my trial and even in the middle of it, I would have called those changes miracles. You see like most of us, I used to perceive the gift of unexpected resources that come to meet a bill or the unexpected job offer as miracles. I would think that these financial changes were the miracles that allowed me to conquer my trial. I was wrong. My vision was clouded.

It is not the gift but the gift giver that is the miracle. I believe a true miracle is that a holy, all powerful, all-knowing God would reach through the fabric of this physical world and down into the bowels of that fallen world to extend love to one wounded, sinful human being. In my helpless, guilty, trapped, hopeless, isolated, forgotten, and judged state, Jesus loved me. When I came to the end of myself, Jesus loved me. It is the miracle of this love that allowed me to conquer my financial trial, not the gifts. Certainly, the financial changes allowed me to emerge from my trial but it was the miracle of love that allowed me to conquer my trial. Conquering a trial has nothing to do with our external world. Conquering a trial is an internal spiritual transformation at the depths of our souls.

The moment that I encountered Jesus with nothing between us, the miracle of love began to transform me. My limited human vision of my trial was changed. I began to see beyond my turmoil. Now I had an expanded spiritual vision that had been purified in the fire of adversity and revealed in the miracle of love. Certainly, I still felt the turmoil of my own financial trial, but I was released from the helpless, guilty, trapped, hopeless, isolated, forgotten, and judged state. I was able to read the Bible but with a dramatic difference. Passages I had read many times before now came to life for me. They captured my wounded spirit, filled my soul, and empowered me in love to see my trial through different eyes. James 2:5: "Listen my brothers, has not God chosen those who are poor in the eyes of the world to be rich in faith and to inherit the kingdom he promised those who love him?" I had been given the opportunity to see my earthly poverty, my trial, as heavenly wealth, faith. Every single follower of Jesus should view themselves as poor in the eyes of the world. But "things" can get between us and Jesus, and we can view our earthly possessions as wealth and lose sight of our true wealth, the miracle of love. The farther I have gotten from my trial, the more I realize I was given a precious gift to have all my earthly possessions stripped away. It was a purification of my faith that gave me a soul-deep encounter with the love of Jesus.

For you see, I absolutely know that Jesus loves me for who I am in his eyes not for what I have or what I do. His love is not manifested in the size of my home or the size of my bank account. His love is not manifested in my career status. His love sees past my human weakness and struggle, to see who I am in him. His love is grounded and manifested in the fact that he died on a cross some 2000 years ago for the sins that I committed some 2000 years later.

My financial trial did not magically end. There were times when I would get discouraged. But I was now empowered by love and I would only need to read the Bible and pray to continue on. "Therefore, we do not lose heart. Though outwardly we are wasting away, yet inwardly we are being renewed day by day. For our light and momentary troubles are achieving for us an eternal glory that far outweighs them all. So we fix our eyes not on what is seen but what is unseen. For what is seen is temporary, but what is unseen is eternal" (2 Corinthians 4:16–18).

There were times when I felt guilty. But rather than sink into self-pity and beat myself up, I now chose to look at that guilt and determine my responsibility. What part of this trial was my responsibility? Inevitably I would come back to one root cause: my lack of faith, which led me to hold on to myself and not Jesus. Only enveloped in the miracle of love could I have seen that spiritual misstep, something we all have in common in the middle of trial.

Here is what I have learned. A financial trial is an extremely fearful journey. It is easy to get worn down and become terrified. Once fear has overpowered you, you will cling to a trial. You will become completely self-absorbed and see nothing beyond your own turmoil. It is a totally understandable situation but also a dangerous one as well. Fear leads us to cling to ourselves and be trapped in a trial with escape as the only option. We may emerge from the trial but as a fearful, bitter person. Fear is holding onto ourselves and faith is holding onto Jesus. Faith is required before we can conquer a trial.

It took me a while to reach solid financial ground because conquering the trial was more important than emerging from the trial. I had to practice holding on to Jesus no matter what I saw in my external world. The more I practiced, the more I learned that this miracle of love was not just for me but for others. I began to see the miracle to love others would empower me to conquer my trial.

The Miracle to Love Others

As we have learned on this journey, the love of Jesus cannot be possessed; it must flow through us to others. Nowhere is that statement more appropriate than in a trial. In order to truly conquer a trial, the miracle of Jesus' love that flows to us must also flow out from us. We must pass the miracle to love others. You have probably heard the statement that you will either emerge from a difficult situation "better or bitter." It is true. Therefore, if you want to conquer a trial "better", you will need to allow the love of Jesus to flow from you. To understand this, we need to return to the story of Job. When God lead Job out of his trial, he had some choice words for Job's friends.

> I am angry with you and your friends, because you have not spoken of me what is right, as my servant Job has. So now take seven bulls and seven rams and go to my servant Job and sacrifice a burnt offering for yourselves. My servant Job will pray for you, and I will accept his prayer and not deal with you according to your folly. You have not spoken of me what is right, as my servant Job has. So Eliphaz the Temanite, Bildad the Shuhite and Zophar the Naamathite did what the Lord told them; and the Lord accepted Job's prayer. (Job 42:7–9)

These men were the friends of Job who provided no support to him during his trial. They said such things to him as "Does God pervert justice? Does the Almighty pervert what is right? When your children sinned against him, he gave them over to the penalty of your sin" (Job 8:3–4). In other words, we know that you are in pain, Job, but your children just got what they deserved: death. These friends just rubbed salt in his wound. Yet God requires Job to pray for them and Job does.

Unfortunately, trials will bring out the worst in human behavior. Job was not unique. We will all experience the judgment, insensitivity, cruelty, and neglect of others during a trial. That treatment will wound you. But if you do not extend love by praying for these people, you will not conquer a trial. You will emerge from it but you will emerge bitter, angry, and revengeful. In order to conquer a trial, we must extend our miracle of love to others. The miracle to love others comes directly from Jesus' words.

> You have heard that it was said 'Love your neighbor and hate your enemy.'
> But I tell you, love your enemies and pray for those who persecute you, that
> you may be sons of your Father in heaven. He causes his sun to rise on the evil
> and the good, and sends rain on the righteous and the unrighteous. If you love
> those who love you, what reward will you get?" (Matthew 5:43–46)

The unconditional love that flows to us must flow unconditionally from us to others. In and of myself, I could not extend love to those people who wounded, judged, or neglected me during my own financial trial. It was only Jesus' miracle to love others that empowered me to pray, forgive and embrace these people in love.

We can learn from the treatment and behavior of others towards us in our time of need. We know the pain that comes from judgment, insensitivity, cruelty, and neglect. Jesus' love will heal these wounds but we need to remember the pain of being judged, neglected, isolated, and kicked. We need to remember so we do not extend the same treatment to others who go through trials. We are all capable of this type of behavior. So remember how it feels and do not pass it on. Instead, we must access the miracle of love for others.

The miracle of love from Jesus that I received in my own trial left a lasting gift for me: long-suffering. I am convinced that judgment, insensitivity, cruelty, and neglect are the behavior that results from an inability to be long-suffering. Long-suffering means that we forget about ourselves and make a conscious decision to extend Jesus' love to another person for the length of a trial. Long-suffering cannot be manufactured. It can only come from the miracle to love others. If we truly experience Jesus' love to conquer a trial, we will be transformed and be able to be long-suffering with others in a trial.

You can extend this love to another mother in a financial trial. Who better to walk with this woman through this type of turmoil than another mother who has experienced love to conquer a trial? Remember, I explained that understanding the path that leads to a financial trial would be useful information. It is useful for other women. We need to share this path. We, as mothers in the Half Family, need to be long-suffering with each other in love. "Praise be to the God and father of our Lord Jesus Christ, the Father of compassion and the God of all comfort, who comforts us in all our troubles, so that we can comfort those in any trouble with comfort we ourselves have received from God." (2 Corinthians 1:3–4)

Long-suffering means that we extend the comfort that Jesus gave us to another woman. It means that we do not judge, neglect, or isolate another mother who is in financial turmoil. It means we extend ourselves unconditionally, selflessly, and sacrificially to meet another's needs. It means we extend the miracle of love with no time limit. It means we see this suffering mother not through human material eyes but through the eyes of Jesus.

And finally, we do not wait to extend the miracle of love until we are out of our own trial. No, we conquer our own trial by extending the miracle of love to others. In and of yourself, this act of love is impossible. It can only be accomplished through Jesus. Therefore, I want to leave you with a word picture that clearly demonstrates the miracle of love.

Jesus is dying a horrible, excruciating death on the cross. He is isolated, forgotten, and judged by society and he is completely innocent. He is going to die. There is no way out. He is hanging between two criminals who have been convicted of their crimes. Yet, one criminal says, "Jesus remember me when you come into your kingdom." Jesus answered him, "I tell you the truth, today you will be with me in paradise" (Matthew 23:42–43).

The miracle to love others is not bound by a trial but empowered by a trial. So look up and find the other women in financial trials. Trust me, there are far too many on this path. Extend the miracle of love to them and in the process you will conquer your own trial.

Love is the only way to conquer a trial. If we choose to let go of everything in our physical world and trust Jesus, we will experience that miracle of love. Jesus' love will not only show us the way out of the trial, but the journey will lead us into the miracle to love others. And you will be one step closer to the wholeness destination.

CHEAT SHEET

Facing and Conquering Trials

The Truth

1. Testing your faith

2. The silence of God

3. The solitary struggle of a trial

The Hope

1. We have hope to face a trial.

2. God is in control.

3. You are not alone.

The Love

1. The love to conquer a trial

2. The miracle of love

3. The miracle to love others

16

Creating a Whole Home

The promise of a "whole" home was the vision that kept me moving forward on my own Half Family journey. As I started down this road, I envisioned a whole home picture to include that perfect husband, a perfect son, a three-bedroom, two-bath house in the suburbs, a new car, and a great job. But as I traveled this boulder-filled, rain-soaked road, that picture began to fade. I did not find that perfect husband and my son was certainly not moving in the direction of perfect. I never did get that three-bedroom, two-bath house in the suburbs or a new car.

It would have been depressing except as this picture faded, a new picture emerged in my mind. Being stubborn, I tried to cling to the fading view. I wanted this illusion to be real, but I could not deny the sense that this new picture was real. It was what I longed for: a Whole Home. It made no sense to me, but each time I emerged from the pain and turmoil of a tough stop on the road, I seemed to be one step closer to a Whole Home. This creation process was not apparent to me in the dark moments on my harsh road. I did not see anything but destruction amidst the boulders, rain, and Chasms. However, I could not deny that each time I maneuvered a difficult spot, something changed in my little Half Family. It took the devastation of landmine explosions and the shattered remains of my life from my own financial trial to finally push me to accept the real picture. And it was no where close to my initial vision.

As I looked closely at that path behind me, my vision cleared. What I saw surprised me. I saw that I had actually been in the process of creating a Whole Home from the moment I chose to step forward and journey this Half Family road. Looking back, I could see the difficult road I had traveled, but I saw something else too. I could see the results of each step on my own Half Family journey. I saw that my Whole Home was being created from the truth, the hope, and the love.

The real picture of a Whole Home was revealed in the condition of my internal world, not the condition of my external world. I saw that a Whole Home is an internal dwelling that travels with you on the road rather than a physical location. This dwelling cannot be destroyed by rain, or boulders, or Chasms. In fact, a Whole Home is purified and strengthened in the times of adversity. A Whole Home does not deteriorate or age but continues to grow in its beauty with age.

You may be clinging to some distorted picture. The old saying that "home is where the heart is" is true. So choose to let go of your own illusion and see that the fulfillment of the promise of a Whole Home is found in the journey. We only need to pause, turn around, and look at the path behind us to see the truth of that statement. We will see that the truth, the hope, and the love have created a new home, a Whole Home. We will discover the truth is the foundation, the hope is the frame, and the love is the roof.

The Truth

Before we took even one step on the Half Family road, we needed a clear picture about the true condition of the road for our journey. We needed to see the Whole Truth Picture, which was difficult to understand and accept but it was a necessary first step.

Remember our Whole Truth Picture? I compared that picture to a mosaic, an art form made up of thousands of small pieces of colored glass or stone that form a picture. If you stand too close to a mosaic, all you see are the pieces in front of you in no recognizable pattern. You know that you are looking at a mosaic, but you cannot see the picture. Only when you stand at a distance do you see it.

As related to the truth, we realized we were sometimes so close to the fragments of our lives and our shattered emotions that we did not see the full picture. Therefore, we took a step back and saw the whole picture, the Whole Truth. We saw the non-personal Cold Hard Facts that represent Real Fear in our external world. We saw our painful wound and our vulnerability to Nightmare Fear in our internal world. We saw our lack of margins that often pushed us into Crisis Management and the danger of the Chasm. We saw the whole road. It was a depressing picture filled with dark, colored stones.

As difficult as it was, we learned that understanding and accepting the Whole Truth was the only way for us to stop stumbling around in the dark on the road. Up until that point, you may have been like me and ignored the truth. You may have seen flashes of it periodically in the dark, but you never saw the Whole Truth. Therefore, you would fall over the truth on the road in the darkness of your ignorance. Ignoring the truth only delays the ultimate encounter with it.

Ignorance leads to reacting to the truth and acceptance of the Whole Truth leads to managing the road. So far I am not stating anything new.

But understanding and accepting the Whole Truth Picture and actually walking through that truth on the journey is entirely different. And it is that difference that we need to examine.

We have traveled through the truth, and it is no longer just a picture that provides a logical explanation for the condition of our road. It is not just words on a page. The Whole Truth has traveled from our brains to our gut and it is now part of us. We have accepted the truth and acceptance has transformed our perception of the truth. And it was an amazing transformation.

At each stop, we made a choice to pick up a dark, colored stone of the truth. As we examined each truth, we chose to accept it. Sometimes it was extremely painful, but always, in the warmth of our acceptance, that dark stone in our hand was transformed into a brightly colored stone. What? Did you miss that transformation? It was a subtle, slow process. Those dark, colored stones of the Whole Truth are now the brightly colored stones of freedom. The truth has set us free. It is a freedom that only comes from accepting the truth. It is this freedom that gives us a new perception of the truth. Look again at the Whole Truth Picture; it is no longer a dark picture that traps us but is rather a brightly colored picture that has freed us.

And it is the brightly colored stones of freedom that form the foundation for our home. A Whole Home is built on the freedom that comes from understanding and accepting the truth. It may twist your brain to realize that from the darkness of our Whole Truth Picture has emerged the foundation for our Whole Home. But it is true. We only need to look back at our journey to see the formation of this solid foundation.

It began with choosing to equip our children for the road ahead. In fact, it was this encounter with the Whole Truth Picture about our children that was crucial to building a solid foundation for a Whole Home.

When we chose to accept the truth that our children were not broken but were wounded, do you know what happened? We were set free from the never-ending cycle of trying to fix our children with gimmicks or that illusive magic wand. We were set free to see their Whole Truth Picture. We saw that our children needed relationship, not gimmicks. We saw the truth that relationship was not an event (fix them) but a journey.

The freedom gained from this encounter with the truth began to transform us from repairmen to the mothers for our children. Choosing to be a mother to a child is a messy journey through a relationship. But that choice was critical because it was and is the first step in the creation of a Whole Home. At the time, you may not have realized the crucial importance of this acceptance step. So I would like us to examine one of the most beautiful stones of freedom hidden in the truth about our children who are wounded not broken.

In accepting this truth, we learned that communicating with and teaching our children has little to do with what we say to them and more to do with who we are to them. Relationships are not created from words but actions. Our children truly learn from our example. Look back at the example of my own experience with my son. He knew when I was using gimmicks to fix him and he resisted the repair job. He resisted because I was not seeing the truth about his condition. I was not meeting his need. He may not have been able to verbalize his need to me, but he internally knew my tactics were off the mark. So I trapped him with me in my endless cycle of trying to fix him: throwing words or gimmicks at him. When I accepted the truth, my words and actions began to move us toward relationship.

We were both set free. My acceptance of the truth allowed my son to move towards freedom. I gave him the freedom to accept that he was wounded. I gave him the freedom to move towards his own hope. Certainly, he needed to make his own choice to accept the truth. But my acceptance gave him the freedom to choose. I gave him the freedom to take this messy, harsh, painful Half Family journey with me. And on this difficult road, he was also gathering brightly colored stones of freedom that were creating the foundation for our Whole Home.

At each stop on this Half Family journey, our children have been watching us. They saw us accept the self-truth about our painful wound and vulnerability to Nightmare Fear. They saw us struggle through forgiveness. They saw us strive to change our unhealthy relationships with our partners. They felt the same pain, fear, and turmoil that we did. They also saw us experience healing, faith, and joy. They have seen us pick up those dark colored stones and struggle to accept the truth. And they have seen the truth transformed into brightly colored stones of freedom that comes from acceptance. They have seen the transformation of their mothers.

Our children are learning from our example. They have their own struggles with truth and acceptance of the road. When they accept the truth about their wound and fear and forgiveness, they too will find the brightly colored stones of freedom.

This freedom that we and our children gained on our internal journey gave us the foundation to withstand the harshness of our external world.

Whether you realize it or not, it was the freedom that we had gained at all the previous internal stops that gave us the courage to face the truth about the Cold

Hard Facts, the Income Gap, the Soft Facts, creating the management plan, and managing the Cold Hard Facts across the Income Gap. The truth that we encountered at each of these stops was devastating at best. Fortunately, we had the freedom that comes from accepting the truth. Now you may not have been able to verbalize that, but you had learned that acceptance was the only way to keep moving forward.

By accepting the harsh truth of our external world, we gained the freedom to know that we did not have to be trapped by our limited vision. We know the truth that our external world is filled with Real Fear. If we try to ignore this truth, the Real Fear will overpower us and narrow our vision. If we accept the truth, we have the freedom to expand our vision. We also know now that we are more than black and white numbers of the Cold Hard Facts. We know our external world is infused with who we are as women and mothers in the Half Family. Each time we accepted another truth about our external world, we added more brightly colored stones of freedom to the foundation of our Whole Home.

But it was the truth and acceptance from our last stop, facing and conquering trials, that provides the cornerstone for the foundation for our Whole Home. In the acceptance of a trial is found the most brilliant stone: it is the source of our freedom. That source is Jesus, the cornerstone of truth that is the source of all freedom. In the pain of a financial trial, we come face to face with that truth. A trial will rip us to the core of our soul. Amazingly, it also gives us access to the fullness of freedom because we will come face to face with the source: Jesus.

We have gathered the brightly colored stones of freedom at each stop on our journey. Each time that we accepted the truth, we were given a stone for our foundation. It is a solid foundation built on freedom. It is this freedom that empowers us to move to the hope that creates a frame for our Whole Home.

The Hope

If we are honest with ourselves, when we began this journey, survival was our main goal. Frankly, my first exposure to the Whole Truth Picture about the condition of my road made me gasp and say out loud, "How will my son and I ever survive this journey?" So I clung to the hope that I would survive. I had no idea that hope would not only guide me to survival, but hope would create the frame for my own Whole Home. Think back to our introduction to hope and my definition of it.

Hope is intangible. You cannot touch hope. For us, I guess I would describe it this way. Hope always follows the Whole Truth. When we shine the light on the

Whole Truth, we also receive the light of hope. And this hope is unique for the mother in the Half Family.

This light of hope was new margins, something extra. If we could get something extra, a foothold on this rough road, we would have hope we could make it to our destination. We needed new emotional, physical, and mental margins to give us a foothold on the rough road and keep us from the danger of the Chasm. We needed something extra, some hope. We need the light of hope found in our Hope Roadmap.

So we used our roadmap at each stop on our journey to wholeness. Certainly, our mindset at the beginning of the journey was survival. In fact, having just faced a financial trial, we may still *feel* that survival emotion, but we now *know* a journey in hope is so much more than survival.

Just like walking into the Whole Truth Picture, we have also experienced an amazing transformation from our hope experience. It is a transformation that has been gradually occurring at each stop. You may have felt the change but not really understood the importance. In fact, if you were like me and held onto the distorted picture of a Whole Home, you may have missed the expanse of hope. Hope has created the frame for our Whole Home. So lets take another look back to see this amazing transformation that has come from each step into hope.

When we began this journey, we were shattered women. We were severely wounded and full of Nightmare Fear in our internal world and our external world was a dangerous road of boulders, rain, Chasms, and Real Fear. Our lives were either driven by our emotions or by the Cold Hard Facts. Either our internal world or our external world drove our decisions. In essence, we were split in two. One day, we would function focused entirely on the demands of our external world. The next day, we would trudge through the emotional turmoil inside completely oblivious to our external environment.

As we have journeyed into hope and used our self-care margins from our Hope Roadmap, we have learned how to merge our internal and external worlds. It was a slow process. Now we no longer live in two separate worlds, external and internal. Our lives are not two pieces. They are merged. And what happens when you put two pieces together? You get one piece: a whole. It is amazing that from each step on this journey, our internal and external worlds have been merged, made whole. As a result, we have been transformed into a whole mother, a whole woman.

We only need to examine our stop at embracing forgiveness to see the beginning of this transformation. When we chose to walk into the hope to forgive others and ourselves, we began to embrace wholeness. Prior to forgiveness, our internal and external worlds were at war. We struggled to contain the boiling, internal anger and hatred towards our partner from spilling out externally on our family and friends. I know that in the middle of forgiveness, your only thoughts may have been to survive the journey. You may have missed the wholeness transformation. So let me share how we have changed. As we accessed the hope of forgiveness, our hearts changed. Anger and resentment melted away with doses of hope. As we embraced forgiveness, our external behavior became a reflection of the condition of our internal world. No longer at war, our internal and external worlds were merged, moving us towards wholeness.

We then took the step towards relationship transformation. When we accessed the hope of unwrapping our ex-partner from our heart, we stopped the missile attacks. Our partner was still in our lives, but he was not our life. We moved toward the hope of healthy relationships. No longer did our painful wound and Nightmare Fear seep into a new relationship. Our external words and actions became a reflection of our internal condition: our partner was no longer wrapped around our heart. Our internal and external worlds of relationship became the same, merged, whole.

Whether you realized it or not, each time that you accessed the Hope Roadmap to make it past a difficult spot, you were being transformed. In the slow, difficult journey through our external world, we chose not to see our lives from the black and white view of the Cold Hard Facts. We chose to access the hope of the Soft Facts and were able to see the colors of who we are as women and mothers. We saw that our external world is infused with who we are internally. As we made the tough decisions to manage the Cold Hard Facts, we were merging our external and internal worlds to create one world, merged, whole. There was no such thing as a separate external and internal world. There was only our world: the same, merged, whole. And our world is a whole mother, a whole woman.

Throughout our journey, I have stated that we are the most important asset. Early on, we needed to accept that statement in order to maneuver the difficult road. It became part of our survival mentality. But now we need to look beyond that view and see there is an even more important reason for this acceptance. We are the most important asset because we are the frame of our Whole Home. Our journey has taught us how important we are, but do you see yourself as the frame of your home? For me it took a powerful story to give me the answer to that question.

It is the story of a poor family in India. I don't even know their names. It was a family that was helped by Mother Teresa. If you are not aware of Mother Teresa, she was a nun who formed the "Missionaries of Charity" which began in Calcutta, India and spread throughout the world. Her mission was to help the poorest of the poor. Or as I like to say, she deliberately, selflessly and sacrificially spent her life meeting the needs of the poor.

In her book, *No Greater Love*, Mother Teresa describes an encounter with a poor, little girl. She took this child in, fed her, clothed her, and gave her a place to sleep. But the little girl ran away. Mother Teresa found her and brought her back to the children's home. She ran away again. Finally, Mother Teresa instructed a sister to follow the child. The sister discovered the little girl was going home to her mother who was living in the street under a tree. The girl had little or no food and there was no warm place to sleep. But it did not matter. Her mother loved her. She was the little girl's family, her home.[1]

Never underestimate the power of a whole mother. Even in those tough stops on the road, in hunger, poverty, homelessness, you are home to your family. And if you continue to access hope, you will be transformed into a whole mother, the frame of a Whole Home. And that type of framing can never be destroyed.

We now have the brightly colored stones of freedom gained from the acceptance of the truth at each stop on our journey. These brightly colored stones of freedom and the cornerstone, Jesus, who is the source of all freedom form the foundation for our Whole Home. We now know that hope from the Hope Roadmap has merged our internal and external worlds to create a whole mother. In this amazing transformation, we have created the frame for our Whole Home, but it is not complete. We need the most critical part: our roof to hold our frame together and protect our Half Family. Our roof is created from the love.

The Love

If you were surprised to find the brightly colored stones of freedom, you will be amazed by the glorious colors of love. This love has led us around boulders, through the rain, and across Chasms. We have experienced the color of love at each stop on our journey. As we have accessed love, we have been given another glorious stone for our roof.

These glorious stones of love are rare and precious because they are formed at the core of our souls in the presence of Jesus. At each stop on our Half Family journey, we were given the opportunity to walk into Jesus' presence and access his love. Each time that we chose to have an encounter with Jesus, we left that encounter one of these stones that would cover and protect our Whole Home.

These rare and precious stones are called joy. Were you aware that you were gathering stones of joy along the way? I wasn't. I knew I was growing in love and

I was changing. I knew love was protecting my Half Family, but I never thought to use the word joy to describe that change. It was only when I spent sometime with Jesus and the Bible that I began to see these rare and precious stones. What is joy?

Joy is a word that is too often thrown around with little regard for the source. Joy is often used to refer to a sense of happiness. It is considered some outward emotional response to praise God. If we limit our perception of joy to those definitions, we will miss its glorious color. Joy is not a feeling based on our external world and neither is joy a feeling based on internal world. Joy cannot be defined in such simplistic terms: it is so much more. Joy lives in a saved soul and grows with each encounter of Jesus' love.

> Surely God is my salvation; I will trust and not be afraid. The Lord, the Lord, is my strength and my song; he has become my salvation. With joy you will draw water from the wells of salvation. (Isaiah 12:2–3)

When we accepted the free gift of salvation, we were given access to joy. Look closely at this passage. "He has become my salvation." Salvation is not just an event. It is Jesus. And each time, we go to that well of salvation born from his love, we do it with joy.

Clearly, joy is not some "happy" feeling that we can manufacture. Joy is a part of the gift of salvation. It lives in the wells of salvation. Joy is a soul-deep knowledge that Jesus loves us. And despite what we see in the external world or feel in our internal world, Jesus' love will sustain us. Think back on your journey and those private moments in Jesus' presence. Wasn't there a sense of protection, peace, and comfort that invaded your soul in those moments? Wasn't there something else? Something you knew but could not quite describe. It was deep warmth. It was profoundly personal. It was pure. It was joy.

As I began to study joy, I could not find a place in the Bible that did not have God or Jesus and joy in the same passages. Joy only comes from being the presence of the love of God. And joy expands as we grow in love.

> As the Father has loved me, so have I loved you. Now remain in my love. If you obey my commands, you will remain in my love, just I have obeyed my Father's commands and remain in his love. I have told you this so that my joy may be in you and that your joy may be complete. My command is this: Love each other as I have loved you. Greater love has no one than this, that he lay down his life for his friends. I no longer call you servants, because a servant does not know his master's business. Instead, I have called you friends, for

everything that I learned from my Father I have made known to you. (John 15:9–15)

If we really examine the passages above, we can see the full definition of joy. As Jesus is speaking to his disciples for the last time before he dies, he is stressing the importance of remaining in him. There can be no love without the presence of Jesus. If we remain in his love, we will find joy. And that joy will be complete if we obey his commands, which are simple. His command is to love others as he loved us. Simply put, if we choose to stay connected and grow in the love of Jesus and allow that love to flow to others, our joy will be complete.

It has been and will continue to be a journey for me to experience complete joy. I have had moments of complete joy. Most of those moments have occurred as I have extended love to my son. When I chose to let the love of Jesus flow to my son, I have experienced it. I found joy that now forms the roof of my Whole Home. As we take one last look back on our Half Family journey, we will find these glorious stones of joy in our encounters with Jesus.

Each time we experienced the Nightmare Fear from our internal turmoil and chose to walk into the love of Jesus, we experienced personal joy. Each time we encountered the Real Fear from our dangerous external road and chose to walk into the love of Jesus, we experienced personal joy. That does not mean that we did not experience pain or even despair. But deep in our soul, we were given the inexplicable joy that can only come from the presence of Jesus.

Think back to the moment you chose to accept forgiveness from Jesus. It was joy. Accepting forgiveness is a journey into joy. When we chose to forgive our partner, our joy was made complete. Now you may not have called that moment joy. For me, the only word that describes that experience is joy, complete joy. It was complete because I was not only extending love to my husband; I was also extending it to my son.

It is true. No longer was I selfishly thinking of my feelings, my need to be right, and my pain. I chose to let go of myself and embrace Jesus' love. I also released my son from my torment in that act of love. Remember, our children are with us every step on the road. When you choose to access the love to forgive your partner, you extend love to your Half Family. Your joy is made complete.

Actually, some of most glorious stones of joy come from our darkest moments on the Half Family journey. Reflect on a time when you were standing on the edge of the Chasm. It does not matter how you got to the edge. You could have been pushed there by the Nightmare Fear in your internal world or the Real Fear from the Cold Hard Facts. No matter what the situation, you were standing on the edge contemplating an escape jump, a selfish action to relieve your pain. Instead you chose to take a step of faith onto the invisible bridge built by Jesus. In that moment that you walked into the loving presence of Jesus, you also made another choice. Do you know what it was? You chose to look up from the edge of the Chasm and look at your Half Family. You knew that escape might ease your pain for a while, but it would wound your Half Family. So you chose to endure the pain and not jump. You not only accessed the love of Jesus for yourself, but you extended love to your child or children. Every single time we make a choice to take a step on the invisible bridge of Faith across our Chasms, we receive the glorious stones of joy. Our joy is made complete.

Take a long hard look at our Half Family journey. As we chose deliberate, selfless, and sacrificial acts of love to meet our children's needs, we were gathering the glorious stones of joy that would create the roof of our Whole Home. Stand back and look at this roof. It is not only dazzling in its color, but it has the strength of God himself. Joy is solid, strong and everlasting.

I personally know the joy that forms the roof of my Whole Home. It is joy that was formed in the fire of adversity. My son and I have a wonderful relationship, but that relationship was not born out of a comfortable external lifestyle free from internal turmoil. That relationship was born in spite of a harsh external lifestyle and internal struggles. It was born out of the love of Jesus that flowed through me to my son. It is the glorious stones of joy found in that love that has created the roof of my Whole Home.

A Whole Home has nothing to do with external factors or a physical location. A Whole Home lives in our internal world and travels with us on our Half Family journey. Its beauty is only enhanced with age. It is created from the solid foundation of the brightly colored stones of freedom, which comes from the acceptance of the truth, the Whole Truth. The truth will set us free. The frame of our home is created from hope. It is the hope that has taught us to merge our internal and external worlds into one: whole. In this merging process, we were transformed into whole mothers. We became the frame of our Whole Home. The roof of our Whole Home is created from the glorious stones of joy. Joy is formed in the core of our souls in Jesus' presence and through his love. And that joy is made complete as we allow his love to flow through us to others. But there is one more aspect that makes a Whole Home. The crowning jewel of the roof of a Whole Home is the joy that comes from knowing that Jesus is our dwelling place. My home would not be whole without the knowledge that Jesus is my home.

CHEAT SHEET

Creating a Whole Home

The Truth

1. Our perception has been transformed: the truth shall set you free.

2. The brightly colored stones of freedom: Jesus, the cornerstone and the source.

3. Freedom is the solid foundation of a Whole Home.

The Hope

1. Hope is more than survival.

2. Hope has merged our internal and external worlds.

3. A whole mother is the frame of a Whole Home.

The Love

1. The glorious stones of complete joy

2. The roof of a Whole Home

17

Half Families Made Whole Through Christ

You are not alone.

Those words were your introduction to the Half Family journey. If you think back to the first time you read that phrase, you may have found some momentary comfort on your dark, dangerous road with no roadmap and no destination. Maybe there was some hope you would survive this journey. If you were not alone, maybe you could make it through each day. Yes, wholeness would be great, but survival was really the goal. I too was only concerned about my survival.

When I began my own Half Family journey, the goal was to be free from the Real Fear in my external world and free from the pain and Nightmare Fear in my internal world. I wanted to be free from my isolated, trapped existence on a lonely, dark road with no roadmap and no destination. Certainly any single mother would want the same.

Unfortunately, any comfort and hope of survival were fleeting in the beginning because this phrase "you are not alone" is not about survival. Those words hold all the secrets about wholeness.

Do you remember our first encounter with the concept of wholeness? There were questions. What is wholeness? What does the destination look like? I did not give you the answers. Instead, here is what I stated. You cannot truly understand or see wholeness until we reach the destination. But I will tell you this: I have been there and it is a marvelous destination. It is a place where you will be healed, whole, and find the desires of your heart.

Do you know why you would not have understood the destination? The answer is your "selfish" vision. I know because I have been there. My intense desire to survive meant that I was consumed with me. So I saw the hope of "I am not alone" through this same vision: selfish. Yes, I started out on the Half Family journey with selfish motives. Quite frankly, I gave little consideration to my son's needs as I started to walk towards wholeness. If you are honest with yourself, you probably felt and acted the same way. You were consumed with Real and Nightmare Fear with no emotional, physical, or mental margins. And you had no Spiritual Margin of Faith because faith and fear cannot coexist. Therefore, in that fearful condition, you clung to yourself, which actually intensified the sense of being alone and the need to survive. To one degree or another, you stepped onto this road with selfish motives: "I do not want to be alone and I want to survive."

Therefore, we had a distorted vision of wholeness. I thought a new husband *for me*, a new house *for me*, and maximum income and minimum expenses *for me* were wholeness. *Wholeness is not a selfish destination, it is a selfless destination.* That is why I did not share the vision of our destination with you.

The amazing thing is that despite our selfish motives, Jesus has led us to wholeness. It is true. From the moment you chose to become a mother in the Half Family, you have been on a transforming journey of truth, hope and love to wholeness. Jesus has patiently, lovingly met us at every step of this perilous road. He has led us through our selfish condition of reacting to the road to making selfless decisions about where to step on the path. And each step has brought us closer to his destination.

It has taken all those steps to lead us to a place of understanding. I am now ready to not only answer the original questions about wholeness, but reveal the secrets to wholeness. As always, we will begin with the truth.

The Truth of…Half Families

From the moment you stepped on the Half Family path, you began a transformation. You began to change from a frightened, isolated single woman. When you chose to take this journey, you chose Jesus as your guide and took one small step of faith onto the Half Family road. You chose to believe that Jesus would be there in that first step. In that choice, you not only gained a guide, but you began to let go of yourself and embrace Jesus. Faith allowed you to look through and past the fear and see him. As you made small choices to stop clinging to yourself and reach out for Jesus, you started to think less about yourself and more about him. The transformation began from selfishly holding onto those words "I am alone" to believing the selfless words "I am not alone."

Yes, believing you are alone is the pit of selfishness. If you reflect for a moment, you know the truth of that statement. Believing your aloneness is clinging to your fear. It is ignoring your children's needs. Actually, believing you are alone negates your children's existence. It will lead you to take escape jumps into the Chasm and ignore the presence of Jesus.

You are not alone and never have been on this journey. Now I am not saying that we did not have moments that we felt alone. There were dark moments on our journey, but we were never alone. We know that Jesus has been with us at each step.

This transformation from selfish to selfless has been a subtle and gradual change in us. It has occurred at each stop along the road. At every single stop on this journey, accepting the truth has meant that we must let go of ourselves. When we accepted the self-truth about our internal worlds, we had to let go our anger, our resentment, our desire to be right, and our needs. We began to see our children and our partner differently not through our own selfishness but from a selfless perspective. Our internal world began to be not so much about "what we need," but it began to revolve around "what others need." We know the truth. We are not alone. Our children are with us, and yes, even our partners are still with us. After all that we have been through together, do you still believe you are alone? Are you still that frightened, isolated single woman who first stepped on this Half Family road? No. The truth has transformed you. You are no longer on a dark, isolated road with no roadmap and no destination. You traveled through the light of truth and used the Hope Roadmap at each stop. The phrase "you are not alone" is no longer about a hope of survival. We know those words are the truth. It is the acceptance of this truth that transforms us from selfish to selfless and leads us to understand the first secret to wholeness.

The First Secret to Wholeness

The secret is that wholeness is not mine to keep. Wholeness only exists as we reach out to other Half Families. I want you to look again at the name of this journey: *Half Families Made Whole Through Christ*. When you started down this road, did you read Half Family or Half Families? In our selfish, frightened condition, we probably read Half Family.

In my "I am alone" condition, I chose not to see other Half Families around me. All I saw was my distorted view of wholeness. I would be whole. I would be healed. I would have my heart's desires. After all I was the one traveling the rough road; I deserved wholeness. But as I journeyed with Jesus, I began to see I was not alone. Not only did I see Jesus, he opened my eyes to the millions of women on the same road. Some were living in utter poverty. Some were deeply wounded.

Some were standing on the edge of the Chasm. Some were free falling into the Chasm. These women were facing similar daily challenges, trials and feeling the same frightening emotions as I. Jesus began to stir my heart. These women needed to know the truth. They needed to know that they were not alone. I could no longer focus on my condition. It would be selfish to cling to the knowledge that I was not alone. I had to share this truth with other women. It was this realization that opened my mind to the first secret of wholeness.

Wholeness was not about me. If I wanted to be healed, whole, and have the desire of my heart, I must choose to give away the truth that I am not alone. I must share my guide, Jesus, with these women. My vision began to expand. This journey was never about the selfish, narrow focus of survival. It was always about selflessly sharing the truth.

Really examine what has happened on our journey. At each stop on the road, the truth has led us to let go of our selfish motives that inhibit the flow of hope and love. Certainly, each encounter with the truth was to light the way for us to take another step forward on this path, but each truth also freed us from some selfishness. And our vision was expanded beyond our own personal, narrow focus. We were challenged to look at our children, our partners and…other Half Families.

The first secret to wholeness is we cannot keep the truth. We need to share it with other mothers in Half Families. Share your journey with these women. Share your Jesus with them. It is a choice. Like every other step on this road, wholeness does not just happen. We must choose to accept the first secret of wholeness

So you must choose. Do you want to cling to a distorted picture that wholeness is yours to possess? Do you want to cling to your perception of being healed, whole, and receiving your heart's desires? Or do you want to experience Jesus' healing, wholeness and receive his desire for your heart? Trust me, Jesus' vision of wholeness is far more expansive than ours. "You are not alone" is not a truth that we can possess; we must give it away. Other women in Half Families need to know that they are not alone.

The Hope to Be…Made Whole

It should come as no surprise that we cannot possess hope. When we choose to share the truth with another woman, we also become vessels of hope to them. How do we share hope? Well, that brings us to the second secret to wholeness.

The Second Secret to Wholeness

We share hope one woman at time. Remember, the phrase is *"you* are not alone." It is not "millions of women are not alone." It is "you." Hope is precious and personal. It must be given in the appropriate doses to one woman in need at one time.

If I had an earthly hero, it would have to be Mother Teresa. She was called by God to minister to the poor, sick, dying, and oppressed people in India. With no personal financial resources, she picked up these unfortunate people one at a time and met their needs. She never was married, never owned a home, or a car. Yet she met the needs of hundreds of thousands of individuals in her lifetime: one person at a time. Jesus miraculously touched these people because one frail woman became an open vessel of hope. We are called to do the same thing.

We do not need monetary resources or an advanced degree or a title or a large organization housed in an impressive sprawling campus of buildings. In fact, in my experience, people with resources and advanced degrees or even massive Christian/nonChristian institutions have done very little to give me hope on my own Half Family journey. It has been the personal, selfless touch from another mother in a Half Family that has given me hope. We have been given the unlimited resource of hope, which never fails to meet any need. All we need to do is be an open vessel to another woman in a Half Family. And there are Half Families all around you. You do not even have to look for them. You only need to choose to become an open vessel and listen to Jesus' leading. He will show you who needs a touch of hope. His expanse of hope changes lives.

When I chose to become an open vessel for another woman, I did not truly understand the resource of hope. I did not understand its power to meet needs and change lives. As a result, I limited the flow of hope. As I began to reach out and touch women, I was overcome with grief about their condition. So many women in this country have such desperate needs in their external worlds. So many women are in such pain internally that hopelessness has driven them to unthinkable escapes. So many divorced and unwed mothers are judged, convicted, and thrown into the prison of rejection by our society. I was deeply grieved and angry. I began to focus solely on reaching out and touching these women in practical ways. Sadly, I lost sight of the unlimited expanse of hope.

I actually stopped writing this book. I became convinced that words would not help these women. How could a book pay a woman's bills or physically hold a woman in her pain or provide acceptance in a judgmental environment? And I missed the power, the unlimited resource, the expanse of hope.

We are called to be open vessels for Jesus to use to meet another person's need. Therefore, the power of hope comes from Jesus, not us. He has an unlimited supply and he knows the expanse that each woman needs. We only need to share it with another woman. If we commit ourselves to being an open vessel and remain in Jesus, we will experience the fullness of the second secret of wholeness.

The expanse of hope is only revealed one person at a time. Never underestimate your touch of hope to a woman who is raw from the ripping and shredding of her partnership. Who better to embrace a hurting woman in hope than one who has been in that position? You understand the Nightmare Fear that boils emotions. You understand the inability to even function in the external world. You know the experience of not being able to stop crying or yelling at your children. You can extend an expanse of hope that moves her past this difficult place in the road. You can become her confidante.

Never underestimate your touch of hope to a woman who does not know how to deal with a terrified, unruly child. Who better to come along side this woman than one who has been in that position? You can give her the hope that her child is not broken but is wounded. You can share the Hope Roadmap with her.

Never underestimate your touch of hope to a woman whose family is hungry. She may be standing on the edge of the Chasm contemplating an escape jump into alcohol or drugs or another man. Even sharing your own meager amount of food with another woman extends an unlimited expanse of powerful hope.

This hope is far beyond survival. Don't make my mistake and limit his expanse of hope to another woman with a limited human perception. Every time we extend hope to a woman in need, we demonstrate that she is not alone. That demonstration is an expanse of hope that changes lives. Therefore, we must be open to be used by Jesus anyway that he chooses. Passionately seek his relationship, his words, and his advice through the Bible and prayer. He will honor that commitment with the flow of hope for another mother.

On a very personal note, if you are one of those few fortunate mothers in a Half Family that is not struggling financially, please be generous with your sisters who are in need. Remember, 80 percent of us are making $40,000 or less annually to support a Half Family and 40 percent of us live in poverty. Please make a choice to sacrifice some of your comfort to bring hope to another woman. Meet a basic need and be long-suffering with her. Come up along side your sister traveler in the Half Family and meet her need for as long as the need exists (1 John 3:16–20).

You never know what Jesus will use to touch another woman. Every experience, every failure, every success, and every emotion that you have had as a mother in a Half Family can be hope for another mother.

Therefore, our Hope Roadmap is not meant to be possessed but rather shared. I encourage you to become a truthful, non-judgmental, closed-mouth confidante for another woman. Show her how to play. Encourage her to exercise and eat healthy. In fact, play and exercise with her. Explain to her the value of a MHD and positive input for positive output. Use hope to demonstrate to her that she is not alone. Be a vessel of hope that leads Half Families to be made whole: one mother, one woman at a time.

Most important, share the hope found in your Spiritual Margin of Faith with her. Become "salt and light" to the women you reach out to and touch with hope and love (Matt 5:13–16). Be generous with your material possessions.

If you choose to extend hope found in our Spiritual Margin of Faith to another mother in a Half Family, you will learn the third secret to wholeness.

The Love…Through Christ

There is no doubt in my mind that you have been transformed by the love of Jesus on this journey. If you chose to accept the truth, access hope, and sit at the feet of Jesus, you are learning the love that can meet your needs. We were transformed with each *Jesus* encounter at each stop of this rough road. We can no longer hold onto the earthly view of love. Jesus has touched us at the core of our souls.

We have experienced "knowing" love on our own Half Family journey. We each have had profound encounters with the love of Jesus. It is a love that is not a feeling but a choice. It is a love that protects and covers our Whole Homes. It is a love that we began to know the moment Jesus spoke to our hearts, "You are not alone."

Just like hope, this love is personal and not meant for mass distribution. If God's purpose was mass distribution, why did Jesus spend his entire ministry touching individuals at their place of need? Jesus' love calls us to be open vessels for the flow of love to another person. We are called to share love with another mother in the Half Family with deliberate, selfless, sacrificial acts to meet her needs.

Jesus deliberately surrendered everything to a Holy God—his wealth, his understanding, and his life to meet the salvation need of every human being.

Every human who has lived, does live, and will live has the opportunity to accept salvation from Jesus. It is a gift for anyone.

Throughout his ministry and all the way to the cross, Jesus did deliberate acts to perfectly meet people's needs. Even the manner of his death was a deliberate act. Think about it, *Jesus died with his arms open.* Reflect on that image. There is powerful symbolism in that simple act. Jesus died with his arms open wide for everyone who had lived, does live, and will live. He held nothing back and became nothing for us.

Jesus' enemies chose crucifixion so he would suffer the worst death, and God allowed crucifixion so Jesus would bring perfect life. What Jesus' enemies sought to use for evil, God used for the perfect, deliberate act of love. What his enemies meant as a symbol of humiliation, Jesus used as a perfect symbol of humility.

I cannot imagine being willing to die for a guilty person. Jesus took on the sin of murderers, thieves, terrorists, slanderers, and gossips even though some of these people would never acknowledge or accept his gift of salvation. Jesus' act of dying was deliberate. It was not a feeling or a reaction. It was not complacent or an afterthought. It was planned and executed deliberately. In fact, Jesus' entire life was deliberate. He did not wait for the needy to come to him. He went into the temple courts, the synagogues, the countryside and yes, even into Samaria. He did not spend his time inside the temple. No, he deliberately sought out the needy, the unloved, the oppressed, the outcasts, the unclean, the sick, the hungry, the homeless, and the criminals.

Think about Jesus' deliberate acts of love for us. For me, this love is overwhelming. It is light years away from our distorted human perspective of love. Only through Jesus can we come close to love. We just need to be an open vessel and follow his example one woman at a time.

When we see another mother in a Half Family in need, we need to take a deliberate step towards her. Do not wait for her to ask for help. I want you to think about your own moments of need. When you were deep in the emotional turmoil of your separation from your partner, how did you feel? Weren't you exhausted, fearful, and terrified? Were you in any condition to ask for help? Did you even clearly know what help you needed? Were you comfortable with letting someone into your internal world of turmoil? If Jesus places a hurting, wounded woman in your life, you need to pray for guidance. Did you get that? We need to pray for guidance on the action we should take, and then we need to deliberately walk towards that woman. We need to forget about our comfort level and choose to get uncomfortable. We need to be deliberate in extending love.

In that deliberate step, we need to be selfless. We all know that the love to meet a need must be selfless, but have we truly internalized that fact? Look again at Jesus' deliberate act of salvation. Jesus died for murderers, thieves, liars, unwed and divorced mothers. Jesus did not select only certain groups of people for salvation. His gift was freely given to all of humanity. The only requirements to receive the gift of salvation are confession of sin and acceptance of the crucified/resurrected Christ.

Think about a selfless act. It is focused on the other person's need. If we focus on ourselves and what we want to give, then we can become judgmental. It is true. We will judge based on our situation rather that the other person's need. Jesus clearly calls us not to judge.

For me one of the most profound examples of this principle is found in Luke 17. Ten lepers whom cried out to be healed approached Jesus. Without hesitation, Jesus told them to go, show themselves to the priests, and they were healed as they went. But only one came back "praising God in a loud voice. He threw himself at Jesus' feet and thanked him—and he was a Samaritan" (Luke 17:15). Jesus knows everything, which means he knew from the beginning that only one would come back to thank him and he knew that one person would be a Samaritan. Still, he did not judge, he selflessly met the needs of all ten lepers. In other words, he did not determine, I will only heal the individuals who are grateful "to me" for this gift. No, he selflessly saw these lepers and he healed them. If anyone was in a position to judge, it was Jesus. We cannot judge anyone. Love is a *selfless* act to meet another person's need.

Surely, when dealing with needy people, we are to use discernment. But there is a big difference between judgment and discernment. Simply put *our* judgment systematically eliminates people from having their needs met, but discernment sees needs through Jesus' eyes, and meets the need. We are to see through Jesus' eyes, not our own limited vision. If we see through his vision, we will correctly *discern* the need.

For example, given the harshness of the Half Family journey, you could certainly encounter a woman who has done an escape jump into the Chasm. Maybe she chose to use her rent money to go on an escape shopping spree and is now facing eviction. A judgmental attitude would say that she got what she deserved and you decide to not meet her need. A discerning attitude would say she made a mistake, but she needs to keep her home. You should probably not give her the rent money but rather pay the landlord for her.

Discernment is used on an individual basis. Judgment paints everyone with the same brush.

It is challenging to demonstrate love through selfless acts to meet another person's needs. There may be times when you feel that the other person is not grateful or that they used you. Great, let them be ungrateful and use you. Believe me, the more opportunity you have to show Jesus' love, the more opportunity for Jesus' healing power to touch them. We are called to see needs through Jesus' eyes, meet needs with discernment, and leave the rest to Jesus.

From a human perspective, it may hurt to meet another person's need. We do not meet a need to get something back or to make us feel good. We should be open vessels for the river of God's love to freely flow through us to others. The glory goes to God, not us. Ideally, we should become sacrificial to the point that we, as humans, are invisible. We should become invisible, so that the women we touch see only Jesus. Let me share the transforming power of a sacrificial act.

I have noticed throughout the gospels that often when Jesus healed someone, he would say, "See that no one knows about this." I used to think that Jesus wanted to teach us to meet needs in secret. Anonymity is crucial, but his acts of healing were done in public. There must have been another reason for Jesus' message.

Then I thought that he did not want these people to reveal that he was the Messiah. We all know this interpretation. Clearly, Jesus knew the perfect timing for this revelation. But in these healing encounters, Jesus did not tell these people that he was the Messiah. So how did they know?

I began to study these encounters in the Bible and looked beyond the words. What happened in that moment of healing? I personally believe that Jesus was teaching us an invaluable lesson in a sacrificial act to meet another person's need.

Think about this example. During Jesus lifetime, leprosy was an incurable disease. Lepers were considered unclean and isolated from society. Amazingly, Jesus healed many of these people by touching them. Jews did not touch lepers. They were outcasts. They lived and died alone, separated from family and friends. Yet Jesus touched them. Jesus was King of the universe. He could have spoken healing words or merely thought them. Jesus saw all the needs of these lepers. These people needed to be physically healed, but they also needed physical contact. They had not felt the warmth of a human touch. Jesus saw their need and held back nothing. He forgot about the culture of rejection. He forgot about his personal safety. He became an open vessel for love to flow freely through him.

Now look from the lepers' perspectives; they wanted to be healed, but never did they expect to be touched. What a lavish gift. They knew the sacrifice that Jesus had made for them. They knew that he held back nothing for them. In that sacrificial act, I believe the man, Jesus, became invisible, so that these lepers saw the glory of Jesus, the Messiah. They saw the Messiah, not the man. Jesus, the man, became invisible so the glory of God was seen. These lepers knew that Jesus was the Messiah because they saw him. That vision prompted Jesus to say, "See that no one knows about this:" see that I, Jesus, the Messiah, am not revealed before the right time.

We are called to meet needs sacrificially. We are called to be invisible to the needy women that we touch. We are called to be a clear glass funnel. When water flows through the funnel, you see the water, not the glass. The principle is the same for meeting anyone's needs. We are the funnel and Jesus is the water. If we remain an "open vessel," a clear glass funnel, the women we touch will see the water, Jesus, and not us.

The Third Secret to Wholeness

We are called to extend love to another mother in the Half Family through deliberate, selfless, sacrificial acts to meet her need. It is this definition of love that has led us to the borders of wholeness. We have reached our destination: although, it is probably not the one you envisioned when we started this journey.

For me, I wanted to reach wholeness and get my heart's desires. As I have traveled this road through the dark places and across many frightening Chasms, my original desires have long since died. I never remarried, never got that house or car or money. But in the death of these desires, I was reborn into Jesus' desires for my heart. I have seen his vision and embraced it. It is the third secret.

Wholeness is not the end…it is only the beginning. It is a journey. Wholeness is not an event, or a place, or a person, or even anything we can possess. It is a path that we headed towards the moment we chose to believe that we were not alone. That simple phrase that drew us to follow Jesus has not only transformed us, but it has transformed our path.

Half Families Made Whole Through Christ

The journey through truth, hope, and love has expanded our vision and changed our path. We know the truth that we are not alone. That truth gave us the freedom to travel through the toughest spots in our internal and external worlds. But freedom has also given us a selfless vision. Our eyes have been opened to the other women struggling with internal turmoil and a harsh external world. They may not know about the Half Family road and only you can share the truth with them. They need to know the truth about the painful wound, Nightmare Fear and lack of margins in their internal world. They need to know the truth about the Cold Hard Facts, the Real Fear, and the Chasms in their external world. Did you know these truths before you started the journey? No, I shared them with you. I shared the truth because it is not mine to possess. You need to do the same. When you reach out to another mother and share the truth, you step onto a new path: wholeness.

Like truth, the Hope Roadmap has provided us with guidance to maneuver our rough road. At many stops, the hope found in our emotional, physical and mental margins has given us the extra space to avoid reacting to our internal turmoil. This hope has given us extra space to find financial solutions in our external world. Hope has been the difference between jumping off the Chasm and stepping onto the invisible bridge of Faith. However, hope is much more than survival, and we will never see the expanse of hope until we choose to give it away to another mother in a Half Family. That means you make a decision to share hope one woman at a time. Become a confidante to another mother. Exercise with her, cook meals together, and play together. Demonstrate to her that she is not alone, and see the expanse of hope.

Be assured, that our Half Family journey would not have led us to our destination without love. Each time we sat with Jesus, read his Word and prayed, we were embraced in his love. It is amazing to *know* love not *feel* love. If you have not guessed by now, I have ruined any perception you had that love is a feeling. In fact, you have begun to be transformed into a open vessel for Jesus love to flow to another person. We are called to extend love to another mother in the Half Family through deliberate, selfless, sacrificial acts to meet her need. Wholeness is a journey in love. And we have only reached the borders of this wholeness path: our new road.

The Journey into Wholeness

Not exactly what you expected? Maybe this wholeness destination has twisted your brain. Maybe you are still holding onto your personal vision of wholeness. Maybe no matter what I say, you believe that man, house, perfect child, new car, great job and lots of money will make you whole. Maybe you do see the vision of the wholeness journey but are not sure where to step on this path. I can understand.

I traveled the Half Family road for a long time before I reached the borders of wholeness. The reality is you cannot start a new journey until you complete the old one. That's right. You may not be ready to embark on *the Journey into*

Wholeness. Only a mother in the Half Family who has taken the *transforming* journey of truth, hope, and love can travel the wholeness road.

How do you know if you are ready? Look back. Have you done any skipping, running, or escape jumping on your Half Family journey? Have you accepted the Whole Truth Picture? Do you use the Hope Roadmap for your tough spots on the road? Do you view your child or children as broken or wounded? Are you still harboring anger or hatred towards a partner? Do you have an unforgiving spirit? Did you skip the stop with the Cold Hard Facts because you are paralyzed in Real Fear? Did you read about the Soft Facts and the management plan, but failed to do the work? Do you react to the Cold Hard Facts or manage them?

Most importantly, have you embraced Jesus as your savior? When we began this journey, I challenged you to let Jesus meet you where you are. He has been faithful at each stop. So if you have not accepted Jesus as your savior, now is the time. Jesus is waiting. I encourage you to find a Christian who can guide you to Jesus and the free gift of salvation or you can email me at www.halffamiles.com. It is your choice. But know this: only followers of Jesus can take *The Journey into Wholeness.* Before you take one step past this point, you need to make sure that you are ready. Be honest about the answers to the questions above. You cannot share with another woman what you have not learned.

When you are ready, we have another journey to take together. It will be challenging, but full of joy. We will grow into a deeper knowledge of God and learn to walk in Jesus' footsteps. We will find ways to meet the emotional, physical, mental and spiritual needs of other mothers. We will build relationships with these women and walk them on their road. It will be a deliberate, selfless and sacrificial journey. Amazingly, it will also be a journey of spectacular blessings for us and provide us with a glimpse of heaven.

For now, make a commitment to complete your present journey. And very soon, you will have a new journey: new book to read.

Half Families Made Whole Through Christ
The Journey into Wholeness

End Notes

Chapter 1 You Are Not Alone

1. U.S. Bureau of the Census, *Family Groups by Type and Selected Characteristics of Householders*, Current Population Survey, U.S. Bureau of the Census, Washington, DC, March 2000.

2. Ibid.

3. *The Urban Institute*, "Millions Still Face Homelessness in a Booming Economy," *The Urban Institute*, February 1, 2000.

4. Eugene T. Lowe, "A Status Report on Hunger and Homelessness in America's Cities", The United States Conference of Mayors, December 2001.

5. U.S. Bureau of the Census, *Family Groups by Type and Selected Characteristics of Householders*.

6. Ibid.

7. Ibid.

8. Cheryl Wertzstein, "Unwed mothers set a record for births," *The Washington Times*, April 18, 2001.

9. U.S. Bureau of the Census, *Family Groups by Type and Selected Characteristics of Householders*.

10. Ibid.

Chapter 2 The Truth about Our External World

1. U.S. Bureau of the Census, *Family Groups by Type and Selected Characteristics of Householders*, Current Population Survey, U.S. Bureau of the Census, Washington, DC, March 2000.

2. U.S. Bureau of the Census, *Child Support for Custodial Mothers and Fathers,* by Timothy Grall, U.S. Department of Commerce, Economics

and Statistics Administration, U.S. Bureau of the Census, Washington, DC, October 2000.

3. U.S. Department of Health and Human Services, *Characteristics and Financial Circumstances of TANF Recipients,* Temporary Assistance for Needy Families (TANF) program, U.S. Department of Health and Human Services, Washington, DC, 2001.

4. U.S. Bureau of the Census, *Family Groups by Type and Selected Characteristics of Householders.*

5. U.S. Bureau of the Census, *Profile of Selected Housing Characteristics: 2000,* U.S. Bureau of the Census, Washington, DC, 2000.

6. Ibid.

7. Ibid.

8. Ibid.

9. U.S. Department of Agriculture, *Official USDA Food Plans: Cost of Food at Home at Four Levels U.S. Average, March 2006,* Center for Nutrition Policy and Promotion, U.S. Department of Agriculture, Washington, DC, April 2006.

10. Linda Giannarellli and James Barsimantov, "Child Care Expenses of America's Families," *The Urban Institute,* December 2001.

11. "Hidden Expenses—The Cost of Ownership," *Smart Car Guide,* 2002, http://www.smartcarguide.com/.

12. U.S. Bureau of the Census, *Family Groups by Type and Selected Characteristics of Householders.*

13. Christie Dawson, "Transit Ridership Report," Third Quarter 2001, American Public Transportation Association, January 2002.

14. U.S. Bureau of the Census, *Family Groups by Type and Selected Characteristics of Householders.*

15. U.S. Bureau of the Census, *Health Insurance Coverage: 2000,* Consumer Income, U.S. Bureau of the Census, Washington, DC, September 2001.

16. U.S. Bureau of the Census, *Family Groups by Type and Selected Characteristics of Householders.*

17. Ibid.

18. Ibid.

19. U.S. Bureau of the Census, *Poverty in the United States: 2000,* Current Population Survey, U.S. Bureau of the Census, Washington, DC, March 2000 and 2001.

20. U.S. Department of Health and Human Services, *The 2001 HHS Poverty Guidelines,* U.S. Department of Health and Human Services, Washington, DC, 2001.

21. U.S. Bureau of the Census, *Child Support for Custodial Mothers and Fathers.*

22. Ibid.

23. Ibid.

24. U.S. Department of Health and Human Services, *Characteristics and Financial Circumstances of TANF Recipients.*

25. U.S. Department of Agriculture, "Frequently Asked Questions," Food Stamps, U.S. Department of Agriculture, 2002, http://www.fns.usda.gov/.

26. Michael Wiseman, *Food Stamps and Welfare Reform,* WR&B Brief No. 19, The Brookings Institution, March 2002.

27. U.S. Department of Health and Human Services, *Characteristics and Financial Circumstances of TANF Recipients.*

28. Ibid.

29. U.S. Bureau of the Census, *Family Groups by Type and Selected Characteristics of Householders.*

30. "Outreach of Reach 2005: Housing Wage Climbs to $15.78," Vol. 10, No. 48, National Low Income Coalition, December 2005.

31. U.S. Bureau of the Census, *American Housing Survey for the United States: 2001,* U.S. Bureau of the Census, Washington, DC, 2001.

32. U.S. Department of Agriculture, *Official USDA Food Plans: Cost of Food at Home at Four Levels U.S. Average, March 2006.*

33. *Food Security and Diet Quality,* Federal Interagency Forum on Child and Family Statistics, America's Children: Key National Indicators of Well Being, 2001.

34. Ibid.

35. *Hunger Study 2006,* America's Second Harvest, The Nation's Food Bank Network, 2006.

36. Giannarellli and Barsimantov, "Child Care Expenses of America's Families."

37. Ibid.

38. U.S. Department of Commerce, *Profiles of General Demographic Characteristics,* 2000 Census of Population and Housing, U.S. Department of Commerce, Washington, DC, May 2001.

39. "Transportation and Jobs," Surface Transportation and Policy Project, 2006, http://www.transact.org/.

40. "Driven to Spend," Surface Transportation and Policy Project, March 2000, http://www.transact.org/.

41. Ibid.

42. "Your Driving Costs in Southern California," AAA, 2001, http://www.aaa-calif.com/.

43. U.S. Department of Transportation, "Table 3-14: Average Cost of Owning and Operating an Automobile," Bureau of Transportation Statistics, U.S. Department of Transportation, Washington, DC, April 2005

44. U.S. Bureau of the Census, *Health Insurance Coverage: 2000.*

45. Ibid.

46. Julie Appleby, "Health Insurance Premiums Crash Down on the Middle Class," *USA Today,* March 17, 2004.

Chapter 5 The Hope Roadmap

1. "High Blood Pressure—Am I at Risk?" American Heart Association, May 18, 2006, http://www.americanheart.org/.

2. Miranda Hitti, "Healthier Foods Often Lose Out to Sugary Ones in Children," January 13, 2005, http://www.webmd.com/.

3. Sue Dengate, "Fact Sheet—Food Additives," June 6, 2005, http://aca.ninemsn.com.au/.

4. "Anxiety Disorders," May 2006, http://www.psyweb.com/.

Chapter 10 Learning How to Wrap Relationships

1. Department of Health and Human Resources, *New Report Sheds light on Trends and Patterns in Marriage, Divorce, & Cohabitation,* Center for Disease Control and Prevention, National Center for Health Statistics, Department of Health and Human Resources, July 24, 2002.

2. Department of Health and Human Resources, *Report to Congress on Out-of-Wedlock Childbearing,* Centers for Disease Control and Prevention, Department of Health and Human Resources, January 21, 2003.

Chapter 11 Facing the Cold Hard Facts and the Income Gap

1. U.S. Bureau of the Census, *Family Groups by Type and Selected Characteristics of Householders,* Current Population Survey, U.S. Bureau of the Census, Washington, DC, March 2000.

2. U.S. Department of Health and Human Services, *The 2001 HHS Poverty Guidelines,* U.S. Department of Health and Human Services, Washington, DC, 2001.

3. U.S. Bureau of the Census, *Child Support for Custodial Mothers and Fathers,* by Timothy Grall, U.S. Department of Commerce, Economics and Statistics Administration, U.S. Bureau of the Census, Washington, DC, October 2000.

4. U.S. Census Bureau, *Family Groups by Type and Selected Characteristics of Householders.*

5. Ibid

6. U.S. Department of Agriculture, *Official USDA Food Plans: Cost of Food at Home at Four Levels U.S. Average, March 2006,* Center for Nutrition Policy and Promotion, U. S. Department of Agriculture, April 2006.

7.   U.S. Department of Agriculture, "Frequently Asked Questions", Food Stamps, www.fns.usda.gov, U.S. Department of Agriculture, 2004.

8.   U.S. Department of Transportation, *Average Cost of Owning and Operating an Automobile,* Bureau of Transportation Statistics, U.S. Department of Transportation, 2004.

9.   Julie Appleby, "Health Insurance Premiums Crash Down on the Middle Class", *USA Today,* March 17, 2004.

10. Linda Giannarellli and James Barsimantov, "Child Care Expenses of America's Families", *The Urban Institute,* December, 2001.

Chapter 16 Creating a Whole Home

1.   Mother Teresa, *No Greater Love* (California, New World Library, 1997, 2001).

978-0-595-40535-0
0-595-40535-5

Printed in the United States
64740LVS00005BA/238-264

9 780595 405350